Memoirs of the
Life, Character, and Labors of

John
Smith

An Itinerant Methodist Preacher

Memoirs of the
Life, Character, and Labors of

John
Smith

An Itinerant Methodist Preacher

by
Richard Treffry, Jr.

KingsleyPress

Shoals, Indiana

Memoirs of the Life, Character, and Labors of John Smith

PUBLISHED BY KINGSLEY PRESS
PO Box 973
Shoals, IN 47581
USA

Tel. (800) 971-7985

www.kingsleypress.com
E-mail: sales@kingsleypress.com

ISBN: 978-1-937428-79-2 (paperback)
ISBN: 978-1-937428-80-8 (eBook)

First Kingsley Press edition 2018

This new edition is based on the fifth edition, as revised by Ellen Smith (the subject's widow), and sold by John Mason, 14 City Road and 66 Paternoster Row, London, 1845. It has been very lightly edited in order to bring it into line with modern punctuation and grammar.

Printed in the United States of America.

Contents

Preface

He who ventures to diverge from the beaten track of his predecessors must make up his mind to be the subject of conflicting opinions. Few who are practically original are so fortunate as to meet with universal approbation; and still fewer so unhappy as to have none to advocate and abet their plans. This partisanship on secular questions, while maintained in a spirit of candour and moderation, is not likely to do injury. Indeed it often serves to evolve collateral truths of even greater importance than the questions at issue; and the judgment of mankind, though it be long before it assumes the character of unanimity, is at length sound and satisfactory. It is confirmed by one generation after another, and ultimately its authority is placed beyond all question. But when the subject in dispute involves the interest of the souls of men, the honour and prosperity of the church, and the glory of God—difference of sentiment, especially among influential Christians, is a momentous evil; and the more practical the question, the greater will be the mischief of allowing it to remain undetermined. In matters of science, repetitions and varieties of experiment are pleasing and serviceable. The vapor which the chemist consumes today without any satisfactory result, he can reproduce tomorrow by a process with which he is perfectly familiar; but the spirit which enters eternity is irrecoverably doomed. In the decision of the questions which affect man's eternal destiny, the urgency of the case admits of no delay. We stand on the margin of our fate, and we must ACT. "A man who gets into the habit of inquiring about proprieties, and expediencies, and occasions, often spends his life without doing anything to purpose. The state of the world is such, and so much depends on action, that everything seems to say loudly to every man, 'Do something,'—'Do it,'—'Do it.'" Whatever, therefore, prevents resolution, promptitude, and diligence, be its aspect of expediency what it may, is *sin*. "While Rome deliberates, Saguntum perishes."

Such considerations give to the following pages an importance to which, as the history of a single individual, they could not pretend. They have been compiled with the humble hope that the development and the advocacy of the principles which they present may somewhat tend not only to remove differences of opinion respecting their subject, but also to stimulate to a higher degree of usefulness those who are capable of serving the church of God.

The admirers of Mr. Smith's character, it is hoped, will detect in the following Memoirs no indisposition to do justice to his great and singular virtues; while on the other hand, the impugner of his views, the author trusts, will not have to complain of wilful indiscrimination or of the absence of candour. He has not the presumption to imagine that his sketch will meet with the unqualified approbation of both classes of readers. It will be enough if neither charge him with disingenuousness or with being wanting in sincere endeavour to promote the truth.

Of the literary character of the work, it may not be improper to add a few words. As soon as its writer understood that there was no probability of any other person undertaking to perpetuate the memory of one whom he so dearly valued, he readily complied with the wish of Mr. Smith's friends that he should become his biographer. He knew that even a very indifferent delineation of his subject, when no better was to be procured, *would* be welcome to multitudes, and *might* be serviceable. The state of his own health, under other circumstances, would have rendered him very reluctant to have bound himself to such an employment; and indeed to this cause may be attributed a measure of the defectiveness of the present work, as well as of the delay in its publication. He has often prosecuted it with a trembling hand, a fevered cheek, and a depressed spirit; and an hour or two in the course of the day has been as long a time as his weakness would allow him to devote to it. As fast as the manuscript has been completed, it has been put into the hands of the printer; and the author has not had the opportunity or ability to give any great attention to the proofs as they issued from the press.

The available materials for the composition of the following pages were not ample. Mr. Smith left but few papers which could assist the undertaking; of these the largest possible use has been made. The author is further indebted to the communications, not only of those friends of Mr. Smith whose names occur hereafter, but also to several others whose views of his character and narratives of his successes have been, for the most part, embodied in the work. To have given at large the statements of each would have induced much repetition and swollen the volume to more than double its present size. To his valuable correspondents, the author gratefully ascribes whatever degree of interest the *materiel* of his work may be thought to possess; their assistance has been very welcome and is most sincerely acknowledged. It ought also to be added that he has submitted the manuscript to the inspection of some very dear friends, whose suggestions have in a few instances served to give a comparative regularity and force to its generally feeble and unequal style. With all the advantages which he could command, however, the picture falls so far short of the reality, and the result of his efforts is so much below the idea which warmed the writer's imagination when he commenced, that it is with deep and painful diffidence he presents it to the Christian public. Yet he thanks God that he has lived to complete his task; and it is his consolation that, however speedily and entirely his labours may be engulfed in oblivion, truth and virtue, the interests of which he has endeavoured to subserve, are imperishable and eternal.

It is only necessary to add that the entire profits of this work will be devoted to the use of Mr. Smith's family.

Penzance
September, 1832

Advertisement to the Fourth Edition

The lamented death of the compiler of the following Memoirs, and a wish to meet the exigencies of a class of readers who possess inadequate pecuniary means, are the assignable reasons for the publication of the fourth edition in its present form. The work has been thoroughly revised, a few alterations have been made, and two or three additional facts have been introduced. With these exceptions, the present is a copy of the former editions.

These pages unfold not merely the life of an individual eminent for piety, or of a minister distinguished both for piety and usefulness; but of one who, having singled out for himself the noblest object that can engage the mind of man, gave himself up unreservedly to work out its accomplishment. That object was *the salvation of souls.* Hence, his life was an exposition of grand principles, illustrated by grand experiments; and the truths he discovered while diligently studying the Word of God he proceeded to verify by the test of trial. He smote the waters with a faith that said, "Where is the Lord God of the Bible?" And the Lord worked with his servant and confirmed the word preached with *signs* following. The Memoir of such a man is, therefore, an inheritance to the church.

During the time this edition has been passing through the press, the father of Mr. Smith, who is alluded to in the first page as still living, has entered into rest. His death was sudden, but he was prepared for his change.

Ellen Smith
Sheffield
March 28, 1840

CHAPTER 1

Cudworth—Sheffield—Barnsley
1794–1812

John Smith was born at Cudworth, near Barnsley, in the West Riding of Yorkshire, January 12th, 1794. His parents, who have both survived him, became savingly acquainted with evangelical truth and united themselves to the Methodist society about the time of his birth. His father has for many years sustained the important offices of leader and local preacher, to the advantage of the church and the honor of God; and his mother, in the quietness and seclusion of humble life, has long adorned her profession and exerted that holy influence which belongs exclusively to maternal piety. From his earliest infancy, therefore, the subject of these memoirs was placed under the directions and restraints of domestic religion, and he was carefully instructed in the verities of God's most holy Word. Nor is there any doubt but that he was privileged by the visitations of the divine Spirit at a very tender age. When between eight and nine years old, he was powerfully affected by concern for his soul, under a sermon by a local preacher of the Wakefield circuit, from Psalm 114:15: "Happy is that people whose God is the Lord." His serious impressions, however, were but occasional and transitory.

In his infancy, he exhibited an ardent and headstrong spirit. The earliest recollection with which his father has supplied me is of an act of singularly wanton and precocious mischievousness, the results of which, had it not been for a merciful Providence, might have been of the most serious kind. Generally, in his childhood, he had not the fear of God before his eyes. His sports were characteristically bold, boisterous, and wicked. He was even accustomed to attend the prayer meetings held in his native village to collect materials for the mirth of his ungodly companions; and, endowed as he naturally was with extraordinary powers of mimicry, he afterwards amused them by striking and ridiculous imitations of the peculiarities which he had observed in the pious persons who conducted those means of grace.

During the time that he remained at home, he was, of course, prevented from the full indulgence of his depraved propensities; but when about fourteen years of age, being placed as an apprentice with a grocer at Sheffield, and of consequence more free from control, he became decidedly wicked. He conducted himself generally in so irregular a manner that, after two years, his master, unable any longer to endure his bad conduct, sent him back to his parents. He then obtained a situation at Barnsley in the same line of business. Here he even gave up attendance at a place of worship and thus broke the last link which seemed to connect him with the principles and example of his pious parents. He associated himself, without restraint, with other ungodly young men, and had his natural corruption increased, and his habits of evil confirmed, by their example and counsels. He imitated their profane language, and learned to blaspheme the God of his father. As far as his means permitted, he became a gambler, and contracted a strong passion for wrestling and other athletic exercises, especially for pugilistic contests. He often traveled considerable distances to attend prize-fights, and actually put himself under the tuition and training of scientific boxers; and his muscular frame and lion heart well fitted him for pre-eminence in such vain and wicked exercises. It is needless to say anything of the deeply debasing society into which these pursuits continually led him. It was congenial with his corrupt affections; and, perhaps, no stronger evidence than this can be found of his perfect estrangement from God and virtue. In short, he was an adept and an enthusiast in vice; and he gloried in the awful distinction which an athletic body and a desperate mind enabled him to maintain among his sinful associates.

Even in this course of sin, however, might be easily discerned indications of the same natural character which afterwards, under the sanctifying influences of the Holy Spirit, contributed to render him so distinguished a Christian and minister. Here was the energy which, in good or evil, allowed him to be satisfied with nothing like a medium of feeling or exertion. Here was the strong, concentrated passion, urging him on by its hurricane power to the utter abandonment of religion, which, in a brighter era of his life, became the impulse of generous sacrifice, self-devotion, and labor. If he now spurned reproof, rejected all care of reputation, and hardened himself against every suggestion of peril on account of sin, he was equally daring and independent when "the excellency of the knowledge of Christ Jesus" became the object of his emulation. The popularity which, by his highly social qualities, he acquired among the vain and worldly persons by whom he was at this time surrounded, was succeeded, in a more honourable period of his history, by the warm Christian attachment of all who had the privilege of his intimacy. It is a melancholy fact, also, that he was a sinner of influence; and there were some of his companions in vanity who, according to human probability, were prevented from the choke of a religious life only by the fascinations of his society. How fully, as a Christian and a Christian minister, he exerted a similar power over those with whom he associated, the succeeding pages will tend to show.

The extreme profligacy of some who have had a religious education is no evidence of their having forgotten the pious instructions of their childhood. In fact, paradoxical as the assertion may appear, their resolute abandonment of themselves to vicious practices is, in not a few cases, a proof of the depth and permanence of their previous impressions. Next to making him virtuous, the best effect of admonition on a sinner is to render him unhappy. Dissipation is an indication of a mind ill at ease. The natural posture of happiness is calmness and repose; and where men are fully stupefied by the influence of sin, the love of reputation and many similar principles of counteraction will frequently tend to make them moderate in their pursuit of forbidden pleasure. On the other hand, where there still remains a considerable degree of moral sensibility, the spirit seeks, in the perpetual hurry of business or of vice, to still the voice of conscience and to overcome the strivings of God's Spirit. This, of course, will be the more apparent in persons of such great power of feeling as was possessed by the subject of these memoirs.

Meantime his parents' patience, counsel, prayers, and tears were not forgotten before the Lord. In the spring of 1812, it pleased God to visit Cudworth with a gracious rain of his Holy Spirit. Several persons were awakened and converted, and, among others, a cousin of John Smith. On Sunday, April 5th of that year, John, with one of his companions, came over from Barnsley to Cudworth. He there saw what had been done for others, and his mind was much affected. In the course of the day, his pious mother conversed with him at large on his miserable condition; and when he was about to return, she said to him, "You are wandering about in search of happiness, but you will never find it till you turn to God." Her conversation produced so powerful an effect on him that he abruptly left her, lest she should remark his emotion. He and his companion had not proceeded far on their journey home before Smith suddenly stopped, and, with a deep groan and a gesture expressive of strong determination, exclaimed, "I am resolved to lead a new life." As soon as he had uttered this resolution, he felt a measure of satisfaction to which he had before been an entire stranger; and he immediately proposed to return and attend the prayer meeting which was that evening to be held at Cudworth. When he arrived at the chapel, the meeting had begun. He entered, however, and almost instantly the agitation of his mind became uncontrollable. He cried aloud and besought the friends to pray for him. The meeting concluded, but he obtained no relief. Several others who were in distress accompanied him to his father's house, where another meeting was commenced. Mr. Smith the elder had been in the circuit fulfilling his appointment as a local preacher. His feelings may be imagined when, on entering his dwelling, the first objects which presented themselves were two of his children, in deep agony of soul, who, with strong cries, were pouring out their hearts before God. One of them was the prodigal—upon whom he had expended so many tears and prayers, and for whom he had undergone such deep anxiety. God heard the prayers of the distressed youth that night, and brought him into glorious liberty, filling his heart with peace and joy in believing. The next day he was again brought into bondage by giving way for a moment to the hastiness of his temper, and for a while he walked in great darkness and disquiet. He was, however, by the advice and intercession of some Christian friends, encouraged again to trust in the atonement of Christ; and the comfort of the Holy Spirit once more returned to his soul. From that time, there is reason to believe, to the day of his death, he walked uninterruptedly in the light of God's countenance.

Perhaps these pages may fall into the hands of some pious parent who has to mourn over the irreligion of a dear child. To such the conversion of John Smith ought to be a source of the highest encouragement. No condition, surely, can be marked by a more obvious alienation from the spirit and practice of Christianity than that in which the mercy of God found him. In his case, there is the strongest illustration of the honor which the Almighty will put upon the labors of godly parents. The Holy Spirit is the giver of pious and compunctious recollections. Christ expressly promised that the Comforter should recall to the minds of his disciples whatsoever he had declared to them during his personal ministry.[1] The instructions of pious parents are treasured up in the secret cells of memory, hidden it is true for a time, and perhaps supposed to be forgotten. But the time will come when the energy of the blessed Spirit will quicken them, and they shall stand forth in the sudden broad light of heaven, endued with accumulated power, to astonish and confound the heart of the careless and ungodly child. It may be in the hour of sickness, or in some other time of darkness; it may be when shame and want shall have driven away the companions of his dissipation. He may be far from the influence of Christian instructors or Christian example. He may have hardened his heart, and stiffened his neck, and given himself over to the companionship of the infidel and scoffer; but there is no condition so remote from piety as not to be within the reach of the mercy of God; and he has promised his Spirit to the seed of Jacob, and his blessing to the offspring of his servants.[2]

---

1. John 14:26.
2. Isa. 44:3.

CHAPTER 2

Barnsley

1812–1813

In seeking to account for the various forms which Christianity assumes in different individuals, much light may usually be gained by considering the condition of each before his conversion to God, and the more remarkable circumstances attendant upon that gracious change. The events preceding and immediately concurrent with this great transition, in the experience of the subject of this sketch, without doubt served to give, to a considerable degree, a color to the opinions and feelings of his subsequent Christian course. It is not unlikely that the enlarged view which he was, at all times, enabled to realize of the fullness and extent of divine mercy was originally presented to his mind by a reference to the extreme degradation of his unregenerate state; and the freeness and urgency of his invitations to sinners, however vile, might have partly arisen from a peculiarly lively sense of the greatness of the grace of Christ exhibited in his own case. Of him it might emphatically be said, as of the woman who had been a sinner—and for the same reason—that he "loved much." The foregoing facts enable us also to account for his strong attachment to prayer meetings, and for the high estimation in which he held them as means of grace. Nor was it the least important feature of the converting operation of God's Spirit in his soul that it was at once powerful and rapid. This was no doubt one reason for the force and frequency with which, in later life, he insisted on the excellency of God's "quick way" of saving men.

One of the first and most striking evidences of the divine change which had taken place in his heart was an insatiable appetite for the Word of God. His long-neglected Bible was now resorted to as a source of the highest delight. On the day after he obtained the evidence of the favor of God, he read about thirty chapters. He kept the sacred volume upon the counter of the shop in which he was a servant, and at every opportunity flew to it with the most ardent desire and relish. He naturally possessed a very quick and retentive memory, and at this time he learned several of the New Testament epistles. The practice of committing to memory large portions of the Scriptures he continued in after years, and found it productive of great comfort and advantage. His earnest love of God's book remained with him during the whole of his life, and his acquaintance with it was remarkably extensive and perfect.

He also became distinguished for his habitual devotion. This was in his case peculiarly necessary. When his former sensualizing and degrading course of life is considered, and the steadfast alienation of his mind from God, as well as the natural strength of his passions, it is not too much to affirm that he required an extraordinary measure of inward religion. Persons of constitutional equanimity and generally moral conduct cannot calculate on the temptations and difficulties which await a babe in Christ of the character of John Smith. The measure of grace which suffices to maintain them in a regular course of consistent, and it may be even eminent, goodness, would have been totally inadequate to a successful encounter with the obstacles which crowded his path. The constant sense of his peril appears to have been exceedingly vivid on his mind. He lived, therefore, in jealous watchfulness, and spent a large portion of his leisure hours in communion with Heaven. In retired fields, in woods and other places of concealment, he was accustomed to wrestle with God till he was copiously baptized by the Spirit. His very intimate friend, the Rev. W. H. Clarkson of Nottingham, states that "one day, soon after his conversion, being under peculiar temptation, he retired into a cavern, where he continued for a considerable time in prayer, till he felt such an overshadowing of the divine presence as quite overwhelmed him; and he has been heard to say that had he not often had such visits from the Lord, he never should have been able to have persevered in the Christian warfare."

Another of the qualities which distinguished his subsequent life, and which now began to manifest itself, was his concern for the condition of sinners. Upon his conversion, he had renounced the spirit and occupations of his former associates; but he did not allow them to hear of the change in his views and feelings merely through the medium of a third party. He took every opportunity of visiting and conversing with them on the concerns of their souls. He artlessly detailed what God had done for him; he reproved their vices, entreated them to abandon their sinful course of life, and assured them of the readiness of the Savior to receive them. His affectionate expostulations were not without success. Two of his former companions he had the happiness of bringing under the influence of divine grace, and of seeing united to the church of Christ, the first fruits of a mighty harvest.

Having become sensible also of the value of mental cultivation, and of his responsibility for the exercise of his intellectual powers, he referred with great regret to the time which had been so entirely lost to improvement of this kind. Under the influence of his new principles, and with his characteristic buoyancy of hope, he diligently applied himself to study, particularly to the study of the English language; and he succeeded in inducing several other young persons in the neighborhood of Barnsley to devote their leisure hours, which had before been spent in vanity or sin, to the acquisition of useful knowledge.

It is not uncommon for young Christians to imagine that there are certain excellencies and habits which, in all their degrees, belong exclusively to a highly matured state of piety; and hence they do not labour to attain those mental and moral qualities which are perfectly within the reach of present faith and diligence. They appear to suppose that religion is a series of novelties and that in the regular sequence of cause and effect they shall partake of them severally and consecutively; that, in short, the elements of exalted piety are, to a certain extent, widely different from those of a less mature spiritual condition. They therefore rest contented, though consciously destitute of many qualities which the Word of God commends, and which the experience of other Christians exhibits; and they live in the vain hope of hereafter retrieving opportunities which they at present neglect, and of obtaining that good to which they do not at present aspire. But where is the Christian who has ever been eminent by the operation or under the influence of such opinions? The most robust man possesses no greater number of bodily members than the infant just born; and from this scriptural analogy, as well as from the testimony of experience, we may conclude that, in general, he only can expect to attain any exalted condition of piety or usefulness who labours to possess all the essential elements of perfection in his spiritual infancy.

There was no characteristic of the most striking and successful part of Mr. Smith's life the germ of which may not be readily discovered at this time. Of course, he obtained more perspicuous and exalted views of the truth; his faith was more powerful; his affections were more spiritualized, refined, and intense; he entered more fully into the designs of God, and enjoyed more perfect access to him in the maturity of his Christian career; but he was even now marked by Christian courage, zeal, activity, and benevolence; by love of God's Word, delight in prayer, simplicity of faith, deep concern for the souls of men, and ardent desire for mental improvement; and these were the identical features of his character which afterwards made his path so bright, and which now shed so pure and untroubled a lustre over his memory.

It amounts, therefore, to almost a moral certainty that, had his views of the rudiments of piety been less comprehensive or less practical—had he contented himself, in this stage of his Christian life, with walking merely on the verge of experience—had he postponed his efforts after an entire Christianity to some remote and indefinite period—had he not, in fine, made religion in its integrity the alpha and omega of his desires and pursuits, he would never have attained the eminence in the church which multitudes afterwards delighted to witness, acknowledge, and admire. The current mistakes on this subject no one more fully discerned, or more deeply lamented, than Mr. Smith. To the compiler of these memoirs, he has often said, "We begin to live too late"—a melancholy truth, equally applicable to those who are laying up stores for futurity, which are now either useless or unemployed, and to those who neglect present opportunities and dream of some virtue in the lapse of time, which shall complete the array of excellencies, for the perfection of which they are not now solicitous.

As Mr. Smith had learned to esteem the employment and cultivation of his mind a religious duty, so, as his piety increased, his desire for this species of improvement became more remarkable. He was now, in several respects, a character so interesting as to attract the notice of some pious persons of considerable intelligence, who probably discerned in him the indications of future service to the church and the world. Having particularly observed his diligence in the acquisition of knowledge, they recommended that he should be removed to a situation more favorable to mental improvement than that which he then occupied. He was accordingly, in May, 1813, placed under the care of Mr. James Sigston of Leeds, being at that time in the twentieth year of his age.

CHAPTER 3

Leeds

1813–1814

The views entertained by the subject of these memoirs on the duty of intellectual cultivation are particularly worth the attention of all who admired his zeal and who emulate his example. Ignorance and mental imbecility, though sometimes associated with Christianity, are no auxiliaries to it. The religion of the New Testament, though it has frequently found a race of men in a state of intellectual prostration, has never left them in that condition. On the contrary, those nations for whose elevation in this particular many unsuccessful attempts have been made by ordinary means, have been gradually raised by the influence of scriptural piety to a commanding situation in the ranks of science and philosophy; and it is not too much to affirm that the world at large has been incomparably more indebted to religion for all that exalts man as a thinking being than to all other causes combined. It has given characters, grammar, and literature to the most ferocious savages. It has converted the wandering barbarian into a peaceable citizen, a mechanic, a philosopher. It has established and fostered the purest forms of jurisprudence and the noblest systems of political government; and it has not only extricated man from the deepest vice, but it has exalted him from the most obtuse stupidity into the world of reason, contemplation, and poetry.

The most excellent talent which the all-wise God has bestowed upon us, next to the capacity for loving and enjoying himself, is the ability to contemplate, and, to a certain limit, to understand his character, both in his Word and in his works; and for the use of this talent he holds us responsible. The instructed Christian also has sources of religious enjoyment to which others are strangers. He possesses the ability to recommend his faith to those whose minds would repel the counsels of less cultivated persons. His views of the divine character are ample and lucid, beyond what others can conceive. He has an armor both offensive and defensive against infidelity, of which others cannot avail themselves, and the elements of a higher steadfastness of character than that of ordinary Christians.

Nor is it any argument against intellectual cultivation that we rarely find it united with the simplicity of piety, power of faith, and fervency of zeal. Were these the characteristics of Christians in general, and were intellectual men the only persons of low spiritual attainments, there would be force and propriety in such an objection.

But, alas! How little is there of these excellencies among the mass of professors! How complex and obscure are their notions of God's plan of saving men! How feeble is their faith, and how cold their charity! That the majority of Christians of cultivated minds are defective likewise is therefore only in melancholy conformity to the rest of the church. It is readily admitted that unsanctified learning is a very great evil, and that the proportion of grace required by each individual depends partly on the number and power of the talents which he is called to devote to the service of God. A half-instructed man also has, without doubt, numerous temptations to self-dependence; but when the requisite and promised influence of the Holy Spirit accompanies the lawful use of study, Christianity assumes a higher and more influential character; and those who thus employ the talent committed to their trust become, in the "great house" of God, not only "vessels of gold," intrinsically valuable, but also "vessels of honor fit for the Master's use."

Some who may peruse these remarks are probably placed in circumstances far more encouraging than he whose character has suggested them. It was not till he had nearly arrived at manhood that he discerned the importance of mental culture and discipline. He had formed no habits of application; in fact, all his previous pursuits had tended to sensualize, distract, and debase him. He had lost the most valuable, because the most impressible and the least occupied, part of his life. His mind had ceased to exhibit the ductility of boyhood; and this was the more important in his case, since he had never possessed

an easily modelled character. Under these disadvantages, it is no matter of surprise that he did not make that high degree of improvement
which others, in different circumstances, may without difficulty realize; and if, at any future period of his life, he was deemed deficient
in intellectual character and attainments, it was not from the want
of a substratum of good sound sense, nor of a correct estimate of the
value of human learning. He has often lamented to the writer of
these pages what he esteemed his intellectual inferiority; and, from
the statement of an early and intimate friend, it appears that, only
a short time before his death, he expressed his regret that he had
not attained that degree of mental improvement of which, had his
circumstances been different, he felt himself to have been capable.
That which would call forth such expressions from a man of such
ardent zeal, and such extensive usefulness, is not surely a matter of
small moment. Nay, more; with his practical views, it is certain that
he not only considered the qualifications in question not likely to
be detrimental to his personal religion, or his service to the church,
but greatly promotive both of the one and the other.

Mr. Smith's situation at Mr. Sigston's academy was highly gratifying to himself; and it is not a little honourable to him that he
was pleased to be considered a schoolboy at such an age. He here
had the opportunity of attending the means of grace in connection
with the excellent society of Leeds. He was brought into association
with some singularly pious and useful characters, and, among others, with the late eminent and deeply lamented David Stoner. Mr.
Stoner was at this time an assistant in Mr. Sigston's academy; and
here a friendship was commenced between them which, I doubt not,
has been renewed where there is no possibility of its interruption.
To the subject of these pages such an intimacy was of great service,
in an intellectual and literary, as well as in a higher sense. Many of
his leisure hours were spent with his excellent and judicious friend
in diligent research; and there can be no doubt that this association was deeply interesting and mutually helpful. Although in some
points of character strikingly dissimilar, there were others in which
they pleasingly resembled each other. Mr. Stoner was of a reserved
temper; Mr. Smith open as the day. The former was melancholic;

the latter highly sanguine. The dark and depressing aspect of subjects in general seemed to affect the one; the bright and cheering
to impress the other. Mr. Stoner was the more intellectually gifted
man; Mr. Smith the happier Christian. The habits of their youth
had been as opposite as possible, and the result was what may be
readily anticipated. Both were gems of the first order, but one of
them had only just been extracted from the mine. On the other
hand, they were about the same age—had each been indebted to the
influence of pious parents—possessed in many respects similarly
stirring views of divine truth—had the same untiring zeal—were
eminently owned of God, and, as the most melancholy part of the
parallel, both were cut off in the prime of life, while their glory was
fresh in them.

In the letter to his parents announcing his arrival at Leeds, bearing date July 15th, 1813, Mr. Smith states that he had been the
subject of powerful temptations. This could scarcely be a matter of
surprise, except to those who are ignorant of Satan's devices. Upon
entering into a situation so novel, being associated with many
strangers, and occupied in a way in some respects unusual, it would
have been wonderful had the case been different. Every new form
of society into which we are introduced calls for the exertion of
those graces of the Holy Spirit which before have perhaps been the
least cultivated, and these exercises are permitted in order to bring
into full action the power of the entire Christian man. As, however,
the subject of these memoirs had entered upon his new situation
in the spirit of simple dependence upon God, so was he enabled to
triumph over his spiritual foes. After having stated his temptations,
his mind, by a natural and pleasing transition, adverts to the joy of
his Christian hope and the abundance of his consolations; and in
the conclusion of his letter he says, "In a short time the warfare of
life will be over. A few more conflicts, and we shall be in glory. I feel
at present truly happy in my God. Tears of gratitude flow from my
eyes for his loving kindness towards me. Pray that God may help
me, for I wish to spend and be spent for him."

In a letter dated September 4th of the same year, he describes his
faith as depending too much on the state of his feelings—an error

to which all young Christians, and particularly persons like himself, of great constitutional vivacity, are peculiarly liable. His testimony of his Christian experience is, however, on the whole very satisfactory. The following is an extract:

> My soul is panting after that mind which was in Christ. In consequence, I meet with many oppositions from Satan; but the Lord is present with me, and supports me constantly under every difficulty. Though I believe that in Christ "all fullness dwells," I do not sufficiently look to him for help and salvation. When I am tempted, I am frequently cast down for a short time; my faith diminishes, and I have not that confidence in God as when everything goes on, or seems to go on, well with me. But when I come simply to the Lord, make my case known to him, acknowledge my weakness, plead the merit of the atonement, and believe on his name, he delivers me from temptation, lifts upon me the light of his countenance, and causes me to rejoice in him as my salvation. I can come to him through Jesus Christ and call him my Father. The Spirit itself beareth witness with my spirit that I am a child of God.

In the latter part of this letter he speaks of having commenced the study of Latin. In this language I believe he made no considerable proficiency. In after years he had a wish to make himself acquainted with Greek and Hebrew, but he found that his other occupations would not allow him sufficient time to gratify this desire. He however succeeded in attaining a perfect acquaintance with his own language; and a gentleman of classical education who enjoyed his intimacy at a subsequent period remarked that of all men whom he had ever known, Mr. Smith possessed the most accurate and extensive syntactical knowledge. He had also a high relish for the best English writers, both in theology and general literature. His taste for poetry was chaste and classical, and he had a feeling of its beauties far superior to that of many more perfectly cultivated minds.

For several months after the above date there is nothing in Mr. Smith's correspondence so striking as to demand insertion here. It will be sufficient to say that in general it affords interesting evidence of his Christian progress, of great artlessness and sincerity, and of

increasing devotedness to God. In the meantime he diligently prosecuted his studies and was deemed qualified to act occasionally as
a teacher in the school. After the midsummer vacation of 1814, he
became a regular assistant; but before this he had begun to preach.
The great and responsible occupation of the ministry he undertook
with much fear and hesitation. The first time it had been arranged
for him to address a congregation, he could not summon sufficient
resolution to fulfil his engagement. At the advice and entreaty of
some of his friends, he a second time promised to make the attempt;
but it is probable that had it not been for the remonstrance of his
friend Mr. Stoner, he would not even then have ventured.

> As the time approached, he yielded again to timidity and retired
> to the teachers' room, intending not to make his appearance at the
> place appointed. Mr. Stoner was in the room. "I thought," said he
> to Mr. Smith, "that you had agreed to preach tonight." "Yes," said
> the other, with much hesitation and embarrassment, "but I must
> give it up." "What!" rejoined Mr. Stoner, with severe and powerful
> emphasis, "do you mean then to ruin yourself?" This pointed ques-
> tion, resting a compliance with acknowledged duty on a regard to
> personal safety, produced the desired result.[1]

The place at which Mr. Smith commenced his public labors was
a schoolroom in Park Lane, where Mr. Stoner himself, some time
before, had preached his first sermon. His text was Proverbs 18:24:
"There is a friend that sticketh closer than a brother." The embar-
rassment which he felt upon this occasion was most painful both to
himself and his hearers. After having proceeded with great difficulty
for some short time, he was compelled to tell the congregation that
he could not address them any longer; and he sat down in a state of
distress, such as may be anticipated from so humbling an issue of
a first attempt. His want of suitable expressions seemed to be the
cause of his failure in this instance; and indeed, for several years
afterwards, he was not unfrequently straitened in his pulpit labors
from the same circumstance.

---

1. Stoner's Memoirs, c. iii

CHAPTER 4

Leeds—Oulton
1814–1816

Although Mr. Smith has left no record of those exercises of mind which preceded his entrance into the ministry, yet from documents of a later date, as well as from the character which he at this time sustained, there is no difficulty in accounting for the reluctance with which he undertook it. His habits of natural feeling will not allow the supposition that his hesitation proceeded from the absence of mere animal courage. The ardor of his piety equally forbids the idea that he wanted the necessary concern for the souls of men. But his mind was deeply impressed by a sense of the seriousness of the undertaking, and his humble views of himself naturally led him to shrink from it. Nor will this be a matter of surprise to any enlightened man. The office of the Christian minister is connected with the highest honor, interest, and peril. It is the institution of God himself for the conveyance and proclamation of the most important message that ever stirred the energies or woke the attention of apostate man. This message has to be expounded, illustrated, vindicated, and enforced. It is capable of an infinite variety of aspects without losing its identity, and is thus to be adapted to the incalculable diversity of human character, intellect, and destitution. Nay, the honor of being "workers together with God" is of itself so great that it is no wonder that they who attentively contemplate it should be overwhelmed by its ponderousness.

The Christian minister is the herald of *judgment*—severe, and irrevocable; *execution* omnipotent and resistless; *eternity*—mysterious and terrible. For a single sinner—isolated from the human family without influence either of good or evil—to be lost is an event to shadow forth the horror of which it would not suffice "for the sun to veil his face, and the moon her brightness, or to cover the ocean with mourning or the heaven with sackcloth." Nor, "were all nature to become animated and vocal, would it be possible for her to utter a groan too deep, or a cry too piercing, to furnish an adequate idea of the magnitude and extent of such a catastrophe."[1] But no sinner can be so separated from his fellows. He is one in an extended series, the moral character of the succession of which he may eternally determine; and the most insignificant of men may thus cast into the balance the poise which shall bring down the destinies of multitudes of deathless spirits. Such are the interests which depend upon a Christian minister. The consequences of fidelity or neglect for ever extend themselves over generations yet unborn. The founding of empires, or the overthrow of dynasties, is lighter than the "airiest gossamer" compared with the amount of good or ill which he is capable of achieving. It is marvelous, therefore, not that some holy men enter upon the ministerial office with great reluctance, but that any should be able to endure the consciousness of a responsibility so tremendous.

The ill success of Mr. Smith's first attempt to deliver a sermon of course tended to increase his indisposition to the work of the ministry, and it was probably some time before he made a second. It was not till the Christmas quarterly meeting following that he was proposed to be taken on the plan as a probationary local preacher. His name was introduced at the local preachers' meeting by Mr. William Nelson, who had been his fellow assistant at Mr. Sigston's, and who was at the time gradually sinking under the power of a disease that ultimately proved fatal. Mr. Smith, who was spending the vacation with his parents, received the intelligence of his having been appointed to preach a trial sermon in a letter from his dying friend, whose case had just then been declared hopeless by his medical attendants. Mr. N., in the conclusion of his communication, says, "It is settled that you are to take my plan. I hope to live to see you return, but that is only known to God." This entrance upon the more regular work of a local preacher must have been very affecting to Mr. Smith. A solemn bequest was thus committed to his trust; and

---

1.   Robert Hall.

if the spirits of those who die in the Lord are allowed to trace the steps of their survivors, the fidelity of the subject of these memoirs must have given a spring-tide of gladness to the heart of him whom he was thus impressively called to succeed.

In the first letter sent by Mr. Smith to his parents after the vacation, dated February 21st, 1815, he gives an account of the death of Mr. Nelson, with whom, in the interval, he had had much profitable fellowship. "I was with him," says Mr. Smith, "a short time before he died. He seemed at that time to experience a good deal of pain. When I parted from him, I said, 'I hope the Lord supports you.' 'He does,' he said with great energy. 'God only knows how long he intends me to linger here in pain, but I am quite resigned. The will of the Lord be done!' He died triumphing in the redeeming blood."

In the same letter, he alludes to his having preached at both the large chapels in Leeds. In the former instance, he preached his trial sermon; and though he states that he was under the influence of much fear, yet he adds a fervent expression of thankfulness for conscious divine assistance. This effort seems to have met with the approbation of those who were present and, among others, of the late Rev. Walter Griffith, then the superintendent of the Leeds circuit, who, being unable to fulfil his appointment at Hunslet the following Sunday, sent Mr. Smith in his place.

In the latter part of the communication to which reference has just been made, Mr. Smith offers a few sentences of judicious and pointed counsel to a young friend on the subject of his studies, which serve to show the deep interest which he felt in the intellectual improvement of those over whom he had influence; and with great kindness and modesty he proffers whatever assistance he might in future be able to afford. Of his own experience he says:

> I thank God for his goodness to me. He still keeps my feet in the narrow path, and I trust will to the end. He often causes me to rejoice in the hope of future glory, and I am hungering and thirsting after a larger earnest of it. I want to be entirely the Lord's.—I think I am in the way of Providence. I have but little time, but I would improve it to great advantage. Lord, help me!

The following is an extract from a letter dated May 24th, 1815:

> I thought I would defer writing for a few days, that I might give
> you a little information respecting the watch-night which was
> held last Monday. In the afternoon we had a local preachers' meet-
> ing, at which I was highly gratified and greatly benefited. At seven
> o'clock, Mr. Dawson preached from John 6:63: "It is the spirit that
> quickeneth; the flesh profiteth nothing." God was with him and
> accompanied his Word to the hearts of the congregation, and we
> had a refreshing season from the presence of the Lord. Mr. D.
> considered the church as the body, Christ as the head, and the
> Holy Ghost as the animating principle. He observed that the
> operations of the Spirit might be seen in the ministers, ordinances,
> and members of the church; ministers, in their qualifications for
> the ministry, their call to the ministry, the principal subjects, and
> the success of their ministry, etc. After the sermon, two excel-
> lent exhortations were given, and five persons exercised in prayer.
> Blessed be God, I think I never felt more determined by grace to
> *live for God.* O for wisdom! O for power from on high! According
> to your request, I have sent you a plan. You will perceive that I
> am still appointed to hold an important office. "Who is sufficient
> for these things?" May I ever hang dependent upon God! Amen.

Mr. Smith's religious friends now considered him as called to
a wider sphere of usefulness, and it was proposed that he should
enter the itinerant work. In these views he appears to have acqui-
esced without any very considerable hesitation. Upon the death of
Mr. Ault, one of the first Wesleyan missionaries to Ceylon, he was
deemed a suitable person to supply the vacancy. He was applied
to accordingly, and evinced the utmost readiness to comply with
the request, provided his parents could be induced to accede to it.
No insuperable difficulty presented itself from this quarter, but the
idea was abandoned in consequence of the questionable state of
his health. Some short time before, he had had the measles. This
disorder had left a cough and other unpleasant symptoms; and a
medical gentleman of the highest character, upon being consulted,
gave it as his opinion that a tropical climate would, under these
circumstances, be unsuitable to Mr. Smith's constitution.

During the whole of the time in which Mr. Smith remained at Leeds, by those not intimately acquainted with him, "he was merely"—to employ the words of an attached friend—"noticed as an amiable, pious youth, whose manners were distinguished by peculiar frankness, accompanied by the signs of an affectionate heart and blandness of disposition." The following is the testimony of Mr. Sigston, whose opportunities for observing him were of course frequent and ample:

> From the commencement he manifested an ardent desire to improve his mind, and especially with reference to the study of divinity. His general deportment was very exemplary, and he will long live in the recollection of several who then became intimately acquainted with him. There was one trait in his character which every Christian minister would do well to imitate—I mean his constant endeavour to promote the salvation of sinners. For this he studied, prayed, and preached; and I have often heard him *agonize* for souls. In this particular, I would humbly pray that his mantle may fall upon those whom he has left behind.

In the beginning of the year 1816, Mr. Smith engaged himself as an assistant in a seminary at Oulton, in the Wakefield circuit. As soon as he entered upon this situation, he interested himself deeply in the spiritual, as well as intellectual, improvement of his pupils. He frequently took occasion to talk to them on religious subjects, both in private and when together. Several were much impressed by his affectionate counsels, and one or two began to meet in class. In a letter to his parents, dated February 20th, 1816, he thus speaks of his engagements and prospects:

> My situation is remarkably pleasant. The duties it imposes on me I find no difficulty to perform. God has dealt kindly with me. "The lines have fallen unto me in pleasant places, and I have a goodly heritage." I have frequent opportunities of meeting with his people, and he has met with me and blessed me. Blessed be God, I trust he has begun a good work in the minds of some of the boys. When I speak to them about the salvation of their souls, some of them frequently begin to weep; and many of them say they never had such feelings before. I have a strong confidence

that R. G. is powerfully influenced by him who hath said, "None shall pluck them out of my hand." He has met in class twice, and is still determined by the grace of God to go forward. Blessed God, thou lovest young disciples; may he be kept by thy mighty power "through faith to eternal salvation." I feel my heart is engaged in the service of God. He has a right to ALL.

The situation of Mr. Smith at Oulton, however, was, in several respects, less favorable to improvement than that which he filled at Leeds. His opportunities for associating with pious people, and especially those of cultivated minds, were much less frequent; nor did he enjoy an equal measure of bodily health. Still his thirst for knowledge was insatiable; and, as far as his circumstances admitted, he assiduously occupied himself with reading and study. He had the satisfaction of maintaining an epistolary correspondence with his friend Mr. Stoner, who was now an itinerant preacher in the Holmfirth circuit. He also became increasingly acceptable as a local preacher. Those of his pupils who had manifested religious desires continued to afford gratifying evidence of their sincerity and resolution; and above all, his own spirit was more abundantly enriched with blessing from on high. "Religion," he remarks in his correspondence at this period, "*demands* my first attention. It *has* my first attention. I hope while I live I shall be employed for God and the best interests of my fellow creatures. Pray that the Lord would direct me into the way in which he would have me walk in this respect." His mind was not yet quite made up as to his duty to the heathen world, although, with unaffected modesty, he states it as his opinion that the wish of the Missionary Committee to employ him would immediately cease if they only knew him better. He concludes his remarks on this subject with the devout ejaculation, "To thy glory may I live, O Lord my God!"

In the course of this year he became quickened to seek the full power of the cleansing blood of Christ, and the utter extirpation of the carnal mind. In a letter to Cudworth, bearing the date October 5th, 1816, he says:

My heart is given to God. I am seeking and longing for all the mind which was in Jesus Christ. Blessed be God, I am encouraged by his gracious promises to persevere in seeking full salvation. I long to experience this purity of heart. For this I pray, read, study, watch, and trust. It is thy work, blessed God! Let me enjoy it. In your prayers do not forget him who blesses God for such parents, and who daily prays for you.

In the year 1815–16 there was a gracious revival of the work of God in the city and circuit of York. At the Conference of 1816, there were three hundred and fifty more members in society than twelve months previously. It was found necessary to erect an additional chapel, and in the autumn of this year the commodious place of worship in Skeldergate was opened. The labors of another preacher were in consequence required; and, application being made to the proper quarter, Mr. Smith was appointed to assist the Rev. Messrs. Lessey, Sr., John Nelson, and Stones, who were already occupied in this interesting field of Christian exertion.

CHAPTER 5

York
1816–1817

The life of every man has its epochs; and perhaps in no class of facts is the providence of God more strikingly illustrated than in the arrangement of those events which, either singly or in connection with a series, give the color to the characters and conditions of men, in this life and beyond the grave. Nothing can be less important in itself; nothing, according to human judgment, likely to be more insignificant in its results than the incidents which thus often direct the course or impel the tide of the most momentous of human interests. It follows that no event, however apparently trivial, should be disregarded; it forms one link in a mystic chain, the connections of which we may not at present discern but which, nevertheless, in its succession, will be connected with our best hope and our highest desire. No adventure, therefore, is so small as not to demand divine direction. God is to be acknowledged in ALL our ways; and it may be that in those very particulars which we foolishly deem too insignificant to require his sanction, he will bring our boasted wisdom to nought, and even allow the "serpent" tasting us, while we "lean on the wall" of our own house.[1] History is rich in illustrations of this subject. The festivities of Babylon proved fatal to Alexander after he had escaped the dangers of a hundred fights. Caesar overcame the barbarians and Pompey, and in the midst of his honors was slaughtered in the senate-house. The delay of a few hours detained in Britain a discontented Puritan, who in the reign of Charles I was about to exile himself to New England. That man was Oliver Cromwell. Bruce the traveler, unhurt by the thousand perils of the sea and the wilderness, was killed by a slip of the foot on his own staircase.

---

1. Amos 5:19.

But while to the man of presumptuous mind there is often latent danger where he least suspects it, to a spirit of humble and conscientious trust in God and reference to his will, divine direction and divine defence are indubitably ensured. While the one stumbles in the broad day, the other walks secure in the thickest darkness; and while the one is overthrown by the most insignificant agencies, the other passes unhurt through the whirlwind and the earthquake. It has never been the happiness of the compiler of these pages to meet with an individual who so fully embodied these views as his eminent and lamented friend. He introduced God into all things; sought his direction on the meanest, as well as on the most important, subjects; and although his life does not exhibit any of those remarkable coincidences which we dignify by the title of "peculiar providences," yet to one who attentively surveys it, there will be no difficulty in tracing the continued leadings of the divine hand—like a stream of silvery light flowing through sunshine and gloom—in all its periods.

An interesting illustration of this feature of his character is found in the following statement, communicated by a person who knew him familiarly. "I remember," says this friend, "his noticing some step which he had taken, in itself right, but in which he had not first of all ascertained the will of God, as the chief error of his religious life, the effect of which he traced through his subsequent experience. Well as I knew him before, nothing ever marked so strongly to my mind the unreprovable and earnest character of the whole of his Christian course as his thus singling out an omission which in the experience of Christians generally would, I fear, have excited little notice and certainly been soon forgotten."

We have already referred to the great epoch of Mr Smith's life as a man—his conversion to God. His appointment to the York circuit was the most important event in the course of his ministry—an event in which it would be scepticism not to recognize the finger of God. Hitherto we have contemplated him only as comparatively an ordinary character and an ordinary Christian; we have now to observe him assuming a higher ground and coming under the influence of those principles which were so remarkable and conspicuous in the succeeding periods of his life. When he came to York, he was in no respect esteemed a distinguished man. His talents were generally considered below mediocrity; in fact, he was not thought qualified for the ministerial duties of a circuit possessing so considerable a share of intelligence. Nor was he extraordinarily zealous; and his preaching possessed nothing of that forcible and stimulating character which afterwards rendered it singular. In addition to this, he labored under extraordinary diffidence; and Mr. Stones states that when it was his turn to preach in the city on a week-evening, he could never summon sufficient resolution to mount the pulpit if one of his colleagues was likely to be present; and in such cases the preacher who was disengaged usually had to occupy his place.

Still he had an active mind and was diligent in promoting prayer-meetings, visiting the sick, etc. What was of still greater moment, he was artless and sincere—a man of one motive and one desire, and he had capabilities for great energy which only waited to be called into action and directed aright. Had the most diligent and acute investigation been employed in reference to his situation at the commencement of the itinerant life, he could not have been placed where, according to human judgment, he would have enjoyed the advantages which surrounded him at York. This circuit has been for many years, in some respects, peculiarly interesting. There is a simplicity, a fervor, a forbearance, and a tenderness in the character of the people which render its recollections very dear to many who have labored among them. At the time to which our narration refers, there was an unusual degree of religious feeling, expectation, and desire in the neighborhood; and these circumstances were highly conducive to a valuable impression on the character of Mr. Smith at this critical period of his ministerial history. York is also inseparably associated with the memory of several eminent saints, of whom the Lord will record, when he "writeth up the people," that they were "born there." Under the influence of one of these, Mr. Smith came in a peculiar degree—I mean the late Mr. Richard Burdsall—a man whose name in that part of Yorkshire is as ointment poured forth.

But that which particularly tended to form the character, both personal and ministerial, of the subject of these memoirs was his association with the late Rev. John Nelson. This distinguished Christian and successful minister discerned in Mr. Smith the elements of an energetic and useful agent for Christ; and though they were then without order, or method, or direction, he gave them an impulse and arrangement which, in the course of a short time, issued in the formation of one of the most powerful and beneficent characters that in recent times has arisen among us.

There are many zealous preachers with whom Mr. Smith might have been associated who would have failed to produce anything like a revolution of his views and habits; and had not Mr. Nelson's character possessed a peculiar adaptation—perhaps I might say, affinity—to the native elements of his own, the probability is that even he would not have succeeded in his attempt to mould a mind so constitutionally daring and independent. It is worthy of remark, also, that Mr. Smith's first impressions were rather unfavorable to the influence which his revered friend afterwards exerted. Nor was it till Mr. Smith had heard him preach several times, and till especially he had seen the working of Mr. Nelson's principles—for he was even now in a degree a practical man—that his prejudice entirely gave way. And then, to render more deep the admiration of Mr. Nelson, which originated in observations on his public ministrations, his youthful colleague was struck with the nobleness, generosity, and tenderness of his nature, his exalted views of the fullness and glory of the atonement, the energy of his faith, the originality of his conceptions, and his extensive and practical acquaintance with human nature. In short, Mr. Nelson became his *friend*, and then there was no difficulty in the case. The noblest natures are the most fully capable of yielding to the power of Christian affection. Love lays his hand on the lion's mane and compels him to submit to the yoke.

The influence of Mr. Nelson and the other Christian friends who at this time contributed to model Mr. Smith's personal Christianity and public exertions appears to have operated in two ways. He became a man of increased fervor and assiduity in prayer. His diligence in closet duties in the first place arose, partly at least, from a sense of constant and imminent danger. Devotion had now become more fully his element. He engaged more frequently, and more at length, in communion with God, and usually had delightful access to the throne of grace. Under the benign and quickening influence of these exercises, his piety rapidly matured; his hunger and thirst after righteousness increased; and he labored diligently, giving up his desires and energies to the pursuit of entire holiness. According to the testimony of his early and endeared friend, the Rev. W. H. Clarkson, with whom he at this time became acquainted, it was in the course of the nine months he spent at York that he entered into the enjoyment of perfect love.

God will always honor a resemblance to himself; and it must be admitted that, in the absence of a considerable measure of this resemblance, no man was ever extensively useful. But it does not follow that a holy minister must necessarily be a very successful one; nor, in the case of the subject of these pages, would that view of his service to the church be the true one which centered exclusively in his personal devotedness to God. "This, indeed," as one of his friends remarks, "is a truth, but it is not the whole truth." The change which Mr. Smith at this time underwent was not confined to a higher attainment of the divine image; it extended itself to his views, his studies, and his style of preaching. The amplitude and energy of the first will be developed in the course of our narrative. Of the second, it may be sufficient to say that he now began to study human nature as it is rather than as it is delineated in books. He discerned the necessity of knowing man in his general character—his weakness, depravity, and capabilities; of acquainting himself especially with the vulnerable points in the sinner's heart; and the varied modes of address, and modifications of personal feeling, by which he might probably lay hold on the most powerful human passions and prejudices. He set himself also to consider the character and circumstances of each of the congregations to whom he was called to minister, and sought in his own heart the indications of the necessities, and the key to the affections of others. He learned the use of prayer as a means of ascertaining the description of truth which was adapted to the conditions of his several collections of hearers. In short, he became a man of bold and successful experiment on human nature, and ceased to estimate all preaching, and indeed all ministerial labor, except as it produced saving effects.

"Previous to his coming to York," says Mr. Clarkson, "he appeared to have studied the artificial science of sermonizing, rather than the divine art of winning souls to Christ. In his fellowship with Mr. Nelson, he got his mind fully enlightened as to the grand design of the Christian ministry, and as to the manner in which it was most likely to be accomplished." Another friend, whose abilities and opportunities for ascertaining the measure of his intellectual stature were of an unusual order, thus speaks on the subject of the style of preaching which he now assumed:

> It was from no inability to construct a regular and expanded discourse, according to the taste and practice of the day, that he confined himself to the simple but fervid and impressive style of preaching which he adopted. At the commencement of his ministerial career his sermons were more elaborate in their structure; but although I forget the particular circumstances which, as he told me, induced him to alter his plan, I know that he was decided by a conviction that in so doing the great *end* of preaching would be more fully accomplished. The change, therefore, was one of principle; and for the sake of this he was content to forego the reputation of advantages which even the spiritual part of the church are but too apt to magnify and deem indispensable, and to acquiesce willingly in being thought destitute of talents which he could not but be conscious were in his power. I know no harder "lesson that humility can teach," or self-denial submit to learn.

Of course all these changes, so material and permanent, were not effected at once. It took much time, much anxiety, much experiment, many tears, and a more maturely instructed faith fully to complete them. But it was at this time that the revolution of character commenced, to the perfecting of which a number of causes subsequently conspired. Among these may be reckoned, as one of influence, what the friend from whom I have just quoted supposes to have been the original cause of the alteration in Mr. Smith's style of preaching. The following is the result of that person's observation on the subject, some years after the date under which we now write.

A conviction where his own strength lay induced him, for the most part, to disregard those homiletical forms which are deemed (perhaps too uniformly so) essential to a public discourse; and the ardor of his mind hurried him at once into the heart of his subject. My own impression is that as his expectation of success was in a peculiar degree from the aids and effusion of the Spirit, the style of preaching he adopted left him more at liberty both to exercise such dependence, and to dwell on, and realize to himself and others, those appropriate truths through which alone he expected the Holy Spirit to work upon their minds; and that it was this consideration principally that dictated the change.

The former part of these observations, however, must be understood to apply specifically only to an early and comparatively immature stage of his ministerial history. In more recent years (as will appear in later chapters) he added to his other excellencies the recommendation of regularity in the form and arrangement of his discourses.

The following are extracts from his correspondence with his parents, and from a few private memoranda of the state of his religious experience. The reader will here find as well the occasional indications of the opinions to which reference has just been made, as evidences of a pleasing measure of advancement in knowledge and love. The first of these extracts is from a letter announcing his arrival at York and the commencement of his labors there. It shows with how low views of himself, with what determination to deal rigidly with his own character, and with what pious resolution he entered on the great work of an itinerant preacher.

To his parents:

Nov. 18, 1816. Various have been the exercises of my mind. I think my confidence in the Lord is a little strengthened. I am more and more convinced of the absolute necessity of being clear respecting my own salvation; and, blessed be God, I am saying, "Lord, I am thine; save me!" The people are very kind. I am only afraid that my coming among them will prevent some other person from coming who would be more useful. I feel, however, resolved to be diligent, to lay myself out for usefulness in every possible way, and to give myself into the hands of God. Never did I need your prayers so much as I do at present.

To the same:

Dec. 28, 1816. Since I wrote to you, I have not been very well. I have had a very bad cough; it has disqualified me, in a great measure, for reading and study. This has made me very uneasy. I have spent some almost sleepless nights. I have thought if God had called me to preach, he would have blessed me with better bodily health. But, blessed be God, I have been much encouraged with seeing and hearing that the Lord condescends to work by me. If it please the Lord to use me, he has a right to me. He shall have *all*: body, soul, time, talents—ALL ... I am reconciled to God by the death of his Son. I am seeking to be conformed to the image of my Savior. Christ is precious to me at this moment. I do not cease to give thanks for you, making mention of you in my prayers.

Jan. 3, 1817. My mind this day has been unsettled. I anticipate many difficulties in the work in which I am engaged. "Who is sufficient for these things?" *I am more fully convinced of the necessity of describing character.* What shall I do to know the hearts of men? How shall I know my own? *This* I must know. Lord, show it unto me, for thou alone art able.

Jan. 11. The Lord has been exceedingly kind to me this day. I have had some precious seasons in private. Never did I feel more— never, I think, so much—of the power of God, as at the prayer meeting tonight. My confidence in the Lord is stronger, but I want a clearer manifestation of his sanctifying presence. O for this killing and quickening word! Mr. Nelson prayed for it tonight.

Here it is worthy of notice that, in the experience of Mr. Smith, not only in the case just quoted, but in multitudes of other instances, a time of refreshing in public was preceded by special visitations in secret. The connection between the two is understood, more or less, by all Christians; but upon his mind it was impressed at all times with peculiar emphasis; and in the following pages it will be found frequently alluded to, in different forms of expression.

Jan. 15. Yesterday and today I have experienced much uneasiness of mind. I wish to please God, but I fear I am not where I ought to be. It matters not what I hear, or what I read; I have to do with

God. It is a personal concern. I shall quickly be gone; then where or what shall I be? O eternity!

Jan. 21. I have had this day a renewed sense of the favor of God and a foretaste of the rest from inbred sin. The blessing seemed to be very near. O that I may be enabled to lay hold of it tonight!

To his parents:

Jan. 23. The Lord is reviving his work in my soul. I am longing for an increased conformity to my Savior. I want more feeling for poor sinners. I must look to him who had not where to lay his head. I must view him in the garden, behold him at Pilate's bar, see him nailed to the cross, hear him say, "Father, forgive them, for they know not what they do," and the heart-rending cry, "My God, my God, why hast thou forsaken me?" It is this that melts the stony heart. God grant that we may be ever properly influenced by it! The Lord has lately brought many souls to himself in York. We are expecting a signal outpouring of his Holy Spirit. O that a gracious shower may very soon descend upon us! I have heard Mr. Nelson preach some such sermons as I never heard before. I never see my littleness as a preacher under any man so much as under Mr. N. He has the unction; this makes him great. He tells me that I must bless God for barren times. Mr. John Burdsall was at York last week, and from him I got some important directions respecting study. He recommended a few books to me, some of which I have procured. I am to write to him in a short time to let him know how I come on, etc.

Feb. 12. My mind has been much composed and stayed upon God for several days past. My confidence in him has been much increased. I feel conscious of my inability for the great work in which I am engaged, but he has all wisdom and power, and in him I trust. If he have called me to preach the gospel, he will qualify me; if not, he will, I trust, show me, and save my soul. Blessed be God!

To his parents:

Feb. 14. My soul is alive to God. Of late the Lord has revived his work in my soul, especially in private devotion. Never was I more fully convinced of the absolute necessity of personal holiness of heart and life. O this being dead unto sin, and alive to God through faith in Jesus Christ! The work in which I am engaged is the most important in the universe, yet I feel encouraged to put my trust in the Lord whose work it is, and who has engaged to give grace according to my day.

Feb. 26. Various, indeed, have been my exercises of mind during the last few days; but, blessed be God, my confidence in him is stronger. O this preaching! I have an increasing sense of my inability. May it drive me to God, instead of sinking my mind into a dejected state!

March 2. I feel happy in God. I can trust in Christ for my own salvation. But I am much concerned about preaching. O that the Lord would give me more satisfactory evidence of my call to this important work! I have, for some time past, thought that I was thrust out too soon.

March 9. My soul is longing, yea, panting after God, yet I want more ardent desires. I long to see souls converted to God. I want more sympathy. I drag my cold and hard heart to Mount Calvary; if the bleeding Lamb cannot warm and melt it, nothing can. I want more of the dying love of Christ shed abroad in my heart. Lord, help me! If thou canst use me, here I am at thy disposal. "Sanctify me wholly, body, soul, and spirit, and preserve me blameless to the coming of the Lord Jesus."

April 3. I am thankful that I am in my closet at half-past nine o'clock. O that I may be able to cultivate habits of regularity! [In allusion to his exercises of mind about preaching, he adds,]—I think, surely, no preacher was ever in my situation. Blessed be God, I can cast my soul on the atoning sacrifice of Christ.

Jesus, to thee my soul looks up.

To his parents:

April 8. O the happiness to know that my sins are put away by the sacrifice of Christ! Of this I have not the shadow of a doubt. I want more of the Spirit; for this I pray, for this I read, for this I believe, and I want to believe more. I must believe for salvation—not be saved and then believe. I have a painful sense of my inability for the important work in which I am engaged; but it is the work of God. He is all-sufficient. If he has called me to it, he will help me; if not, he will send me home again, and he will save me. I am in his hands, bless the Lord! I never was more sensible of the necessity of experiencing the truths of the gospel in order to preach them successfully to others. A *conscious* salvation is absolutely necessary.

The preceding extracts furnish a very inadequate idea of the anguish undergone by Mr. Smith in reference to the ministerial work. This was only known to his own heart, and to him by whom the depths of man's severest feeling are as perfectly understood as his lightest and most transient emotion. As an illustration of the extreme character of this distress, it will suffice to say that, with all the consolation which his faith could command, and all the support arising from confidence in God—which it does not appear that he ever lost, even in the time of his greatest conflict—he was nevertheless so overwhelmed by the exercises of his mind that, as he afterwards confessed, life itself was burdensome, and he wished himself a tree, or anything but a being endowed with sensation. On one occasion, as he told the writer of this sketch, having heard a strain of very touching music, he longed to be changed into some plaintive instrument, which might, without reproof or restraint, continually breathe forth its melancholy tones.

It is probable that Mr. Smith's views of the importance of the Christian ministry were, in the first place, as penetrating as the measure of his piety would allow. Had they been more impressive at an earlier period he would scarcely have been able at all to have endured them; and at all hazards he would most likely have refused to engage in an occupation so responsible. Yet that he was from the beginning convinced of his call to the work seems sufficiently obvious from his yielding to Mr. Stoner's remonstrance on the subject,[1] which would have been without significance or point had not he to whom it was addressed been conscious of the obligation

1. Page 28, above.

of the case. But his perceptions afterwards became so expanded and comprehensive that he was in the highest degree dissatisfied with his original views, and seriously doubted whether an impression so feeble as that which he at first experienced could be really a divine designation to the ministerial office.

It may rationally be questioned whether any person of Mr. Smith's temperament ever became in a high degree a minister of the Spirit without some such exercises as those to which he was so long and painfully subjected. It is readily admitted that there are some diligent and devoted ministers who have never known much, if anything, of such misgivings of heart. They have never had that poignant and distressing consciousness of their own inadequacy; that earnest and continued wish, if it were possible, to withdraw themselves from a situation of so much personal hazard, and connected with such high trust and accountability. These, however, are for the most part men of equable temper, to whose minds a state of repose appears most congenial. But on the other hand, it seems necessary that persons of sanguine temperament, of great ardor and buoyancy, should undergo a process of a more permanently impressive order. When, therefore, they have made every effort towards ministerial usefulness—when the powers of their minds have been exerted to the greatest possible tension—they are, by a sudden and prostrating burst of divine light, given fully to see how amazingly short they fall of what the ministerial office requires, and how utterly vain, considered of themselves, are all their exertions. Such a revelation, to a man of even and gentle temper, would cast him into despair; while in the case of the others, nothing less will save them from a degree of self-confidence, or from being satisfied with a comparatively low measure of devotedness and success. A powerful and consoling view of God's sufficiency usually comes afterwards and is accorded in proportion to the patient diligence with which the former exercises have been undergone, and the degree of self-renunciation which they have succeeded in producing.

Independently also of the *appropriateness* of these trials, as the means of preparing a minister of the Spirit, sanctified mental conflict is of itself greatly conducive to ministerial usefulness. No man was ever distinguished except by successful engagement with difficulty. The very terms which men employ to express their most exalted notions of honor usually involve the idea of opposition. Where there is no contest there can be no triumph. No Christian was ever eminent who had not many obstacles; no Christian minister who had not to wrestle with powerful temptation. Temptation, according to Martin Luther, is one of the ingredients which go to make a minister; and so essential did he deem it to the completeness of the character, that he associated it with the high and unquestionable duties of study and prayer. The fellowship of Christ's suffering produces conformity to his death; the fellowship of Christ's glory, in its fullness, is promised to him who *overcomes;* and, as well on earth as in heaven, the most splendid order of saints are those "who have come out of great tribulation."[1]

Nor is it difficult to trace, even in the very scanty description left by the subject of these memoirs of the state of his Christian experience, the immediate and practical results of the painful exercises to which we have now been adverting. One of the most observable of these is a strong desire for a more deep feeling of compassion and sympathy—more of the tender yearning of his blessed Master. As Christ suffered being tempted, that he might be able to succor those

---

1.   The reader will readily forgive the introduction of the following simple yet striking illustration of this subject from the pen of an eminent and singularly devoted French pastor:

I have before me two stones, which are in imitation of precious stones. They are both perfectly alike in color; they are of the same water, clear, pure, and clean; yet there is a marked difference between them as to their lustre and brilliancy. One has a dazzling brightness, while the other is dull, so that the eye passes over it and derives no pleasure from the sight. What can be the reason of such a difference? It is this: the one is cut but in a few facets; the other has ten times as many. These facets are produced by a violent operation; it is requisite to cut, to smooth, and polish. Had these stones been endued with life, so as to have been capable of feeling what they underwent, the one which has received eighty facets would have thought itself very unhappy, and would have envied the fate of the other, which having received but eight, had undergone but a tenth part of its sufferings. Nevertheless, the operation being over, it is done for ever. The difference between the two stones always remains strongly marked; that which has suffered but little is entirely eclipsed by the other, which alone is held in estimation and attracts attention.—*Memoirs of John Frederic Oberlin,* pp. 128, 124.

who are tempted, so did this faithful servant of Christ seek to obtain a higher qualification for his work by the influence of sanctified mental suffering; and he was thus enabled afterwards to comfort others with the consolation which he himself had received of the Lord. But the result of these trials, which bore more immediately on his ministerial character, were of still higher importance. The revelation that he now obtained of the greatness and seriousness of the office of a Christian preacher appears never to have left him. Henceforth he was a man of one object; and no demand involved too great labor, no sacrifice was too severe, no opposition too determined and complicated to deter him from diligently pursuing it. On the other hand, no man could more deeply feel the futility of all labor of itself, or seek more diligently for the aid of the Holy Spirit, upon every religious work, how small soever it might appear. To be a *minister of the spirit* was his highest ambition and his constant aim; and how fully he became such may be found recorded in multitudes of living epistles seen and read of all men.

In the month of May he was, by a slight illness, laid aside from his work for some short time. This affliction was probably sanctified to the tranquilizing of his mind; at least, after this, I find in his papers and correspondence no indication of those continually distressing anxieties on the subject of the ministerial work that previously preyed upon his spirits; and though his discouragement was not entirely removed, yet, as the following extract from a letter to his parents will testify, it was associated with greater calmness of feeling and more established resolution and hope.

> York, May 29, 1817. Of late I have had many visits from the Lord, especially in private. Mr. Bramwell once said, "If you wish for any great and lasting blessing, expect it in private." Many here speak very clearly on entire sanctification and I believe give satisfactory evidence that they are in possession of that blessing. Who is a people like unto this people? The District Meeting commenced on Wednesday. I was rather afraid that the list of books which I had read since I became a traveling preacher would have incurred the censure of the meeting; however, it was quite the reverse. I hope to be more diligent than ever. I still anticipate almost insurmountable difficulties in preaching. I am ashamed of my sermons, but I

yet hope. This hope, how it encourages—animates—strengthens! Mr. Nelson is as valuable to me as ever.

The following extract, dated August 20, 1817, will furnish a still more clear and satisfactory view of the state of his mind. It is from a letter addressed to the niece of Mrs. Nelson, Miss Ellen Hamer, who afterwards became his wife, and is now his mourning widow.

> O maintain holy familiarity between your soul and God. Make him your friend and associate. Cast all your care on him; he careth for you. I am glad that you have such an encouraging view of the fullness of the promises. Examine yourself by the Word, your experience by the promises, and your conduct by the requisitions. My soul is alive to God, and I am longing to be more conformed to the image of my Savior. I am determined by the grace of God to aim at souls. A minister of the gospel is sent to turn men from darkness to light, and from the power of Satan to God. I feel myself a poor, weak, unworthy, insignificant creature, but if the Lord please to employ me, he can make me useful. In him I trust, and they that trust in him shall never be confounded.

Then, in allusion to Miss Hamer's engagement at the time in a young ladies' boarding-school, he adds the following concise and pithy directions:

> As it respects the business of the school, maintain your authority, be attentive, do your pupils all the good you can, be an original in teaching, use familiar illustrations, make everything pleasing, and you will succeed.

CHAPTER 6

Barnard Castle

1817–1818

At the Conference of 1817, Mr. Smith was appointed to the Barnard Castle and Weardale circuit. His colleagues were the Rev. Messrs. Rogerson, Sr., and Elliot. He was now more fully thrown on his own resources, and he had ample opportunity of ascertaining the value of his new views and principles. His circuit was in many respects favorable to the experiment. It was of considerable extent, and the people were simple and lively. They had little of that false delicacy which in other places might have proved at this period a source of considerable discouragement. In general, they appear to have valued the zeal and labors of their new minister, and to have in a degree cooperated in his plans. From the beginning he was gratified with the field of usefulness in which he had been placed. A finely diversified country also presented to him those sources of delight which, to an observant and devout mind, the loveliness of creation never fails to open; and on the whole he entered upon his work with tranquillity of mind, and a religious resolution to give himself wholly to the duties of his sacred vocation.

Although separated in person from his friend Mr. Nelson, he still maintained an epistolary correspondence with him. Mr. Nelson's first letter is so pointed, so characteristic, and so paternal, that I think none of my readers will deem the insertion of an extract from it irrelevant to our present subject.

York, Nov. 7, 1817. MY DEAR BROTHER—I received your welcome epistle. I bless God for strengthening your body and soul, and also giving you to see some fruit. The gospel of God our Savior, preached in faith, will be followed with signs more interesting than even taking up serpents or drinking deadly poison and sustaining no harm thereby. Always go sword in hand and beg of God the power of the Spirit, while you raise it to his glory, that prejudice with every opposition may be cut down. Eye your Captain; hear his voice; follow closely; be deaf to the voice of the enemy. Now is your time to play the man. Do not study until your head aches. Lay your plans short but clear. Look always for divine aid; and after you have spread the net, close it with great care, that you may there and then bring some to shore. I lately heard a good sermon; the net was well spread, and at the close the righteous were encouraged and the wicked threatened; but no attempt was made to catch a fish. We had better catch a few fishes with a little net than dash with a great one and let them all slip under or by the side. Preach in the Holy Ghost; and before you dismiss your audience, offer them salvation now. Remember *first* to convert, and then the good fruit will *follow*; only, the rebel must lay down his weapons, yea, all of them, or he will not succeed with his Prince; but they may be all dropped in a moment. Never lose sight of present salvation, nor of God who is to work it. Give him all the glory. Should any attempt to praise you, dart immediately to God, "Lord, I am thine; save me!"

My soul is kept in peace and purity. I have some good times in the new chapel. We are all peace. Would to God we had prosperity also. We had better be saved in a storm than lost in a calm. God bless you. Write soon. I am, etc.

In a letter to his parents, dated September 3rd, Mr. Smith, after stating his safe arrival, proceeds:

The day after, I set out for Weardale. I went about twenty miles to a place called High House. I had a very pleasant journey, and was much pleased with the romantic scenes which presented themselves to my view. It is the finest dale that ever I saw. I arrived safe, and met with a hearty welcome. I preached on Saturday night, and again on Sunday morning and afternoon. You would have been astonished to have seen the congregation: there are but a few houses about the chapel, and yet there were well towards a thousand people. It is the largest chapel in the circuit. The people of Weardale are rather languid. The pressure of the times has had an unfavorable influence on their minds; but they hope to rise. They are celebrated for music up the dale; many of the women sing sweetly. I came to Barnard Castle yesterday. I went to see my colleagues, and we had prayer together.

I am much pleased with the circuit and people. My health, I hope, will be established. My soul is alive, blessed be God! I feel myself as a little child, and I have a child-like *confidence*. By the grace of God, I will aim at souls. I know you pray for me, and God answers you. Pray on. Mr. Nelson prays for me; God bless him.

About the same time, I find the following private memorandum:

I feel deeply humbled under a sense of my unfaithfulness. Still I am encouraged to put my trust in God. By his grace, I will aim at converting and saving souls. O for more fellow-feeling! I think my views of the plan of salvation are clearer, but I want more of the Spirit. My health is better than I expected. Yesterday and today, I have been unwell. May the Lord pardon my imprudence and help me to act with caution in future!

Caution was, indeed, the more necessary at this time, since his constitution was in a critical state; and in addition to much travelling, he not infrequently had to preach thrice on the Sabbath, and on every evening of the week besides. It would have been a happy circumstance had his care of his health (the duty of which he was always most ready to admit) extended itself fully to his public labors. Unless, however, he had entirely exhausted his strength and felt the immediate results of his extreme exertion in great debility; or by some other token equally palpable was made sensible of having acted imprudently, he does not appear to have been aware that he was at all injuring himself. The gradual undermining of his constitution was the natural consequence; and thus to the church and the world was early lost the light and guidance of a fair star from the moral hemisphere. At the commencement of his labors at Barnard Castle, however, his health was generally very good.

Under the date of September 27th he writes to his parents:

I am as well as I ever have been since I had the measles; and I have had I think more signal manifestations of the divine presence since I came to Barnard Castle than I ever had. O unite with me in blessing God for his continued and increased goodness. "Bless the Lord, O my soul, and all that is within me bless his holy name.

Bless the Lord, O my soul, and forget not all his benefits!" I see there is nothing like entering into God's design concerning us. He wishes to make us *perfectly holy* and to fill us with all his fullness. We should aim at this; not merely to get to heaven, but to be as fit for heaven as we can be, and to have as much of heaven as we can have while in this world. In order to achieve this, we must believe much. Let us give credit to God's Word, and realize the blessing in the promise. Let us behold as in a glass the glory of the Lord and be changed into the same image from glory to glory as by the Spirit of the Lord. Let us look on him in Jesus Christ; at his love, till our hearts are set on fire; at his purity, till we are made pure. It is by holding communion with God that we are transformed into his likeness. Let us come with childlike simplicity and confidence. Let us plead the blood!—plead the blood!

Blessed be God, it is good news. We are poor, helpless, hell-deserving sinners, but Jesus hath died for us—for *me*. O the sweetness of this!—for *me*. This makes me love God. It constrains me. Let us constantly feel this:

> O for a heart to praise my God,
> A heart from sin set free!
> A heart that always feels thy blood
> So freely spilt for me.

How insignificant the world seems when we have much of God!

In another part of the same communication he speaks of his happiness with his colleagues; and having now had the opportunity of judging more fully on the subject, he says, "I believe some part of the circuit will be very severe in winter, but I hope it will agree with me. At present the country is delightful, far more so than the neighborhood of York,"

To Miss Hamer:

Sept. 30, 1817. I am glad that you are longing for a full salvation. Bring it to a point. I urge your petition. He still says, "I will sprinkle clean water upon you, and you *shall be clean*." Has he not power? Yes, he is almighty to save. Is he not willing? Yes, for "For this purpose the Son of Man was manifested, that he might destroy the works of the devil." Does he not require us to be holy? Yes, for without holiness no man can see the Lord. And he says,

"Be ye holy, for I am holy." O, then, be sensible, you *must* be holy; acknowledge that you cannot make yourself holy, and be assured that he is willing to make you holy, and I hope this will induce you to say, "I will not let thee go until thou bless me."

His anxiety on the subject of preaching had not yet entirely left him, as will appear from the following extract from his private papers, under the date of October 16:

I am humbled on account of my vileness, my ignorance, and unfaithfulness. I am much concerned on account of my inability for the awfully important work in which I am engaged. If the Lord be not with me, I shall sink. If he has called me to the work, he will stand by me; he will be my helper. Lord, help me to get into and abide in thy will. Good is the will of the Lord.

It sometimes consists with God's good pleasure, and perhaps it is a special act of divine sovereignty, to apply with peculiar power to the minds of his people, while engaged in devotion, some appropriate portion or portions of Scripture. Those to whom such communications are granted are frequently persons in circumstances of trial or in some other condition that demands more than ordinary direction and comfort. Only those who have heard the voice of God can form an idea of the stability and repose which it communicates to the spirit. The subject of these memoirs was at this time privileged by this emphatic adaptation of Scripture truth to his condition.

In two several instances, while engaged in prayer, passages of God's Word were applied with divine power to his mind. The one was Proverbs 3:6: "In all thy ways acknowledge him, and he shall direct thy paths." The other, Matthew 6:33: "But seek ye first the kingdom of God and his righteousness, and all these things shall be added unto you." Their united influence on the one hand soothed, and on the other, stimulated him. From this period I cannot understand that he was ever disturbed on the subject of his call to the ministry, and the following extracts will readily be admitted as indicative of the quickened state of his personal piety. The most interesting feature of the first is the emphasis with which its writer speaks on the subject of humility—that virtue, the perfection of which is perhaps, of every other in the Christian character, the least enjoyed and the last attained.

To his parents:

> Oct. 22, 1817. O what humblings I have had of late! My soul has been in the dust before the Lord, and at the same time I have felt the confidence of a little child. I love to be in this state. In your class, press the necessity of purity of heart; show that it is received and retained by faith; show it to be a privilege. O what a happiness to be delivered from *all* anger, peevishness, pride, malice, etc., and to be filled with gentleness, patience, humility, love, etc.! Let us feast ourselves on Jesus. Let us contemplate him, our infant Savior, in Bethlehem, and be humbled. Let us listen to him—"Foxes have holes, and the birds of the air have nests, but the Son of Man hath not where to lay his head"—and be humbled. Let us look at him washing his disciples' feet, and be humbled. Let us walk with him in the garden, view him prostrate on the ground, sweating great drops of blood, hear him crying, "If it be possible, let this cup pass from me," and be humbled. Let us behold him on the cross, and be humbled; yet still let us be confident.

And this is evangelical humility, since that alone can consist with confidence. Nothing can be more anti-evangelical than the doctrine which makes inbred sin necessary to the production of humility. The lowliness of mind which the gospel commends is the lowliness of love, and not the depression which results from the consciousness of our own depravity.

In another part of the same letter, Mr. Smith thus speaks of the work of God:

> The work of the Lord is prospering, especially at Barnard Castle. Glory be to God! A spirit of prayer is given. Last Tuesday week four souls obtained liberty; on Sunday night, after preaching, two or three, and last night, one. There seems to be a good work on the minds of many. O that God would pour out his Spirit upon us in an abundant manner! There are several seeking purity of heart; this gladdens me. I am expecting to see good days. You are in a deplorable state at Cudworth—so many backsliders, so many who have been pricked to the heart and yet will not turn to the Lord. O do not cease to cry to God! Make an effort; do not be ashamed

to be a fool for Christ's sake. You will remain low if extraordinary exertions are not made. Extraordinary effects are not produced by ordinary means.

The soundness of these views will be appreciated by all who have made themselves conversant with the indications of a prosperous and promising condition of the work of God. One of Mr. Smith's principles was that the world was to be benefited through the agency of the church, and that no signal manifestations of divine power in awakening and conversion were to be expected except through a quickened state of piety among believers. In the foregoing extract, he refers to the means, through the divine blessing, upon which we may rationally anticipate the salvation of sinners and the enlargement of the tabernacles of the faithful. These are: increased desire after holiness, the spirit of prayer, and extraordinary effort among the people of God. And if those who are most holy are likely to be the most concerned for the salvation of men, and to have most of the power of the Holy Ghost; if God *will* hear the voice of his elect, who cry day and night to him for the outpouring of the Spirit; and if they who are most scripturally diligent and energetic *must* be the most successful; it follows that the principle to which we have just alluded, with the practical illustration which accompanies it, is in the most perfect manner borne out by Scripture and matter of fact.

The converse also must be equally true, that where no sinners are converted, a church must be either defective in its views or low in its attainments. Where there is no influence diffused without, the principle of piety is certainly languid within; where there is no *shining*, there is little *burning* light; where souls are not saved, Christians in general must be imperfect in the character or degree of their personal religion. The building up of believers on their most holy faith was a principal object of Mr. Smith's ministry, but he never considered this species of labour successful except as its results were indicated in the conversion of sinners. That edification he justly deemed of a very low and questionable order which was not accompanied by a spirit of intercession for those who were without God, by "the work of faith and the labor of love." He rationally argued that where there were no answers to prayer, the throne of grace could not be very ardently importuned; where there was no outpouring of the Spirit, the promise of the Spirit could not be very determinately pleaded; where there was no exertion for perishing men, there could not be much of the bowels of Jesus Christ. And whether that Christian society can be correctly esteemed in a high and advancing state of improvement where prayer is cold and cursory, where faith is weak, and love is listless, it requires no great sagacity to determine.

They will have a very partial and incorrect view of Mr. Smith's ministry who suppose that its benefits were wholly confined to those who were awakened and converted through its instrumentality. It is true that he embraced every opportunity of attempting to rouse the consciences of such as were hardened by the deceitfulness of sin; but he anticipated extensive success, even in this respect, only as the faith and intercessions of God's people were brought to accompany his efforts. His labors, he knew, could be succeeded or frustrated by them alone. Hence he strove primarily to obtain the quickening influences of the Spirit upon them; nor was he unsuccessful. Had it been possible that his exertions for the conversion of sinners should have proved utterly unavailing; had he never succeeded in awaking the most transient alarm in a stupefied conscience, or the smallest desire after goodness in a depraved heart; had he never plucked one brand from the fire, nor ever pointed a penitent to the blood of Christ; still his memory would be blessed in our Zion for the many instances in which, through his instrumentality, the Spirit was "poured upon us from on high, and the wilderness" became "a fruitful field," and what was once esteemed a " fruitful field," in the comparison, was "counted for a forest." In short, the retrospect of his labors furnishes the most satisfactory sanction to his favorite opinion on this subject, that *he most certainly and perfectly edifies believers who is most ardently and scripturally laborious for the conversion of sinners.*

Mr. Smith's experience continued to be, in general, happy and prosperous. In one of his letters at this time, he says: "I am sometimes oppressed with an overwhelming sense of the goodness of God. My cheeks are moistened with tears of gratitude, and I can call God my Father with such a divine sweetness." In another, "You may be sure that the enemy has been very busy with me. But, blessed be God, I feel power to cast my helpless soul on his mercy through Jesus Christ." Again:

> I have a praying heart and a child-like confidence, but I want to be delivered from all distrust. I can feelingly say, "Christ died for *me*, and ever liveth to make intercession for *me*." Yet I see I know but little, I enjoy but little, compared with what I might know and enjoy. But I wish to proceed; my privileges will unfold, my prospects will brighten. I expect to meet with difficulties, but my Savior says, "Be of good cheer, I have overcome." In his strength I am strong. I have had some refreshing seasons of late in private; these greatly encourage me.

In consequence of the prospects of good things in Barnard Castle, Mr. Smith was betrayed, at the latter part of the year, into exertions too great for his strength; and the result was that for several weeks he was very unwell and compelled entirely to relinquish his beloved employment. This affliction, under such circumstances, was particularly trying to him; but he says of it, in one of his letters, "Upon the whole, I think I have learned some important lessons; it is good for me that I have been afflicted." Of his labors and prospects at this time, he remarks: "Blessed be God, I am encouraged, because I do not altogether labor in vain. The people in Barnard Castle are rising, and increasing a little. I am increasingly attached to them. O that the Lord may fully qualify me for my important work!" At the beginning of 1818: "I feel a disposition to labor for souls. The people, I mean the society, have got a grand impulse; and I trust the work is going on. Ride on, my God! May every house be visited and every heart feel thy power." A few weeks afterwards: "The people in Barnard Castle are alive to God, and the prospects in some parts of the circuit are rather cheering. We want a shower of heavenly blessing."

In the early part of the year 1818, a revival of the work of God took place in his native village. On this occasion he writes to his father as follows:

> I am glad to hear of your prosperity at Cudworth. Only keep the people in action, and you will get on. There is no standing still.

O let us come to God for great blessings. He is willing to save the world. We must make a noble effort in the name of God, and we shall not labor in vain. The gospel, preached in faith, must do execution: "Cry aloud, spare not, sound an alarm in the holy mountain." Offer a present, free, and full salvation, and you will see signs and wonders. Blessed be God, he is doing great things for us at Barnard Castle. On Sunday last, four souls got into liberty; on Tuesday night, at the prayer meeting, seven more. Many, I believe, are awakened; and I expect the work will go on. My soul is alive to God. I am longing for more of the life and power of godliness. I wish to feel what I preach.

To the same:

April 7, 1818. Blessed be God, he is carrying on his work in my soul. Of late, I have had some precious seasons, both in public and private. I want more of the spirit of prayer. There is nothing like getting filled with the Spirit before we go to the house of God, and then pleading with God in the presence of his people. The Lord is deepening his work in the hearts of professors among us, and awakening and converting sinners. Last Tuesday night, at the prayer meeting, there were six souls set at liberty. On Sunday night, I preached a funeral sermon from John 9:4. At the prayer meeting afterwards, the Lord brought three into liberty, and I believe many others were much affected. "This is the Lord's doing, and it is marvelous in our eyes."

To the same:

April 27, 1818. God is still carrying on his good work among us. I was much pleased with a woman at Staindrop, who was converted as clearly and in as scriptural a way as ever I knew any one. I saw her the next day; she was still praising God. I asked, "How was it that you were made happy?" She said, "While you were showing Christ as a Savior, and telling us to believe on him, I thought, 'I can believe, I can believe!' Something said, I was to *repent* longer yet, but I said, I think I can *believe*—I do believe! *It came,* and I believed that God had pardoned all my sins." On the Tuesday following, a woman came from the same place to Cockfield on purpose to get her sins pardoned. At the prayer meeting, after preaching, she was enabled to believe on Jesus Christ to the saving of her soul; and she went home rejoicing in God. O let us go on in the name of the Lord and expect present effects; yea, let us be restless for the salvation of souls. We shall not labor in vain. What condescension in God to use such unworthy creatures in the accomplishment of his designs! The walls of Jericho fell at the blowing of rams' horns. Of late I have had many visits from the Lord. I can venture on Christ for deliverance from sin; but I want to be filled with all the fullness of God, to have the mind of Christ in me. O urge your members to purity of heart! Much will be done by a single act of faith in the blood of Jesus.

To Miss Hamer:

July 10, 1818. Let us look attentively into our hearts, look into the written Word, and look up to God for the light of the Spirit to shine upon the heart and the Word. Whatever we discover in us contrary to the Word, let us bring it before the Lord (for we cannot take it away ourselves) and plead with him until we feel power to venture on Jesus for its destruction. When God speaks to the inmost soul, "Be clean," all corruption and defilement shall depart, and purity shall be diffused through the soul. Let us not be discouraged, however frightful our hearts may appear, and however feeble and helpless we may feel; Jesus's blood is all-cleansing. Jesus's grace is all-powerful. Jesus is ours by faith. God offers him to us. O let us lay hold of a whole Savior! Let us force ourselves to the foot of the cross, lift up our eyes, and look to Jesus, till our hearts are pierced to the very bottom with his dying love. Let us continue there till his love has melted us down, that we may receive and retain the impress divine. "Be ye perfect, even as your Father which is in heaven is perfect." "Be ye holy, for I am holy." "For this purpose was the Son of God manifested in the flesh, that he might"—what? Subdue the works of the devil? Weaken the power of sin in the heart? No; but "that he might *destroy* the works of the devil." O then let us say as God says, "Destruction—complete destruction—to sin!" Faith, which is a *continued* and *conscious act,* will preserve us pure. Let us cry day and night to God for this faith—perfect faith. We shall meet with much opposition. The world cannot do with this; the devil hates this; but few professors will do with this; but *the will of God! the will of God!* Make good use of your time; live by rule; love Jesus with all your heart; be solicitous to have those committed to your care early converted to God. I am, etc.

Mr. Smith this year attended the Conference which was held at Leeds. A principal reason which induced him to do so was a wish to converse with, and receive instructions from, the venerable William Bramwell. Of the manners of this eminently useful minister, Mr. Smith's prepossessions were rather unfavorable; and he thought it not improbable that his inquiries would be met with something like austerity. At every expense, however, he resolved if possible to gain the information which a man of Mr. Bramwell's character would alone be able to communicate. Like the Athenian who said to his opponent in council, "Strike, but hear me," so he, with his characteristic disregard to everything but improvement, was willing to be rebuked if he could but be instructed. He had several opportunities of being in Mr. Bramwell's society. On one occasion, if not oftener, he was accompanied by Mr. Stoner; and in this interview the distinction between the two friends must have been sufficiently marked. Mr. Smith asked a variety of questions on the subject of Christian experience, and the best methods of carrying on the work of God. He stated at large his own difficulties and plans, proposing inquiries on each as it was mentioned. Mr. Bramwell looked surprised, but replied in a concise and generally in a satisfactory manner. Mr. Stoner in the meantime sat by, listening with profound attention, and in unbroken silence; and, as he afterwards confessed to him, wondering at the readiness with which his friend succeeded in drawing forth the lights of an experience so deep and varied. In the course of a few days after this conversation, the treasures of Mr. Bramwell's ardent and manly heart were for ever sealed to all earthly inquirers by the hand of death; and it was an act worthy the close of so signally useful a life thus to cast his garment on one who already emulated his spirit and who subsequently, to so great a degree, inherited his success.

The period which Mr. Smith spent at Barnard Castle he at this time described to Mr. Clarkson as having been the happiest year of his life. He had been rendered very useful; his talents were more fully developing themselves, and his character was becoming more perfectly formed. It would, therefore, have been agreeable to all parties for him to have been re-appointed to that circuit. The only reason which prevented this arrangement was the state of his health, which, by a situation so northerly, and a climate occasionally so severe, had in several cases already been injuriously affected. It was thought, therefore, that the southern coast of England was more adapted to his present circumstances; and he was accordingly appointed to the Brighton circuit, under the superintendence of the Rev. F. Calder.

CHAPTER 7

Brighton
1818–1819

To a man of nervous mind and resolute decision nothing seems to give so great an increase of determination as the absence of all encouragement from without. A feeble spirit will falter in such a situation; but the necessity of relying on his own resources makes him who is capable of elevation truly great. Where mighty interests—the interests of truth and eternity—depend upon the principles which such a one has espoused, or the plans which he has adopted, his perseverance under discouragement is the highest moral sublimity, the truest and most illustrious heroism. No test of strength of mind is so severe or so infallible. An obstinate man may be rendered confirmedly pertinacious by contradiction; but it is the attribute of nobleness and greatness alone to triumph over neglect, indifference, or neutrality.

The removal of Mr. Smith to the south of England was, at this period of his life, the most happy arrangement which could have been made for the establishment of his principles and the completion of his character. The societies to which he was now introduced, it is true, were able to discern and value ministerial zeal and diligence. They possessed many members of great personal devotedness, whose piety was silently but powerfully influential, and whose hearts longed for the prosperity of Zion. But the appearance among them of a man of Mr. Smith's peculiar views and singular modes of operation was in many respects a phenomenon. They had no previously formed standard of ministerial character by which he could be measured; there was no class under which he could be ranged. They required time fully to comprehend the man and his principles. They were at first startled and confounded and, of consequence, unable to come to any correct or even sober judgment concerning him.

Meanwhile, he was of course without any considerable cooperation on their part. He was alone—a man "to be wondered at." It was now to be tried whether he would sink into an ordinary character, or whether he would become more established and eminent than he could have been with the assistance and encouragement which, in the northern parts of the kingdom, he might at all times to a considerable extent have secured. It was a crisis of fearful importance. Is it too much to say that the destinies of multitudes of immortal men were suspended on its issue? And if those philanthropic spirits who serve "the heirs of salvation" contemplate with the deepest concern the moral crisis of the history of an individual, with what anxiety must they watch the turning-point in the character of a minister, and especially such a one as John Smith! All glory to God! The decision in his case was worthy of a strong and enlightened mind. How many will for ever adore that grace which at this time wrought effectually in him, the revelation of the great day alone can determine.

The following extract from his private papers will serve to show with what pious and humble feeling he entered upon his new situation:

> Brighton, Sept. 1, 1818. I am ashamed before the Lord on account of my unfaithfulness; yet I feel encouraged to put my trust in him. He is a God of boundless mercy. I have an affecting sense of my own inability; the Lord must undertake for me. I wish to be useful. By the grace of God, I will aim at souls. The people here seem very kind but the place is very gay. I know not how to proceed. Lord, direct and strengthen me, and deliver me from the fear of man. O that this may be a growing year to my soul, and a year of general prosperity throughout the circuit!

In his superintendent, Mr. Smith found a true and staunch friend, who discerned and estimated his real character and worth, and who has amply contributed to these pages, principally characteristic notices of the present period.

At the commencement of his ministry at Brighton, Mr. Smith seems particularly to have dwelt upon the high calling of believers, with the hope of producing among them that quickened feeling which, as has been already noticed, he deemed essential to permanent prosperity in the church of God. He particularly insisted on the necessity of Christian perfection, and that so frequently and emphatically that at the conclusion of one of his sermons on the subject, a member of the congregation met him at the foot of the pulpit stairs and accosted him with, "So, Mr. Smith, you have given us the old thing over again!" "Yes," said he, with his accustomed benignant smile, "and till all your hearts are cleansed from sin, you shall have it still over and over again." Nor were his labors in this respect without encouragement. In one of his first letters to his parents, dated October 8th, he says, "I trust we shall have a revival of the work of God. We have had a few drops; several seem to be longing for purity of heart."

The following interesting testimony of the state of his own experience, and the fullness and force of his views of evangelical truth, is also from the same letter:

> Blessed be God, he is carrying on his good work in my soul. He has of late poured upon me a spirit of wrestling prayer. He has also astonishingly answered my prayers. I hang upon him continually, and he keeps my soul in peace. There is nothing like getting into, and keeping in, action. Let us be constantly at work. We shall soon have done. The night is coming on apace. If our work be done, we shall have a calm night. The Lord still inclines me to offer and urge a present and full salvation. The gospel offers nothing less than a full salvation. We want the faith that cannot ask in vain—a holy panting, labouring, hungering, thirsting—and this *constantly.* Self-denial is absolutely necessary. Do not hear much of "I am unworthy" in your class. God does not save us because we are worthy but because he is bountiful. God knows that we are unworthy, and therefore offers us the blessings of salvation *freely.* Should we not be nearer the truth if we were to say, "I will have a little sin to remain; a little pride, anger, love of the world, etc.?" O let us say as God says, *Destruction to sin!* And we must have the *whole man* engaged constantly in the service of God or we shall soon be tainted again.

Under the date of Nov. 2nd of this year he writes thus to Miss Hamer:

Last Monday morning J. P. died of a cut which he had received the week before. I saw him the day before he died. I said, "Is the Lord precious to you in your suffering?" He replied, "I have a steady reliance upon him." "Do you think you will die?" "I have not thought much about it; but if I were to die now, I should go to heaven." He was nearly eighteen years of age, had met in class about five years, and for three years had had a constant sense of the approbation of God.

While I have been pleading with God, I have seen such a fullness of Christ that I have been encouraged to cast my poor soul upon him. The Lord is very kind to me, but I am like a child who cannot rest except when his father is saying, "My dear child, I love you." I want more faith. God has given me the greatest proof of his love in giving his only-begotten Son to be the propitiation for my sins. I *must* believe whatever I feel. *All prayer* will secure us constant victory. Stand firm, and Satan cannot harm you. He is a chained enemy. Do not put yourself within the reach of danger, and, "having done all, stand." Mason's *Self-Knowledge* will do you good.[1] Read your Bible much.

Of Mr. Smith's personal attachment to the Word of God, and its influence on his ministry, the testimony of Mr. Calder is very striking:

The whole force of his mind was directed to the object for the accomplishment of which he undertook the Christian ministry— presenting God's truth to men in order to effect the salvation of those who heard him. And while he was fully capable of luxuriating in the riches of literary pleasures, he steadily and conscientiously avoided that species of reading which, though innocent in itself, was not immediately connected with his great work. He would frequently remark to me, in relation to any work of a generally interesting character, "Yes, it is very good, I have no doubt. I shall be glad to read it at a future period, if God spare my life; but I must read my Bible more. I must devour God's book, or how can I know his mind? I do not legislate for others, but I must be allowed to follow my own views on this subject." The result was a distinctness of conception on the subjects of evangelical and

---

1.   John Mason, *A Treatise on Self-Knowledge*. Edinburgh: Manners & Miller etc., 1810.

experimental religion, accompanied by a simplicity and perspicuity of statement, I had almost said, unique in its kind. His style and manner of preaching always accorded with the great end of leading men to God; it was emphatically scriptural and, in the best sense of the term, highly theological. Indeed he was a great divine, if understanding God's Word makes a man such, and especially understanding and exhibiting God's mode of saving a sinner.

His memory was extraordinary, and I believe it would have cost him very little trouble to have committed any moderate sized volume to its storehouse. To God's book his pious and devout heart turned as to an ever-living fountain of truth and light, to satiate and delight his soul. He usually read twelve chapters, or the whole of a Scripture book in a day, and committed a portion of it to memory. In consequence of being short-sighted, and not able to read when traveling on foot, he was accustomed to repeat some considerable portion of the sacred oracles as he itinerated his circuit; and when I informed him on one occasion, in a village where he met me to assist in holding a missionary meeting, that he must preach before the public meeting commenced, it being his appointment, he smilingly replied that he had no sermon to preach, but that he would go into the pulpit, and repeat the epistle of St. James, having just done so on the road as he walked to the village. I need scarcely add that we had not the epistle so repeated; yet it ought to be stated that amongst those causes which contributed to the wonderful success attending his ministerial labors, the aptitude with which he could use the sword of the Spirit may be deemed not one of the least. To souls in distress on account of sin, his quotations of Scripture, as suited to their state, were singularly appropriate and attended with blessed effects.

His own views of divine truth might, with great propriety, be described as those of a minister of the Spirit. His mode of presenting the subject of God's love to man, his willingness to save sinners, the value of the atonement, and the power of faith to secure personal salvation, as known in its different degrees of justification, or entire purity, might well entitle him to the designation of a master in Israel.

Notwithstanding his simplicity, plainness, and vehemence, the congregations at Brighton increased considerably soon after his arrival. Some, no doubt, came from motives of curiosity; many were

surprised, and a few were terrified. His own feelings may be readily gathered from the following sentences from a letter to a friend
written in the beginning of November:—

> Our congregations increase at Brighton, but we are not got into
> the way, I am afraid, of looking for present blessings. This is of the
> greatest importance. He cannot do many mighty works because of
> our unbelief. In the circuit, I had a prayer meeting after preaching
> in every place during my last round; we saw nothing very particu-
> lar. Perseverance—*we must have souls converted!*

He appears constantly to have lived under the influence of this
last sentiment. Whether in the pulpit or in the closet, in social interaction or alone, he never lost sight of the great design of his mission.
"Of that species of preaching," Mr. Calder observes, "which only
produced intellectual pleasure, he had a holy abhorrence." Nothing
can be more characteristic of the man than his remark to a friend, on
sermons in which power of intellect or imagination is almost exclusively predominant: "They *achieve* nothing, Sir." Perfectly capable as
he was of appreciating what was refined and intellectual, a sermon
which achieved nothing, however characterized by taste, argument,
eloquence, or even abstract and generalizing theology, was to him
merely as the play of the painted fly in the sunshine, whose parent
is a worm and whose life is a day.

> The importance of the object of his vocation held his faculties
> in a state of excitement which was too rigid to be affected by
> lighter interests. All his subordinate feelings lost their separate
> existence and operation by falling into the grand one. There have
> not been wanting trivial minds who have marked this as a fault in
> his character, but he is above their sphere of judgment. The invis-
> ible spirits who fulfil their commission of philanthropy among
> mortals do not care about the objects we so much admire; no more
> did he, when the time which he must have devoted to them would
> have been taken from the work to which he had consecrated his
> life. Such a sin against taste is very far beyond the reach of com-
> mon saintship to commit. It implied an inconceivable severity of
> conviction that he had *one thing to do;* and that he who would do
> some great thing in this short life must apply himself to the work

with such a concentration of his forces as, to idle spectators, looks like insanity.[1]

Mr. Calder continues:

Where the results which he desired did not attend his own ministry, he would spend days and nights almost constantly on his knees, weeping and pleading before God, and especially deploring his own inadequacy to the great work of saving souls. He was, at times, when he perceived no movement in the church, literally in agonies, travailing in birth for precious souls till he saw Christ magnified in their salvation. He was accustomed to say that a preacher ought to have restless solicitude on the subject of fruit; that God demands this of us, and that wherever it is found it will secure his approbation. How far he was right, let the case of Jeremiah testify, who said, "If ye will not hear it, my soul shall weep in secret places for your pride, and mine eyes shall weep sore, and run down with tears"; or indeed the Prince of preachers, in his weeping over Jerusalem.

To his parents, who were now as desirous to receive his counsels as they were formerly anxious that he should listen to theirs, he thus writes:

Nov. 13th, 1818: Have your enemies *without;* allow them no place within. Open the door of your heart wide. Invite Christ, yea, beg of him to come in, and dwell, and take up all the place—to be Sovereign. He will put down all rule and authority, and bring every thought into subjection. Hear what he says, "Behold, I stand at the door and knock: if any man hear my voice and open the door, I will come in to him, and sup with him, and he with me." Do you believe him? He is more ready to enter than we are to receive him. The devil will rage when he appears, but we must tear ourselves from ourselves, the world, and the devil. When Jesus Christ fills the soul, the commandments of God are not grievous. You know there are many who say, "I desire, I would wish, I would wish above all things to serve the Lord." Now suppose a man to fall down in your street, and you were to hear him say, "I desire, I would wish, I

---

1. A passage from Foster's *Essays*, pp. 126, 127, accommodated to the present subject by an intelligent and familiar friend of Mr. Smith

would wish above all things to get up!" What would you say? Why, "Man get up, do not sit whining there. Try—make the attempt."

God commands us to be holy; we cannot make ourselves holy. He has promised to make us so: let us enter into his designs. Be close with your class; tell them they *must* be saved from sin. You are right respecting looking to Jesus. This is the way to get, keep, and increase in purity. Let us look *intensely, steadily,* and *constantly* to Jesus; then we shall be pervaded with the rays of his glory, and reflect his image in the world. "We all, with open face beholding as in a glass the glory of the Lord, are changed into the same image from glory to glory, as by the Spirit of the Lord." Through mercy I continue pretty well. The Lord has blessed me with some signal revelations of his love in my soul since I came to this place. Yesterday Mr. Adams (who is going on a foreign mission) and I had a blessed time in brother D.'s chamber at Lewes. While we were pleading with God and throwing ourselves on his mercy and protection, he came down and blessed us abundantly. O it is a good thing to plead with God! We want more Bramwells, Longdens, Nelsons. God can "do for us exceeding abundantly above all that we ask or think." I have had many conflicts. Christ is strong and at hand to deliver. Praying that God may bless you with his great salvation, I am, etc.

P.S. How comfortable we are in our family! Mr. Calder is nothing but kindness to me.

Of Mr. Smith's humility and watchful jealousy over himself the following private memorandum will give some idea.

Dec. 6, 1818. I am more fully persuaded of the necessity of look-ing constantly to Jesus in order to be preserved from falling, yet I am afraid I am not sufficiently sensible of the great evil of falling. Gracious God, deliver me not up to vile affections! I wish to be more diligent in redeeming the time and in my studies. I am persuaded that much depends on this. I have been one of the most unfaithful of all the servants of God, yet I am encouraged to come to him, because I "have an advocate" with him, "Jesus Christ the righteous," and

> Jesu's blood through earth and skies,
> Mercy, free, boundless mercy cries.

In still further illustration of these amiable and Christian qualities, Mr. Calder relates the following incident:

> During Mr. Smith's residence in Brighton, a certain female became deeply distressed on account of her condition as a sinner. He deemed it right to pay her several visits in order to instruct and pray with her. The husband, a violent, unconverted man, was greatly incensed at these intrusions and, it was said, put Mr. Smith out of the house by violence. After his departure from the circuit, this man was converted; and he then greatly deplored his treatment of our friend. In London, I subsequently adverted to the man's behavior, saying to Mr. Smith that I understood he had thrust him out of the house. "No," said he, "he did not do that; but I saw that he was under the power of strong feelings, and I apprehended that he was about to lay hands upon me. I therefore left the house, not afraid of him, but afraid of myself, not knowing to what I might have been tempted had he touched me."

Nor did his low opinion of himself refer merely to those moral accomplishments which were the most remote from his natural character. It extended itself to the qualities in which, by the united influence of nature and grace, he seemed most fully to excel. How severe, for example, is the following piece of self-accusation!

> Dec. 11. I have not had that lively sense of the presence and favor of God, the whole of this day, which I wish to enjoy. I am deeply sensible of my ignorance and of my want of ability for the work of the ministry; yet the Lord is all-sufficient, and he will qualify and help. I trust I shall be more diligent than I have been. *I have to lament my instability in everything.* I have not prayed against it as I ought to have done. By the grace of God, I will make a renewed effort.

Under the same date as the foregoing he writes thus to Miss Hamer:

> I am glad that the good Spirit of God continues to strive with you; but I would just say, do not let him strive: *yield* to him. Be led by him at all times. Be as much in private as possible. Come to the throne of grace with boldness. God's having given his Son is an *infinite* and everlasting proof of his willingness to save us to the

uttermost. O get transforming views of Christ; these you must get in private. Do not rest without the constant enjoyment of the perfect love of God. Get deeper baptisms, signal revelations of the love of God in your heart. Experience the Word; feel that you have the same Spirit that inspired the sacred penmen. Of late I have had severe and peculiar temptations; and, blessed be God, I have had strong and peculiar consolation and support.

In reference to the work of God, he adds:

Our prospects in the circuit are very cheering. Congregations increase; the people in many places are greatly quickened, and some are brought out of darkness into God's marvelous light. Last Tuesday night, in one of our country places, there were many in distress; and several professed to be made happy. On Wednesday night also there were some in distress. O! If we were always filled with the Holy Ghost before we go to the house of God, we should see signs and wonders.

Mr. Smith's letters to his parents usually contain a few words specifically addressed to his mother; and as she was often much afflicted, they commonly suggest some topics of consolation. The following is a specimen:

Dec. 22. Your bodily indisposition has a tendency to weigh down your spirits, but cast body and soul on Christ. However you may feel, trust in Christ. Cast your burden on the Lord, and he will sustain you. Like as a father pitieth his children, so the Lord pitieth them that fear him. The father attends to the *afflicted* child *because* it is afflicted; and we have not a High Priest who is not touched with the feeling of our infirmities, etc.

Nothing could be more sober and scriptural, nothing farther removed from the visionary and enthusiastic, than Mr. Smith's sentiments on the subject of Christian consolation. One of his friends relates that "to a person suffering from debility, he said, 'You must not make joy the criterion of your state, but confidence in the *truth* of God. It would be a miracle for you to rejoice.' And again, to the same person, 'Now do not be giving way to despondency because you are weak. I used to do it, but I know better now. I use my privilege, and rejoice.'"—Meaning, of course, by the term "rejoice" in this latter case, not to describe the abounding of active delight, but the calm satisfaction arising from an unshaken sense of God's fidelity.

In the letter from which the above is extracted, he elsewhere remarks:

> Let us plead with God for deeper baptisms. We want more of the Spirit. This should be our grand petition—*the Spirit*. He will purify, transform, strengthen, comfort; yea, all is in the Spirit. Give God no rest. How soon can he come down and shake the mountains and dash the rocks to pieces. We may be assured if we are not saved, the hindrance is in us. Let us take hold of our fellow-creatures, consider ourselves one with them, and plead with God for them. Blessed be God, he is beginning to work among us in different parts.

The preceding extract displays one of those grand principles to which Mr. Smith was so much indebted for his usefulness—*sympathy; the taking hold of our fellow-creatures and making ourselves one with them.* To this, indeed, the most obvious forms of love to souls and exertion for their welfare are distinctly referrable. No man feels the value of the soul of another who has not been made sensible of the worth of his own soul. No man discerns the malignity of sin in the world who has not felt its bitterness and terror in his own heart. No man is awake to the peril of the ungodly who has not trembled under the sense of personal danger. No man forms a correct estimate of the value of the atonement who has not had the blood of Christ sprinkled on his own conscience. In proportion as religion becomes a matter of deep personal interest will be the concern which a man feels for the salvation of others. God might have employed (had it consisted with his wisdom) a race of intelligences superior to men as the heralds of his truth; and had luminous perceptions of his character and sensitive jealousy for his glory been the sole qualifications required for a minister of Christ, there is no question but that they would have been inconceivably better fitted for this office than any human beings. But they could have possessed no sympathy with those whom they addressed, and herein would have lacked an essential element of the ministerial character. God has therefore appointed sinners to be instructed and awakened by the instrumentality of those who have themselves been in the darkness and sleep of sin. Men are to be exhorted to repentance by those who have themselves repented. Christ is to be proclaimed as a Savior. The duty of proclaiming him, therefore, rests on those who experience his salvation; and heaven is to be offered to the spirits of the faithful by these who personally enjoy the lively hope of possessing it.

With these arrangements, so fitting in themselves, the whole of Christianity is in the most perfect harmony. Christ, as our great High Priest, was rendered perfect by being invested by our nature and our sympathies, and having that nature tried, and those sympathies fed, by undergoing the same temptations to which we are subjected. He was incarnated not merely that he might make an atonement for sin, but that his human nature might be filled with horror on its account, and might enter into a full perception of the infinite peril of sinners. These impressions he received with such weight in the garden and on the cross that his soul was exceedingly oppressed with amazement and agony. And now being for ever glorified at the right hand of the Father, the memory of these causes him to long for the salvation of an apostate world with infinite passion, till "of the travail of his soul he shall see the fruit,"[1] and his boundless desire shall "be satisfied."

> The great principle of vicarious suffering which forms the center of Christianity spreads itself through the subordinate parts of the system, and is the pervading if not the invariable law of Christian beneficence. He who, with a due sense of the greatness of the enterprise, devotes himself to the removal of the moral wretchedness in which human nature is involved, will find the sad quality of these deeper woes is in a manner reflected back upon himself, and that to touch the substantial miseries of degenerate man is to come within the infection of infinite sorrow. And this is the law of success in the Christian ministry, that highest work of philanthropy. Every right-minded and heaven-commissioned minister

---

1. Lowth's translation of Isaiah 53:11.

of religion is baptized with the baptism wherewith his Lord was baptized; and he knows that, by the great law of the spiritual world, the suffering of substitutes enters into every procedure of redemption.[2]

Some eminent ministers have been possessed by so great a jealousy for the honor of God and by so determined a resentment against sin that their minds have been shaded by sternness rather than softened by compassion. But there was a native softness and susceptibility about Mr. Smith's affections which, when sanctified by the power of grace, would have peculiarly disposed him, had he been merely an ordinary Christian, to have wept with those who weep. And while on the one hand, as will be hereafter shown, he never forgot the claims of the divine purity, and thus invested with an extraordinary power his denunciations of sin, he preserved the full flowing tide of human feeling; and the condition of sinners inspired his heart with an unutterable pity. He entered so fully into their misery and peril, and had so poignant and distressing a sense of the malignity and heinousness of their violations of the law, as to be often indescribably oppressed. In illustration of this part of his character, Mr. Clarkson says that he held the opinion "that sin must be repented of by someone, and that if sinners would not themselves repent, the people of God must repent in their behalf. It was therefore a settled principle with him to 'confess the sins of the people.' And I remember to have heard him remark that 'unless a preacher carries about with him a daily burden, he is not likely to see many sinners converted to God.'" That he himself carried about this burden, Mr. Calder's testimony will be sufficient to evince. This gentleman remarks, "I have often seen him come down stairs in the morning, after spending several hours in prayer, with his eyes swollen with weeping. He would soon introduce the subject of his anxiety by saying, 'I am a broken-hearted man; yes, indeed, I am an unhappy man; not for myself, but on account of others. God has given me such a sight of the value of precious souls that I cannot live if souls are not saved. O give me souls or else I die!'"

---

2. Isaac Taylor, *Natural History of Enthusiasm.*

And as the sympathy which he felt for sinners was unusually strong, so was it also peculiarly practical. This was strikingly manifested in the case of penitents. "When you are with people in distress on account of their sins," he sometimes said to the compiler of these memoirs, "you must not only pray for them, but you must throw yourself into their circumstances. You must be a penitent too. They must pray through you, and what you say must be exactly what they would say if they knew how."[1] He carried out the same principle into the matter of faith. "It is possible," said he, more than once, "to believe for a penitent." In confirmation of this opinion, he has related instances in which, when he has been laboring to exert this faith of sympathy, actual faith has arisen correspondingly in the mind of the sinner; and the power of God and the joy of salvation have burst upon both as they simultaneously appropriated the atonement of Christ.

To his parents, Mr. Smith writes:

Jan. 25, 1819. I was very glad to hear that my dear mother gets more bodily strength, and with it an increase of the power of faith, power to trust in God. They that trust in him shall never be confounded. I was very glad to hear that my dear and respected father has got a greater victory over his spiritual foes, a more *settled* peace, and that he is blessed in his labors. What encouragement! Labor on. "There is no work in the grave." The work is glorious, the reward will be great. *Will be*, did I say? It *is* great. Preach in faith. Expect that God will work, when, in obedience to his authority, you go to offer salvation to perishing sinners. In prayer, plead with God; and in preaching, plead much with the people. We do little *now* unless we get the people into action. Through mercy I am in a tolerable state of health and am choosing God for my portion; goodly portion! Satisfying portion! Good Mr. Spence of York once said to me, "Give *all*, and take *all*." Thank God, I feel power to give him my undivided heart, and I expect to be filled with all his fullness. The Lord has astonishingly blessed me of late, and he will bless me. He has saved

---

1. In *The Life of Henry Longden, Minister of the Gospel; Compiled from His Memoirs*, p. 44, there is a case mentioned which beautifully illustrates this method of treating a penitent.

My eyes from tears of dark despair,
My feet from falling into hell.

Wherefore to him my feet shall run;
My eyes on his perfection gaze;
My soul shall live to God alone;
And all within me shout his praise.

The following statement of the way of salvation, from the same letter, is very simple and happy. It is a specimen of the form in which Mr. Smith greatly delighted to propound the truth.

Jesus Christ is the gift of God to a lost world. "It hath pleased the Father that in him should all fullness dwell." Faith is the condition on which we receive the blessings of the gospel. I am a lost sinner. Jesus is offered to me. I trust in him and am saved. I *continue* to trust, and am continually saved. God testifies this by his Holy Spirit. So all the way through, in every situation and in all circumstances, if we only trust in Christ, we cannot be confounded. What is it that I want? It is in Christ, and Christ is offered to me. Then I must take what I want in Christ. Nothing but a want of this faith can prevent me from enjoying the blessing. This completely strips man and puts the honor on God's grace in Christ. This is the gospel, good news, glad tidings. "Glory to God in the highest, on earth peace, good will to men."

O for a trumpet voice,
On all the world to call.

Of the progress of the work of God he remarks:

I think we are rising a little throughout the circuit. My dear colleague has had some glorious seasons. At Framfield a number of praying souls were met together to spend a day during the Christmas holidays. Mr. C. had to go that way; he called and preached to them. While he was preaching, the power of God came down. Several cried aloud for mercy. I suppose there were twelve in distress, and one of the local preachers was enabled to believe for entire sanctification.

At the district meeting held in London in the month of May, Mr. Smith was appointed to assist in conducting a watch-night at

City Road Chapel. The whole of the preceding afternoon he spent in earnest entreaty for the divine blessing upon the meeting. He had great enlargement in delivering an exhortation on the occasion; and while he was afterwards engaged in prayer, the influence of the Holy Spirit descended in an unusual manner. The effect was extraordinary. Some cried aloud under a consciousness of their sin and peril; some were unable to repress exclamations of praise to God; while others were so overwhelmed as to be obliged to retire from the chapel. Among these last was a baker who had been accustomed to follow his business on the Sabbath day. His alarm was so powerful that he was bowed down towards the earth, and it was with great difficulty that he succeeded in reaching his own house. When he retired to bed, sleep had forsaken him. He arose in inexpressible agony, and casting himself on his knees, wrestled with God for about two hours, when the Lord pardoned his sins, filled his heart with joy, and his mouth with thanksgiving. His wife also soon experienced the same blessing, the immediate result of which was that they altogether relinquished baking on a Sabbath day and sacrificed the gains of iniquity, which amounted to one guinea per week. "I had an interview with them," says Mr. Clarkson, "about two years afterwards, and they assured me that the Lord had so prospered them in their business that they had been gainers ever since."

Mr. Smith was at this time a stranger in London; and the day after the occurrence of this remarkable scene, he became the subject of pretty general conversation among those who had been present. His character was of course freely canvassed, and the opinions respecting him were very various. Even among his brethren assembled at the district meeting there was this diversity of sentiment. This was what Mr. Smith everywhere expected; and though it never deterred him from what he considered his duty, it was often a sore trial to him that his labors were not appreciated by some of those whom of all men he most honored and loved. In this feeling there was nothing selfish, except, indeed, so far as he identified himself with the work of God. He was personally independent of the opinions of men, of how great influence soever they might be; but where hearty cooperation was withheld by any who had the ability to assist his plans, he felt that injustice was done to the cause of Christ, and hence his regrets. It is proper, however, to remark that it was a very rare case for him to be known without being in the highest degree esteemed, both personally and ministerially. It is only, therefore, to cases of casual fellowship, such as the foregoing, that these remarks apply.

In the course of the district meeting, some conversation took place on the decrease in the number of our members during the preceding year, and several measures were suggested to prevent the recurrence of so melancholy a circumstance. Among those who spoke on the subject was a preacher of the highest character and influence, who had known Mr. Smith before he entered on the itinerant work, and who highly estimated his devotedness and ardor. After having alluded to several other particulars, he added, with much emphasis, "If we all possessed the burning zeal of the brother who addressed us last night, we should not have to lament any diminution of our societies." This remark, from such a quarter, had a happy effect upon the minds of those who had previously been unacquainted with the worth of the person to whom it referred. To Mr. Smith himself it was highly gratifying; it was so full a recognition of the value of the spirit which he took such pains to cherish, that he subsequently recollected it with much thankfulness. "I have reason to believe," says Mr. Calder, "that he often afterwards remembered Mr. B., where it is of most importance that we should not forget our friends." Many other instances might be cited in which Mr. Smith's singular excellence was acknowledged by men to whose opinions the highest deference is due. The venerable Walter Griffith, for example, under whose auspices Mr. Smith commenced his labors as a local preacher, met with him some years afterwards and with profound delight wept over him as he said, "You, my dear brother, have from the beginning preserved your simplicity"—adding much more in the way of approbation and encouragement. But his character demands not the applause of men, as it cannot be affected by their censure. Some may have been induced, by the testimony of those whom they respected, to offer him a measure of their approbation; but his dearest lovers are such as knew him most familiarly, many of whom are men too fully of his own stamp to be materially influenced, except by the distinct personal perception of worth and virtue.

The following is an extract from a letter to his parents, dated June 11, 1819:

My health is better considerably than when I came to Brighton. The rides, air, etc., agree with me very well. I may yet be strong to labor. All things are at God's disposal. His will is heaven to me. The Lord is carrying on his work in my soul. I have, I expect to have, conflicts with the powers of darkness; but the Lord is my helper and defence. "The name of the Lord is a strong tower; the righteous runneth into it, and is safe." God is everywhere. Faith realizes his presence—the presence of a Father—and will not a father protect and defend his child? Will he not provide for him and give him tokens of his affection? I want more of the simplicity of faith, and I am aiming at it. We frequently attempt great things without capacity to do them. What should we say to a person who wished to plough, sow, buy, sell, and to transact a great deal of business, when at the same time he was so unwell that he could scarcely walk across the house? We should say, "You really cannot do what you wish; you must go to the doctor; you must have something to remove your weakness." The depravity of the heart renders us incapable of doing God's will; it is a disease; it is debility; it pervades the system. But there is "balm in Gilead"; there is a "Physician there." Thanks be to God! "The Lord thy God will circumcise thine heart, and the heart of thy seed, to love the Lord thy God with all thine heart, and with all thy soul." "I will sprinkle clean water upon you, and ye shall be clean; from all your filthiness, and from all your idols will I cleanse you." If he speak health and soundness into the soul, we shall be capacitated to do his will. We shall do well to wait at his feet till he speaks. I am looking for a deeper baptism of the Holy Ghost. I am greatly encouraged by what God has already done for me, and by his numerous exceeding great and precious promises secured to them that believe. It is well to dare to take God at his word, to venture on the promises as well as we can, notwithstanding all opposition and difficulty, until it is easy to lay hold of the blessing, to claim it as ours in all its fullness and glory. We cannot believe too much; we cannot believe too soon. A man who is in perfect health naturally desires to be in action; he does well to be in action. When God has written his law in the heart, his commandments are not grievous. The sum is this: the first business of a diseased man is to get cured... Our prospects in this circuit continue cheering. I have seen the grace of God displayed in the conversion of sinners since I wrote to you.

Mr. Smith excelled in pastoral qualifications and duties, and was often distinguishedly useful in private society. As Mr. Calder relates:

Kindness was peculiarly prominent in his moral constitution and gave to his piety the most interesting forms of sweetness and benignity. And this induced an individual, who was no mean judge of religious character, to observe of him, that he had the piety of a certain distinguished saint and minister [who has already been alluded to in these pages], with more of the milk of human kindness. Hence the absence of all austerity from his manners. Of this, children seemed to be conscious, and soon attached themselves to him with peculiar fondness, which he amply returned. In this respect he resembled the founder of Methodism and, I may add, the Founder of our holy religion also. Not satisfied with merely doing the work of the pulpit, he deemed it right to acquaint himself with, and frequently to visit, every family connected with the society. An unconverted individual in such a family became the subject of his peculiar solicitude, and he was placed upon his list to be specifically remembered before God, with many tears and persevering intercessions. This ceaseless concern for the children and servants of our people was attended with glorious results. My house was frequently the scene of holy triumph; for if a visit was paid to me by any of the children of our friends residing in other parts of the kingdom, they became the objects of his peculiar regard. By his kind and affectionate behavior, he first ingratiated himself into their favor, and then, watching the effect of his admonitions, he was restless till they obtained the mercy of God. Never shall I forget the case of one of the sons of the late Mr. B. of London, upon whom, while paying a visit to my house at Brighton, Mr. Smith commenced a serious attack on the subject of his salvation. This was followed up from day to day till the young man became duly impressed with the importance of religion; and not long after, our departed friend called me into his study to join with them in praising God for having bestowed upon this person a sense of pardon. He shortly after returned to his family "a truly converted character," and subsequently became a zealous local preacher. The daughter of one of our London friends was brought to God in a similar manner.

Another incident which occurred about this time will serve to exemplify the same subject. Having to go to a distant part of the Brighton circuit, Mr. Smith stayed to dine at an intermediate village. After dinner, an interesting and intelligent servant girl of about fourteen years of age, who was engaged in the room in which he sat, arrested his attention. "Come hither, my dear," said he, in his usually serious and impressive manner; "I wish to speak to you." She immediately came, and looking very earnestly in his face, awaited, with an appearance of great interest, what he had to say. "Do you know that you are a sinner?" he asked. Heaving a deep sigh, she replied, "Yes, Sir." "Do you know that you will be lost unless your sins are pardoned?" "Yes, Sir." "Are you unhappy?" "Yes, Sir." "Do you ever pray?" "Yes." "Do you *say* your prayers, or do you ask God for what you feel you want?" "I say my prayers." "But you could ask me for anything you wanted, could you not?" "Yes, Sir." "Suppose you were a very poor girl, and went to Mrs. S. to beg, you could tell her of your distress, and ask her to give you something?" In a voice full of emotion, she replied, "Yes, Sir." "Well, you are a poor distressed sinner. God pities you. You can ask him to forgive you. Shall I pray for you? What shall I pray for?" The poor child could not reply for weeping. They then kneeled down, and in a very few minutes she began to cry aloud for mercy and to confess and bewail her sins in a remarkably fluent and affecting manner. She continued to cry till God revealed his Son in her heart. The change in her countenance and accents was astonishing. She praised God in a loud and joyful voice and with a faith that greatly surprised Mr. Smith, who stood at her side, interceded for her relations, for all sinners, and for the world at large. Her gratitude taught her new and eloquent language. With extraordinary emphasis she said over and over again, "Jesus has died for me! Jesus has died for me! Blessed Jesus! Blessed Jesus!—my God!—my Father! God pities me; God loves me, and I love my God! O, when shall I be with thee in glory, to praise thy name for ever and ever?" etc. She continued on her knees for more than an hour, and her state of rapture was so extreme that, as Mr. Smith afterwards said, it seemed as if it had been impossible for her to have survived so overpowering a revelation of the divine love.

In the month of July, Mr. Smith visited Chichester to assist in the opening of a new chapel and remained there for several days. His labors in that city were honored by God. He preached one evening from 1 Peter 3:13: "Who is he that will harm you, if ye be followers of that which is good?" and had great liberty of speech. During the concluding prayer, the influence of God descended on the congregation in a remarkable manner, and several groaned audibly under the burden of their sins. Mr. Smith cried out, "Now let your hearts yield!" and began to pray again. He then came down from the pulpit, and Mr. Hiley, the resident preacher, continued to plead with God on behalf of the distressed. Mr. Smith, in his usual way, immediately addressed those individuals who were seeking salvation, and exhorted them to trust in Christ for a present deliverance. Arrangements had been made for letting the seats in the chapel, but all other business was forgotten in the urgency of the cries of penitent sinners; and the meeting was protracted to a late hour. Nine persons were ascertained that evening to have been brought into the enjoyment of the pardoning love of God, and many others still remained under deep and painful concern for their souls.

Mr. Smith thus writes to his parents, Aug. 5, 1819:

> My soul is kept in peace; frequently I am filled with holy triumph, and I rejoice in hope of the glory of God. "The lines are fallen unto me in pleasant places; I have a goodly heritage." "Bless the Lord, O my soul, and forget not all his benefits." It is reasonable that I should devote myself to the service of God. Thank God, I have this power. I do present myself to him "a living sacrifice," and through Christ he accepts of me. I am engaged in a work in which my soul delights, the preaching of the glorious gospel of Jesus Christ. It is an awfully important work, but those whom Jesus Christ appoints to it, he engages to help and support in it. I will trust in HIM.

CHAPTER 8

Brighton Continued

1819–1820

At the Conference of 1819 Mr. Smith was re-appointed, with his friend Mr. Calder, to the Brighton circuit. His feelings, in reference to the past and his hopes for the coming year, are stated in a letter to Miss Hamer, dated August 14:

> During the year that is past I see much cause for shame and confusion of face; but O, it has been a year of mercy! What long-suffering! What signal outpourings of the Spirit, both in public and private! What displays of the grace and power of God among the people! I cast my unworthy soul on the mercy of God, through the mediation of his Son Jesus Christ. I trust in him for pardon, and holiness, and heaven. I wish that all I have and am may be a sacrifice acceptable to God through Jesus Christ. I trust we shall see glorious days. It stands in the power of God. "Ask, and ye shall receive, that your joy may be full." I am thankful to God that a few, during the past year, have got demised from all sin. I trust that God will raise up many more witnesses in this circuit of his power to save to the uttermost…. On Monday night, a woman got into liberty at the prayer meeting. That night also a poor lad that goes with a crutch was weeping in the chapel yard after the prayer meeting on account of his sins. A few of us went with him into the chapel again, and God removed his burden and caused him to sing for joy. These are encouraging displays of God's mercy. I hope we shall expect greater things. We may have, yea, we *shall* have, if we ask.

The following expression of filial feeling is very interesting. Gratitude to parents or other earthly benefactors is in itself so pleasing that the generality of mankind dwell upon it as something intrinsically complete and satisfactory. Mr. Smith, as will be here remarked, employs it to a higher ultimate object; and this application of the

89

natural charities of man's heart to the production of a stronger faith in God is delightfully characteristic. It displays a mind searching diligently the ordinary trains of human feeling for the most holy purposes and stretching beyond the creature, however fair and venerable, to the Fountain of all purity, perfection, and love:

> Oct. 1, 1819. Your kindness towards me aids me much in my approaches to God. It is said, "If ye then, being evil, know how to give good gifts to your children, how much more shall your heavenly Father give his Holy Spirit to them that ask him." I think—what is it that my parents would not do for me? What is it that they *have* not *done* for me? They have provided for me, wept over me, prayed for me, dealt tenderly with me, forgiven me and, under God, have been my spiritual parents too. They cared for my soul as well as my body. God regarded them and crowned their efforts with success. Their kindness has been a flowing stream. Well, God is my heavenly Father; he cares for me; there is no evil in him. He is full of pity and compassion. He has given his Son. He is willing freely to give all things. I may come to him with confidence. I do come with confidence, with the confidence of a little child; and he blesses me. He gives me his Holy Spirit. Of late I have had such revelations of the love of God in my soul, such baptisms of the Holy Ghost, as I never had before, and such as I had no conception of. God is not only able, but willing, to do exceedingly abundantly above all that we ask or think. "Open thy mouth wide, and I will fill it." We want more faith; power implicitly to rely on what God has said—to take God at his word.

> Faith, mighty faith, the promise sees,
> And looks to that *alone*.

I see more clearly than ever that God *himself* is the portion of his people. All the promises lead into God. Faith looks at them as living springs, always sending forth something fresh. There is an infinite depth in the promises. Let us daily, through the promises, by faith, draw more of God into our hearts. "If any man thirst, let him come unto me and drink." "The water that I shall give him shall be in him a well of water, springing up into everlasting life." I am happy, increasingly happy in God. God is my portion. "Bless the Lord, O my soul." "Christ *is* in me, the hope of glory." I have the earnest of heaven in my heart. This is my treasure. I esteem everything else as nothing in comparison of this. I long that every child of man should participate in the same blessedness.

> What shall I do to make it known,
> What thou for all mankind hast done?'

Thanks be to God, he is blessing us in some parts of our circuit. Some are rejoicing in perfect love; others are gasping for it. And although in some places we are low, God can, and I trust will, raise us. We must *pray*. "Ask, and ye shall receive!" Bless God for such words as these. How are you coming on in your class? What number in society? What prospects in Cudworth? Are the backsliders quite dead? "Come, O breath, from the four winds, and breathe upon these slain!"

Our next quotation from the same correspondence is beautifully illustrative of Christian perfection—beginning and ending in humility, and including delight in Christ, devotedness to God, joy in the Holy Ghost, heavenly-mindedness, confident desire, trust in the atonement, and victory over temptation. The writer appears to labor for expression and to feel the inadequacy of all human language. It is no matter of surprise that, with the enjoyments to which he alludes, he should long to see others in an equally elevated state of salvation:

Nov. 29. Thanks be to God for his continued and increasing goodness to me, the unworthiest and most unfaithful of his servants. What shall I say about my soul? O my dear parents, Jesus was never so precious to me as at present. He is the fairest among ten thousand and the altogether lovely. My soul is penetrated with his excellencies. All I want is in him, and he is mine. I have power to give him my whole heart, and I have the witness that he takes it. His Spirit dwells in me, and reveals to me the beauties of my Savior. I "rejoice with joy unspeakable and full of glory." My "conversation is in heaven." My treasure and my heart are there. God fills my soul. I know that he has taken away the body of sin. In obedience to him, I reckon myself "dead indeed unto sin, but alive to God through Jesus Christ." God is my portion. His fullness is mine. Yet he is "able to do exceeding abundantly above all I ask or think." I am looking for fresh discoveries of his glory. My soul thirsts for God. I never needed the blood of Christ more than I do at present. But I have it, and I never made so much use of it as I do now. I have been mightily assailed by the powers of darkness, but Jesus is my protector. Protected by omnipotent love, what can harm me? "Thou wilt keep him in perfect peace whose mind is stayed on thee." I wish to live in the act of casting my helpless soul upon Christ. I am thankful for your prayers and for the prayers of God's people. I have the prayers of some who have power with God. I am filled with shame when I turn my eyes backward,

> But lo, from sin, and grief, and shame,
> I hide me, Jesus, in thy name.

God is working among us. Many of the people are rising. Several are panting for entire sanctification. Their expectation shall not be cut off; God will speak for himself. He will raise up in this antinomian country, I trust, many witnesses of his power to save from all sin and to keep in that state. My spirit is filled with grief at the prevalence of iniquity around us. I find relief in Christ. "He is the propitiation for our sins, and not for ours only, but for the sins of the whole world." O my dear parents, be solicitous to have all the salvation of the gospel; labor, pant, struggle, believe, and "be filled with all the fullness of God." Give my kind love to your class, and tell them from me that Jesus is waiting to do all they desire for the salvation of their souls. Honor him by trusting in him.

The beginning of the year 1820 was marked by a considerable increase of religious feeling in the Brighton circuit, and Mr. Smith had the high satisfaction of seeing the grace of God displayed in several instances of clear and striking conversion. The following is an example: Calling one day on Mrs. M., a pious lady of Lewes, he there met with her niece, who was under concern for her soul. He engaged in prayer with peculiar sweetness and was afterwards led to speak of the excellencies of the Savior and the happiness of those who are united to him. His word was accompanied by special unction, and Miss —, the young person before alluded to, was so powerfully affected that she arose from her seat and, casting herself on her knees, began to plead with God in earnest prayer for the blessing of a present salvation. In a short time, hope sprang up in her heart. She exclaimed, "I *will* believe," and instantly the Comforter came. She rose and cried, "The Lord has washed away my sins for the sake of the blood of Christ"; and in an ecstasy of gratitude and triumph, she flung herself on the neck of her rejoicing relative, exclaiming, "It is you that have brought me to this!" with similar expressions of joyful feeling. They then united in the praise of a pardoning God. If my information be correct, two other persons in the same family were, a few days afterwards, through Mr. Smith's instrumentality, made partakers of the blessings of saving grace.

In a letter to Miss Hamer, dated Feb. 5, 1820, Mr. Smith thus speaks of his own experience:

> My soul is kept in peace and purity. Glory be to God! What charms there are in Jesus! "Unto you that believe he is precious." I believe; and God testifies that he approves of my faith by continually sending the Spirit of his Son into my heart, crying, "Abba, Father." "I am grafted in the true vine. Life flows into my soul and shows itself in buds and fruit; love, joy, peace, etc. I wish to be filled with the fruits of righteousness, which are by Jesus Christ to the glory and praise of God." "I hunger and thirst after righteousness." Blessed are such. My soul longeth after God. He is all my desire. I am yet but foolish in using the means, especially prayer. I want more of Bramwell's spirit, more of Longden's spirit, more of Nelson's spirit. It is to be had. I believe I shall have it. Lately God has signally blessed me in visiting the sick. "It is better to go to the house of mourning than the house of feasting." My soul has been filled and expanded. The excellencies of Jesus have been more fully revealed. It is good frequently to visit the abodes of the afflicted, especially when Jesus gives us sympathy for the afflicted. I long for more sympathy. I must go to Jesus for it. As man, he was full of it; as God-man, he is the fountain of it. Jesus, come and live in me, that I may, like thee, go about doing good!

With his accustomed affection, Mr. Smith thus writes to his parents in the following month:

> Eastbourne, March 27. Last Friday evening we had a love feast at Brighton. I, with many others, bore a public testimony to

the power of religion. Of course, I could not but mention, with gratitude to God, the influence which the example, instructions, entreaties, etc., of my parents had had upon my mind. A few, to the praise of God's grace, testified that the blood of Christ cleansed them from all sin. I hope that many more will be speedily brought into this glorious liberty; although, in this part, those who profess it are opposed and considered to be in a dangerous error. Thank God, there are some in various parts of the circuit who are clearly convinced of the necessity of a clean heart and who are longing and seeking for the entire destruction of sin. The Lord is very favorable to me. My health is as usual, and I am enabled to believe in Jesus Christ to the saving of my soul. Christ is increasingly precious. I want stability and firmness in the grace of God. God will establish me. The Word of God is precious. I feast upon it. I am persuaded the more implicitly we give credit to it, the more of God we shall enjoy and diffuse.

To the same, he thus writes, May 19:

God has possession of my heart. Christ not only visits me but dwells in me by faith. Christ is all, and Christ is mine. His excellencies exert a continual attraction. The world is unmasked to me. I see it unsuitable for the portion of my soul. It is unsatisfying and perishing. But Christ possesses everything that is suited to me. He is the eternal God. I choose him for my portion. Yet I want more divine power. This must result to me from deeper and more glorious revelations of the excellencies of Christ in my soul, by the Holy Ghost. O that I may ever lie at the foot of the cross and feel my need of and have the merit of the death of Christ!

> Weaker than a bruised reed,
> Help I every moment need.

I am kept no longer than I am kept by the *power of God* through faith. But does he not say, "Fear not—I will never leave thee; I will never forsake thee?" Amen, my Lord. Never leave, never forsake me!

Of the work of God he remarks, in the same letter:

The state of this country affects me. I wish to be strong to labor. I know that it is God the Holy Ghost that converts and saves souls. But God works by the instrumentality of men, and in all ages of the Christian church he has signally owned and blessed extraordinary exertions. I wish to aim constantly at precious souls and to look for *present effects*. I anticipate better days. God is at work. Several are entering more fully into God, and he, I trust, is preparing them to be useful; but we want a union of effort—then something signal will be done.

The following incident, related by Mr. Calder, will serve to illustrate Mr. Smith's disregard to ordinary opinions and manners in the prosecution of what he considered his duty. A woman at Brighton who was very ill had been several times visited by him. Her husband was an ungodly fisherman and, had he dared, would personally have opposed the efforts of Mr. Smith for the conversion of his wife. Being, however, unable to summon sufficient resolution to meet the pointed admonitions of his most unwelcome visitor, he sent for a woman notorious for profaneness and vulgarity to guard the sick chamber. The next time Mr. Smith called, as he was about to go upstairs, she sprang on him, and seizing him by the collar of his coat, protested that he should not proceed any farther. All his entreaties and expostulations were utterly useless. He at last said, "If I am not allowed to see her, I must kneel down here and pray for her." With a tremendous oath, she swore that he should not. He then saw that it was in vain to continue the contest, and returned to Mr. Calder in deep distress. After having related the whole affair, he wished to know whether, when he had been put out of the house, he had not done wrong in not immediately kneeling down in the street before the door and there interceding for the sick woman, and whether it was not his duty now to return and do so. "It was with the utmost difficulty," says Mr. Calder, "that I could prevail on him to abandon the intention."

The same friend has supplied also the following relation, which is equally characteristic.

Mr. Smith, on one occasion, was seated at table directly opposite to a lady of family and respectability, who, though in theory acquainted with the truths of the gospel, was destitute of its saving power. According to his custom, he embraced the opportunity of addressing her on the subject. She was greatly offended, and expressed her resentment in a manner scarcely suitable either to her sex or her rank. When she was silent, Mr. Smith, with a look of expressible kindness, replied, "Madam, you may spit in my face if you please, *but you cannot prevent me from loving your soul.*" The lady was deeply affected. A few years afterwards, she was taken ill, was attended by the Methodist preachers, and died a true penitent.

At the Conference of 1820, Mr. Smith, after having undergone the usual examinations with credit to himself and satisfaction to his brethren, was admitted into full connection.[1] Immediately afterwards he was married, and in a few days proceeded with Mrs. Smith to the Windsor circuit.

---

1. His public and formal admission did not take place till the Conference of 1822.

CHAPTER 9

Windsor

1820–1821

Mr. Smith's new situation was in several respects peculiarly responsible and trying. Until this time, Windsor had formed a part of the Hammersmith circuit. There were but three places besides the circuit town in which societies had been formed, and in each the congregation and number of members were very small. Villages and towns presented themselves on every side, containing a large mass of population, very inadequately, if at all, supplied with opportunities of evangelical instruction. Perhaps there are few districts in England which, with so considerable a measure of wealth, intelligence, and influence, present so many indications of spiritual destitution. In our own societies also there was at this time great and manifest torpor. Many who had a name to live were dead, and not a few who maintained a decent profession had never known the regenerating influence of the Holy Spirit.

To those who do not know the perversity of human nature, it might have been anticipated that, in such a state of things, the labors of Mr. Smith would have been hailed with a universal welcome. It should be particularly noted that he was now no theorist, however he might have been esteemed such at an early period of his ministerial life. Many of those to whom he was now called to minister must have been acquainted with his devoted zeal and his considerable success; and all might, without difficulty, have ascertained how far his experiments had previously tended to the accomplishment of the great object of the Christian ministry. Yet, to employ the testimony of one who was intimately acquainted with him at this period:

> His efforts by some individuals were, for a time, neither understood nor appreciated. This circumstance rendered the struggles

of his faith far more painful to himself, while it delayed no less the general blessing for which he ardently longed. It appeared to me as if settled unbelief, though only in a few, weighed down his own faith much more than the coldness and indifference of a far greater number. It seemed to hang upon him (and think I have heard him so describe it) "as a dead weight," encumbering and retarding his spirit, when it was struggling to get free and ascend to plead with God for the congregation. Under the pressure of such a feeling, I have even known him to call upon such as were indisposed to believe to quit the chapel, with a tone and manner of solemn earnestness which must have thrilled through every mind.

His own heart, however, was fixed. His principles were too firmly established within to be materially affected by the variation of circumstances without. As indifference could not quell them, so the resistance of unbelief served more fully to confirm them. To the friend from whom I have just quoted, who, on one occasion, lamented the obstructions which presented themselves to his success, he replied in his own laconic and decisive style: "I *know* the plan on which I am acting; I have tried it, and found its success." And this was sufficient for his own mind. Before a spirit of his decision, others of a less determined character naturally gave way; and though the blessings which he sought were retarded, they were not ultimately prevented. Indeed, as the following extract from a letter to his parents will show, he was not without early and unequivocal tokens of the divine approbation upon his efforts.

Windsor, Sept. 15, 1820.—I am going to Uxbridge today, God willing, a place nine miles distant, formerly connected with Windsor, but which has been given up about two years. I was there last week making the necessary inquiries. I believe it is a providential opening, and I anticipate much good. Several are longing for the bread of life. Last Tuesday night I visited a place near Windsor where I hope good will be done. When I came, I saw that very little indeed *was done*, and also that much needed *doing*. I was almost ready to despond; but I recovered myself by considering that the work is God's, that he has all power, and that he is willing and solicitous to save the whole world.

Last Sunday afternoon it pleased God to set two souls at liberty while I was preaching from, "Come unto me, all ye that labor and are heavy laden, and I will give you rest." One woman got down upon her knees while I was preaching, and kneeled until we concluded. I then hastened to her and said, "Woman, are you happy?" She said, "I am." "When did you receive this happiness?" "While you were preaching," she said, "I believed that God had pardoned all my sins." I then called upon the friends to sing, "Praise God, from whom all blessings flow," etc. They who were going out stopped and assisted us to praise God. The other woman did all she could to conceal her emotions, but she was observed by her leader, to whom she confessed that God had then set her soul at liberty. I was not acquainted with this until afterwards.

Last night I was renewing the tickets. A young man was present who had not found peace. I told him God was ready to pardon him then. While I was at prayer, he began to be in deep distress, and cried aloud. I concluded that those who wished to go might have an opportunity, and requested any who were so disposed to remain with us. The young man continued on his knees, unwilling to rise without a sense of pardon. I and one of the leaders remained with him until, after a smart struggle, it pleased God to set his soul at liberty. He then sang, "O Lord, I will praise thee; though thou wast angry with me, thine anger is turned away and thou comfortest me." We all triumphed in the mercy of our God. I do not intend to despond. God can, and does, and will work. We have a few in this place, truly pious, who long for the prosperity of Zion. The people are *very kind* and are solicitous to make us comfortable. We are in good health, through mercy, and are trusting in God for a full salvation.

Immediately after his coming to Windsor, Mr. Smith's mind was painfully affected by the numerous and glaring instances of the violation of the Sabbath which presented themselves on every hand. Among other means which he adopted for the diminution of this evil were regular weekly visits to the shops of Sabbath-breakers. Wherever he found in his neighborhood articles exposed for sale, he entered, and with affectionate firmness remonstrated with the parties to whom they belonged, on the sin and danger of their conduct. The reader will readily anticipate the fact that though his admonitions were very troublesome to such persons, yet their success was but partial. Some success, however, it is gratifying to record, did attend them.

A daily prayer meeting at five o'clock in the morning, and a similar meeting after the Sunday evening preaching, were some of the methods for the revival of the work of God which Mr. Smith employed, almost from the time of his arrival at Windsor. They were attended by the happiest results. His estimation of these means of grace has already been intimated, and to them, he, in common with the most successful ministers of modem Methodism, was greatly indebted for his usefulness. As one of his familiar friends relates, in special reference to this period of his life,

> In different places, and according to the different circumstances in which Mr. Smith found himself, or the people among whom he was stationed, his plan of action, in reference to that revival of the work of God which was everywhere his *first* object, was doubtless subject to various modifications. But in general, I suppose, as it pre-eminently was wherever I have witnessed his labors, the fruits of his ministry were most decisive and abundant in meetings for prayer.

These were usually to him seasons of extraordinary physical as well as spiritual effort, though there were interesting instances of a different class.

> On one occasion, after returning from a meeting where nine persons had obtained entire sanctification the same night, he remarked, "I was not equal to strong exertion, and chiefly said— Thy blood was shed for this very purpose; cleanse them, Lord!"

But it was not only by his own individual exertions that Mr. Smith acted upon others. Among the numbers converted by his ministry, there were always some who imbibed his views and spirit, and who engaged themselves after his example, in "holding forth the word of life." It was, indeed, part of his *plan* to form and encourage others to work for God. He aided them by his counsel, sympathy, and prayers; maintained a correspondence with them when separated, and made occasional visits to London and elsewhere, in order to assist their exertions; so that it is not only the instances in which he was immediately and directly the instrument (numerous as these were) that are to be recounted when we number up the spiritual children whom the Lord gave him; nor are we to annex to these only those remote effects which usually ensue in the private circle of individuals newly converted to God; but we are bound especially to add to them those cases in which he was a spiritual father, in scarcely the *second* degree, because occurring under the instrumentality of men who were not only his own children in the gospel, but who continued to act under his direction and looked expressly to him for counsel and encouragement.

Nor was it merely among the host of souls of whose conversion he was the direct instrument that he found the partakers of his spirit and the willing agents of his plans. The Christianity of many others he succeeded in modeling. To occasional and untaught fervor he often gave principle and direction, and kindled scriptural and persevering zeal in hearts which before had been comparatively cold and inert. It was especially in meetings for prayer that such characters were formed. There was in his atmosphere, at these times, a moral stimulus so powerful that sincere minds could scarcely fail to catch a portion of his heaven-descended spirit. Here they saw his principles brought into actual practice, and the value of his plans attested by their skilful and anticipated operation. Every such meeting was a series of striking and triumphant experiments; and it was thus, mainly, that there was formed that class of individuals whom he, from the most prominent feature of their character, was accustomed to designate "the praying men." Of the majority of these, the probability is that, had it not been for his influence, they would have remained—however personally upright and sincere—of little service to the church of God. Hence, in attempting to form an estimate of the extent of his usefulness, it is necessary to include not only the persons to whom reference has been made above, but those also to whom, through the subordinate agency of men whom he had *trained,* he was, in a more remote but no less certain sense, the instrument of conversion. Had he done no higher service to the church of God, this alone would have been sufficient to entitle him to peculiar honor. The traveler looks with deep interest upon the rock which pours forth the waters of the infant Nile; with how much more profound emotion ought he to contemplate the mighty river itself, as through its numerous channels it diffuses universal fertility and abundance!—the fitter emblem of the zeal and wisdom of the subject of these pages.

By the Minutes of Conference, Mr. Smith was appointed to exchange regularly with the Hammersmith preachers. On his first visit to that circuit, he witnessed on several occasions the exertion of the saving power of God. At one place, two persons obtained mercy under his sermon. One of them, a woman who sat in the front of the gallery, rose up as soon as he had done preaching, and publicly testified of the salvation which she had received; and these were but the prelude to yet more extensive success in that neighborhood. Meantime, in his own circuit, he diligently pursued his plans. He frequently preached out of doors,[1] when the weather permitted, especially in places to which he had no other means of access. He succeeded in establishing societies in some villages that had never before been visited by the Methodist preachers; and on every hand, pleasing prospects of usefulness began to present themselves.

Mr. Smith's friend, from whom I have already quoted largely, relates that:

> Among those who engaged his particular attention and care were the soldiers of the regiments of Life Guards who were successively stationed at the neighboring barracks. To many of that fine body

---

1. In this duty Mr. Smith was several times exposed to the violence of wicked men. Having once engaged to preach near a sand-bank contiguous to one of the villages which he was in the habit of visiting, he was informed before he set out that several mischievously disposed persons intended to be present and interrupt the service. He was not, however, to be deterred from his purpose by the apprehension of danger. The congregation assembled; he gave out a hymn and prayed. In the meantime the mob had conveyed an empty cart to the summit of the bank, designing when the attention of the people was occupied to drive it violently down the steep. The principal agent in this piece of wickedness, however, by some means got entangled with a chain or some such thing, and was thrown down with so much force as to be personally injured. This retarded the progress of the cart; the preacher and his audience had the opportunity of getting out of the way, and no evil ensued. There were also other instances in which attempts to molest him and his congregations proved equally unsuccessful.

of men he was made eminently useful. He felt for their naturally exposed situation, and rejoiced in their profession of godliness, as marked by more decision, and maintained under severer temptations than ordinary. Nor was he, I think, insensible to the *manly bearing* of these Christian soldiers. Certainly, if there was any quality he admired that was not in itself religious, it was *manliness* under all its forms. We love to see the feelings of the man thus disclosing themselves in the Christian. And thus I remember being pleased when the habitual current of his thoughts and conversation was interrupted (though but for a moment) by a natural expression of pleasure at the interesting appearance of some Eton boys, whom he seemed to regard with just the sort of complacency which a father might have expressed had they been his own. Several of these pious soldiers also were men of no common faith and prayer, and active in promoting such meetings and using such means as were calculated to spread religion.

Of the work of God among this interesting class of persons, Mr. Smith thus speaks in a letter to his parents dated Jan.11, 1821:

On the Sunday evening before Christmas day, a Corporal in the Horse Guards found peace. He was awakened about three weeks before at our chapel. His father is a Methodist at Cleckheaton. Last Tuesday week he had an affecting discovery of inbred sin, and the whole of the week longed for a clean heart. This morning, at our half-past five o'clock prayer meeting, God cleansed him from all sin; and he made confession before all present—such a confession I think I never heard. I hope he will be very useful. On Christmas day, another soldier and his wife were awakened while I was praying in our chapel. The Wednesday following they came to our house with Corporal E., a pious man who obtained entire sanctification about three weeks ago; and it pleased the Lord to set them both at liberty. Several other soldiers are earnestly seeking pardon.

Among those for whom Mr. Smith was peculiarly interested was a Corporal who once enjoyed religion but who had forsaken God and his people. His wife was a pious woman. She mourned deeply on his account, and perseveringly prayed for his restoration. It was one day impressed on Mr. Smith's mind to visit this man, and accompanied by Mrs. Smith he walked as far as the door of his house, where he met his wife. "Well, Mrs. B.," said he, "where is your husband?" With much concern, she replied, "Yonder he is, going to the races." "I will follow him," he said, and without entering the dwelling, hastily set off in the direction indicated. The Corporal soon perceived that he was pursued, and quickening his pace, succeeded, before Mr. Smith came up with him, in getting into a ferryboat which would have taken him across the river to within a few minutes' walk of the racecourse. The boatman, however, had to put back for another passenger. This brought him near the friend whom he so much wished to shun, who solemnly accosted him with, "Did you pray about it before you set out?" The inquiry fastened on his conscience. He went to the races and was wretched. "Did you pray about it before you set out?" still seemed to ring in his ears. He soon returned home, but he could not succeed in dislodging the arrow which was fixed in his heart. When Mr. Smith next visited him, he was in deep distress. Mr. Smith invited him to unite himself to the people of God. He did so, and never rested till the Lord healed his backslidings and restored him to his favor. He became a useful character, and for some time has been, as he now is, an active class leader in the regiment.

In the letter from which our last extract was made, Mr. Smith thus speaks of the work in general:

> I have still to lament an almost general want of effort in these parts. It is lifting work to get the people to God, but help is laid upon one that is mighty to save. When the Spirit comes, there must be a moving. We are encouraged to expect his Holy Spirit, not only by the sure Word of promise, but also by what we receive. Thank God, there is a striving among the people. Some are teased and are ready to leave the society, or at least have had thoughts of it; but others are looking to God, panting, laboring for God. Several are on the point of receiving entire sanctification, and a few have received that blessing. Others have obtained pardon. The last time I was at Uxbridge, two souls found peace, and one the time before, who shortly afterwards was cleansed from all sin as he and I were praying together in his bedroom. He has just begun to preach, and I hope will be useful. For two years he was a

backslider. This day fortnight, I and my wife went to take tea with brother S., whose wife a short time ago was a persecutor.... On my return from Stoke, after preaching, I thought God would save her. After a few inquiries, we began to pray. The power of God came upon her. She groaned for mercy; and after a struggle, God set her soul at liberty. Her husband found peace a few months before. A young woman found peace at one of our morning meetings, about a fortnight ago. God, you see, is working. Since I wrote last, I have changed with one of the Reading preachers. At the prayer meeting after evening preaching at Reading, four or five found peace. But it is rather strange work in these parts for souls to be in distress and to get liberty. I hope it will not continue so, and that it will not be opposed, but desired and labored for. My soul is happy in God. I am looking for a greater personal salvation and for glorious out-pourings of the Spirit upon the people. I confidently expect them.

Many notices of facts similar to the foregoing occur in Mr. Smith's correspondence of this period; but as they are not connected with any details, I forbear to insert them. The following extracts from his private papers will show how fully he maintained the simplicity of his piety:

Windsor, June 8, 1821. On all created objects is written, in legible characters, *vanity!* I believe the report, and turn from the creature to the Creator, the Fountain of happiness. He is accessible through the incarnation, sufferings, death, and intercession of his only begotten Son, whom he hath set forth "a propitiation for the sins of the whole world." I come to him through Jesus Christ and thankfully avail myself of the blessings which he freely offers. I rest on Christ for the pardon of my past sins, for the destruction of the body of sin, and for God as my portion. He gives himself to me. I am his; he is mine. I present my dear Ellen to him and depend upon Jesus Christ for his blessing upon her also. God is her portion. I pray that we may be a blessing to each other, to the church, and to the world. The people around us are in a deplorable state. We want general and abundant outpourings of the Spirit. I want more sympathy.

June 9. God reveals himself to me as a Fountain of mercy. I have increasing power to lay hold on his truth. This is the result of the fresh baptisms of the Spirit with which I have this day been favored. I have an increase of sympathy; glory be to God! I will endeavour to be *anxiously* careful for nothing. God is blessing my dear Ellen. She is precious in his sight. We shall have more of the mind of Christ. Amen.

June 10. My soul is at rest in God—is centred in God. My desire is to him. All my springs are in him, and he is in me "a well of water, springing up into everlasting life." In endeavouring to water others, I have myself been watered. In the right of Jesus, I claim the promise of the Spirit. God admits my claim—he must— "he spared not his own Son." O, how astonishing is the love of God! How astonishing are the blessings to which he invites! But he offers them. I will, I *do* accept them. I have spoken plainly and affectionately to the people. May God give the increase, for Christ's sake! Amen.

As a still more striking illustration of the scriptural character of Mr. Smith's piety, I quote the following remarks of the friend whose communications have already so enriched these pages:

Of all that he did or suffered, of all that he experienced or enjoyed, *faith* was the great, the animating principle; and the truth of God (which is nothing more nor less than the reality of things) was the groundwork and basis of his faith. To *believe*, as it constitutes the whole of religion—the highest attainments of which are only a development of that all-comprehending principle—constituted the substance of all his exhortations to others, and the scope of all his own prayers and exertions. To the efficacy of faith he set no limits. "If," said he, "a man were as black as a devil and had upon him all the sins that were ever committed, if he would but begin to *believe*, God would raise him." Again I have heard him say, "That is the way I rise. I will not suffer myself to dwell on my unfaithfulness; if I did, I should despond." I have known him quote, with great seriousness, a remark of Mr. Wesley, to the effect that most persons perished through *despondency*. On my asking him as to his confidence of final salvation, he replied that he had "no doubt whatever on the subject"; but to prevent misconception, he added, "Not that I have any *peculiar* assurance of it; but I know I shall get to heaven because I am *determined to believe*." And as he set no bounds to the efficacy of faith, so he appeared to set none to its application. When I have been engaged in writing a letter, he has called out to me, "Write in faith!"

But the daily victories of faith were accompanied with daily conflicts. "We may suppose," said he, "that believing is difficult work, because the blessings of salvation are suspended on it, and they are great." Speaking to him of Brainerd's life and his eminent piety, he replied, "He *labored* for it; and all that are eminently pious, *labor* for it." At another time he said, "Ah! that is the way; to be always at it—to be on full stretch." When I spoke to him, on one occasion, of the *quiet* manner of some eminent Christians, he appeared to acquiesce in the sentiment that it is not equally an effort to all to believe; but to himself, he said, it was a conflict. We are, however, to remember that his life was a continual struggle of faith to raise others; and all the opposition, not only of their unbelief, but of Satan himself, must have been set in array "to resist him."

Of the efficacy of his own faith, the number of conversions which took place under him, and of which "the greater part remain unto this present," is an incontestable and abiding monument. But those who knew him must remember many evidences equally conclusive to themselves, although less capable of being attested and verified to others. I have myself seen a whole congregation so perceptibly quickened in their devotions on his entrance into the chapel, though unperceived by everyone, that it could be imputed to nothing but the earnest exercise of his faith; and I have found, on inquiring whether it were not so, that he had been employed in an act of faith for the people as he came in.

In the month of June he paid a visit to his friends at Brighton and was deeply affected, to use his own words, "with the goodness of God in the kindness of the people." On the Sunday evening on which he preached there the Spirit of God descended powerfully on the congregation. Many were deeply convinced of sin; fifteen or sixteen persons obtained pardon, and the meeting was continued till nearly midnight. On the following day he attended the quarterly meeting of the circuit at Lewes. In the evening he preached, and the Lord granted the congregation a baptism of fire. His subject was the love of God to man; and he urged on his hearers the duty of loving God in return, from the consideration that this alone would fit them for heaven. For himself, he said, in his own pathetic style, he did love God, and he intended to get to heaven. He then appealed to the people whether they would go with him. Pausing as for a reply, there was of course profound silence; and every heart seemed filled with the deepest emotion. Then turning to his friend Mr. Calder, he said, in a thrilling tone, "Brother Calder, will you go to heaven?" As well as he could articulate for weeping, he replied, "By God's grace, I will." "Hear him," cried Mr. Smith with a loud voice, "he says he will." And then, as if putting a seal to a solemn covenant, he feelingly added, "Amen—and now for all of you. God is here to receive your vow, and help you to fulfil it." The effect was magical; awe appeared to rest on every spirit, and multitudes testified that they had never before observed such an impression from simple and anointed eloquence.

Nothing can convey to the reader who never witnessed the exertions of the man the degree of intense fervor to which he was wrought by the time he had finished his sermon. He seemed rapt, inspired; and, to a certain degree, his auditors were carried with him. He then called on the Rev. John Pipe, who had succeeded him in the Brighton circuit, to pray. The Spirit of intercession had come on him also, and with extraordinary earnestness he besought God to bless the *circuit*. Full of confidence and ardor, and forgetful of everything but the amplitude of the petition, Mr. Smith pronounced an "Amen" like the sound of thunder. A second petition that God would bless the *nation* elicited a second and still louder "Amen." But when he who prayed, extending the exercise of his faith and charity, called on God to bless the *world*, Mr. Smith uttered, at the extreme of his voice, an "AMEN" which thrilled through every heart and seemed to infuse the energy of his faith into those who heard it—"making," says Mr. Calder, "the three most memorable amens that I, or I think any human being, ever heard." When the first service was concluded, he proceeded to assist in carrying on the prayer meeting, and had the happiness of seeing, that night, about twenty souls delivered from the burden of their sins, as were two more by his instrumentality on the following morning.[1]

It might naturally be supposed that much animadversion would follow this singular scene. On the contrary, however, so fully was Mr. Smith's—shall I call it—*unique* character understood, and so highly was his worth appreciated, that little surprise and no displeasure was awakened even in the town. All inquiry was silenced by, "It was only Mr. Smith come to visit his old friends."

Yet Mr. Smith was no enthusiast. They who deem him such either do not know the indications of the character and the signification of the term, or they grievously misunderstand the man to whom they venture to apply it. His principles were as sound and sober as his vehemence in employing them was extraordinary and resistless. Indeed his mind was essentially unimaginative and deficient in the inventive faculty. It was distinguished by its strength of common sense, shrewdly observant of human nature, endowed with a keen sense of the ridiculous, and remarkable for its natural and healthy cheerfulness. Is it too much to affirm that there never was, and that there never will be, an enthusiast made of such materials? "Enthusiasm is a term, not of *measurement,* but of *quality.*" It does not describe what is *intensely* good but what is essentially evil. It is the religion of the imagination and not of the heart. There is no antidote against it so infallible as that which was possessed in a peculiar degree by the subject of these memoirs—simple, earnest, scriptural, and absorbing piety. This in him was strikingly practical. It was not made up of reveries and visions or maintained by occasional impulses and frequent abstraction. He knew nothing of those speculations without which enthusiasm must die, which tickle the fancy but leave the heart untouched; pleasant enough to the contemplation, but practically worse than useless; like the phosphoric lights of a damp summer evening, which play around

---

1. The following note from his private papers appears to have been written immediately on his return home: "June 28. I am thankful that I went to Brighton. I have gained a blessed increase of personal salvation. O that I may grow in grace constantly! I hope I shall have more sympathy for the people in this circuit. I have more already than I had when I went to Brighton. This is the result of that increase of grace which I have received. Glory be to God!"

objects, but have no power to enter them, and only serve to scare the traveler, or lead him astray. His religion pervaded all the occupations of common life. It was elevated and impassioned, but without the slightest taint of fanaticism, either of doctrine or experience. It never revolted from the most ordinary subjects and engagements. It presided in his home as well as in the sanctuary; and, to use a common but expressive phrase, it *wore well* in all the rubs of the world.

If, however, by enthusiasm be meant the single, devoted, unwavering pursuit of one object; the concentration of mighty and sanctified affections; the laboring night and day, with many tears, for the salvation of men; the literally counting "all things loss" for Christ; the expecting the fulfilment of the promises of God in their most ample sense; the ready and constant preference of the interests of eternity to those of time, however worthy to be consulted: if, in short, the loving God with all the heart and serving him with all the strength be enthusiasm, John Smith *was* an enthusiast. But the term which describes such a character, far from being a term of reproach, is a title of the highest dignity; and there is no instructed Christian who would not covet to gain it, or would not glory in it when acquired. To use the words of Mr. Smith's attached friend:

> He who best secures an end which many aim at may well be presumed to have employed the best, and therefore the most rational, means. And consequently, since the salvation of souls is the end of the Christian ministry, his known and eminent success, compared with that of most others, may well establish the superior fitness of the means employed by him. In other words, it transfers the suspicion of enthusiasm to those who imagine that a pointless generalizing harangue on some theological subject, that the mere "letting off a sermon" is to convey "life from the dead" and to demolish the bastions of Satan and unbelief. The "gentle theologues," whose nerves are strung with such exquisite sensibility that they are alarmed at the slightest ripple on the dead calm of human affections, and yet expect to accelerate the period when "the sea shall roar and the fullness thereof," are the real visionaries. "And we who mourn that an Elijah is taken from us," and would fain catch something of his spirit, will be content that it shall be said of him, "Whether he were beside himself, it was for God; or

whether he were sober, it was for our cause; for the love of Christ constrained him."

But nothing can more decisively show the thorough sobriety of his judgment than his sentiments on that very subject in which ignorance or prejudice might be disposed to allege that he went too far. It is common for persons to conceive of, and expect, the influence of the Holy Ghost, only as some undefined and inarticulate illapse promised in answer to prayer. It is even rare to hear truth pointed out as the appointed and ordinary medium of operation to the blessed Spirit, and yet it might easily be shown that this is the doctrine of the New Testament.[1] Nothing can more clearly evince the rational and scriptural character of Mr. Smith's piety than a saying of his on this one subject. "The Spirit," said he, "blesses in the *truth:* therefore get to know the states of the people, and apply *appropriate truth.*" Could a sentiment be mentioned or even imagined that would be a better test of sound general views? And whatever he did or said was in harmony with it. The law and the testimony furnished the rule by which he acted. Whether he encouraged the penitent to believe, or the believer to expect entire sanctification, his exhortation was to "lay hold on the *truth* of God." In the spirit of the same views he always inculcated that "God would not go out of his own order." Perhaps a calmer school of theology is not always equally scriptural.

---

1. See, for example, John 8:32: comp. 2 Cor. 3:17, 18; John 17:17; Eph. 5:26: comp. Titus 3:5; 2 Thess. 2:13; 1 Peter 1:22, 23: comp. James 1:18, etc., etc.

CHAPTER 10

Windsor Continued

1821–1822

"Already, in October, 1821, fifty persons had received the blessing of pardon in the Windsor circuit, and scores in the Hammersmith circuit had obtained the same salvation; there prevailed everywhere a more earnest spirit of religion, and the piety of various individuals had acquired, through Mr. Smith's example, a deeply interesting and useful character."

Such is the statement of the friend from whom I have already quoted so much at length as to the spiritual prosperity which presented itself almost immediately after the re-appointment of Mr. Smith to this circuit. Writing to the same person about this time, he thus exhorts him:

> If I do not see you, present yourself as a hell-deserving sinner before God. Acknowledge the goodness of God in the gift of his Son, *whether you feel it or not*. Rest your soul with your sin on the atonement and mediation of Christ, and wait for the Holy Ghost. Claim the Spirit. The promise is to you. Everything must yield to his working. Do have the Spirit, in spite of hell and yourself. God is for you. Wait, O wait, my dear brother; God will come. He will make you unspeakably happy.

The following is an extract from a letter to Mr. Calder, dated October 22:

> I was much pleased with your letter. God is teaching you *by his Spirit* some important lessons. The same lessons are taught in his Word and have been taught by wise and good men; but we want the Spirit. We must have the teaching of the Spirit, or after all we shall be foolish. I thank God for what he is doing in you and by you. Be in the will of God; *know* that you are in it fully—constantly. Perhaps you will have to spend hours on your knees or

upon your face before the throne. Never mind. Wait! God will do great things for you if you will yield to him and cooperate with him. O play the man! Dwell in the clear light. I am hoping that God will make you a great blessing; but you must be a *burning* and shining light. The fire must come from heaven. You have free access. Nelson says to me "Remember, men must be *saved first.*" Be determined not to rest unless souls get into clear liberty. We have a deal to say to them, but they must be *saved.* O what numbers among us are not clear in pardon! Let us agonize to get them into liberty. Maintain simplicity. If you spend several hours in prayer daily you will see great things. I long for you. I do not cease to pray for you. You and your family are closely connected with my mercies. When I think of *them*, I think of you; so that as long as I have piety, I shall not forget you. I am resting on the atonement and intercession of Jesus. God gives himself to me. His Spirit is in me. O what rest is connected with an indwelling God! The abominations of the people around me fill me with grief. I can only find relief in the mercy and power of God and in the merits of Christ. Many of our people are very ignorant of the way of faith. When the power of God is mightily upon them, they do not lay hold of what they want. Until there be a taking hold of God, we cannot expect much signal work.

In the beginning of the year 1822, Mr. Smith assisted at the anniversary of the Canterbury chapel, of which circuit Mr. Calder was at this time superintendent. Among the preachers assembled on the occasion, much concern was felt and expressed on account of Mr. Smith's extraordinary and, as they could not but too truly augur, destructive exertions. It was agreed that he should be the subject of serious remonstrance, and that his new and interesting ties to society (he having recently become a father) should form the ground of expostulation. His old and valued friend Mr. Methley, who at that time traveled in the Canterbury circuit, was to be the spokesman; and he was to be followed up by the serious and affectionate representations of the rest. While they were at supper, Mr. Methley opened the business, and Mr. Smith, laying down his knife and fork, listened with the most patient and respectful attention. As soon as the former had ceased, he burst into a flood of tears, and literally sobbing with grief, at length replied, "What you say is all correct. I ought to put restraint on myself; but O, how can I? God has given me such a sight of the state of perishing souls that I am broken-hearted and can only vent my feelings in the way I do—entreating them to come to God and pleading with him to act upon and save them." Still weeping as in an agony, he continued, "Look round you, my brother; do you not see sinners going to hell? And when I thus see and feel it, I am compelled to act." To this pathetic statement there was no reply; all the company were melted into tears; and Mr. Methley was so deeply affected that, unable to restrain his emotions, he abruptly rose from the table and left the house.

During this visit, Mr. Smith was, as usual, made the instrument of the conversion of a considerable number of persons; and among others, of a young lady, the daughter of one of our principal friends in a neighboring town. Mr. Calder states that, of all the results of Mr. Smith's labors in private which he ever witnessed, this was the most interesting. It appears that she was very much afraid of meeting Mr. Smith, lest he should address her on the subject of personal religion. While he was at Mr. Calder's house, however, she was prevailed on to call. As she had apprehended, he immediately began to converse with her on the necessity and desirableness of a present salvation, until she was completely subdued. For three hours did the friends present incessantly wrestle with God on her behalf, and at the close of that time her soul was filled with peace and joy. She returned to her home a new creature, and from that time has walked worthy of her Christian profession.

This, however, was only an earnest of the extraordinary blessing which attended his labors during the next few days, which he spent in the metropolis and its vicinity. Previously to this, God had begun a good work in London west through the instrumentality of some pious soldiers who, while stationed at Windsor, had obtained the blessing of entire sanctification and had imbibed Mr. Smith's spirit and been taught his plans. He had visited them a few weeks before, and had seen the arm of the Lord gloriously revealed. He now witnessed, to use his own words, "the greatest work he had ever seen." In the course of a very short time, there were, including the fruits of his former visit, nearly seventy individuals pardoned and about sixty made profession of having attained purity of heart. In the same week he also received a letter giving an account of a revival in what is now the London East circuit, of which, under God, he had been the first mover. In his own circuit, too, several interesting conversions occurred about the same time. "So mightily grew the Word of the Lord and prevailed."

Mr. Smith's house was frequently resorted to by persons under the awakenings of the Holy Spirit, and scarcely a week elapsed in which it was not the scene of devout exultation on account of the liberation of some captive soul. One afternoon a stranger called in deep distress. Mr. Smith invited him to take tea, and inquired into the means by which he had come under religious concern. He stated that his name was D—, that he was a publican at Hampstead, and that for many years he had given himself up to the love and practice of vice. He never attended any place of worship, was a gambler, a hard drinker, and in short, a sinner in almost every conceivable way. One of his companions in riot, having left his house in a state of intoxication, had fallen into a river and was drowned. This accident roused him to alarm and inquiry, which was increased by the discovery that his own mind was so weakened, probably in consequence of intemperance, that he was unable to keep his accounts. He thought that he was about to lose his reason; and while under the influence of this distressing apprehension, the enormity of his past sins was powerfully presented to his mind, with the fear of something more awful than even madness. In this state, he recollected a pious person whom he had formerly known; to him he applied for counsel, and this friend brought him down to Windsor that he might receive the benefit of Mr. Smith's direction and prayers. Such was the account which he gave of himself, but his distress was so great that before tea was concluded, he was down upon the floor; and it was a solemn spectacle—to see a large muscular man prostrated by extreme anguish, while he groaned and prayed in unspeakable disquietude. It happened to be the night on which Mr. Smith met a class which he had formed, to the members of which, after the ordinary conversation had concluded, he introduced the case of this penitent, and requested their intercession on his behalf. At the same time he urged him to the exertion of faith in Christ and the expectation of a present salvation. The struggle was continued for a considerable time. At length Mr. Smith perceived that the man was relaxing in his efforts. "What, will you give it up?" said he. Mr. D. complained of exhaustion. "You have danced for whole nights together," was the reply. "That's true," said the other, and with renewed energy he began again to cry to God; nor did he rest till about eleven o'clock, when his guilt was removed, and he rejoiced in the assurance of the divine favor. The following morning, as he and Mr. Smith were walking out, he suddenly stopped and cried, "O, my load is all returned!" In vain did Mr. Smith tell him that this was only an effort of the tempter; in vain did he remind him of the peace which he had before enjoyed. He remained almost on the verge of despair the whole day. The religious services of the next, which was Sunday, seemed to produce no beneficial effect on his mind. In the evening prayer meeting, he was again made the subject of special intercession. One of the friends employed to him an argument similar to that of Naaman's servants: "If the prophet had bid thee do some great thing, wouldst thou not have done it?" "Yes," said he, with an air of desperate energy, "I would stand and be shot." The meeting was continued to a late hour. His strength was exhausted, but his soul refused comfort; and the next day he returned, promising that he would try to believe all the way home. He immediately disposed of his inn and retired to a private house at Hoxton. For some weeks his despondency continued; but at length the Comforter returned, and he wrote to Mr. Smith, giving him an account of his deliverance. A short time afterwards he took cold, fell into a rapid consumption, and died in peace.

And here, perhaps, may be inserted with propriety the following instances of the happy effects of the Sunday evening prayer meetings at Windsor. On one occasion, when a remarkably good influence appeared to rest on the congregation, and several persons were penitentially seeking pardon, Mr. Smith remarked a woman standing near the door and looking at what was going forward with much apparent curiosity and surprise. Her garb indicated much poverty, and it afterwards appeared that she gained a miserable subsistence, partly by gathering and selling water-cresses. She had attended the chapel a few times before, but her ignorance was extreme. Mr. Smith went up to her, and said, "Woman, get down on your knees and begin to pray." She immediately knelt down and asked, "What shall I say, Sir?" "Ask God to give you true repentance," was the reply. The poor woman, for the first time, opened her mouth in prayer: "Lord, give me true repentance." She had not long uttered this petition before it was in a measure answered, and she came under the gracious influence which was in the meeting. She began to tremble, and with great anxiety inquired, "What shall I do now? What shall I pray for?" "Ask God to have mercy upon you," said Mr. Smith "Lord, have mercy upon me, a poor sinner," cried she, "a guilty sinner!" Who need be told the sequel? She was that night clearly converted and filled with the love of God. When Mr. Smith was about to leave Windsor, she came, with many others, to look once more on him who had proved her best friend; and so deep was her emotion that when he extended his hand to her, she fell down on her knees, filled with a gratitude which she could not express. Mr. Smith was deeply affected, and no doubt that moment amply repaid him for all his labors in that circuit.

The following is an extract from a letter written in April, 1822:

I should say a good deal about the Lord Jesus if I had not the pleasing prospect of seeing you so soon and of talking about him. However, he is precious to my soul. I rest on him, and I do not rest on him in vain. God *is* my portion. All my springs are in him; they never fail. Still I am tardy. O how powerfully I ought to be attracted by his excellencies! May he quicken me! Be determined to make use of Jesus, lay claim to his merit, and take for your own. He is God's gift to you and to the world. In the right of Jesus, claim the Spirit. Expect to be filled. Do expect and wait. All is yours. Offer yourself to God as you are, with all your badness, and believe that he takes you through Christ. Do believe. God will bruise Satan under your feet shortly, and your badness shall yield to the working of the Spirit. O, believe! The Word of God is sure. He cannot lie. I hope to see you shortly, to weep with you if you weep, to rejoice with you if you rejoice.

Yet though Mr. Smith had an ever ready sympathy for the afflictions of his friends, it was in behalf of those who had no tears for themselves that he wept most frequently and bitterly. "Some," says he in one of his private papers, "are so base that they do not weep. Hardness and hard-heartedness are their characteristics. From them we expect nothing tender or even good. Some cannot weep; grief has so stunned them; the fountain of tears is walled in. These strike us, and for them we weep, because they cannot. Some weep for mankind and God. This is to be imitated. Think it not unmanly to weep. The God-man wept over Jerusalem. Is there not a cause? Will it be useless? 'Put thou my tears into thy bottle; are they not in thy book?' This grief tells with God." Nor was it merely the misery and peril of sinners which induced his tears, but principally his tender jealousy for the divine honor. Of God's purity and glory he had an awful and penetrating sense, and that aspect of sin which most deeply affected his own mind was its rebellious and treasonable character. He felt in respect of it what he affirmed primarily of heathen idolatry: "It is a system of rivalry to God." Often, from the pulpit and elsewhere, was he accustomed, with a voice which almost always faltered when he approached the subject, to exclaim, "God is dishonored in *his own* world." While he cherished a melting pity for sinners, his nobler feelings still made him the advocate of the divine perfection and gave an indescribable cordiality and intensity to his abhorrence of iniquity. In his public services, as well as in the devotional exercises of the social circle, it was scarcely possible for a person of discernment to hear him speak of the threats of the law without perceiving that his mind was deeply impressed with their rectitude and fitness. He not only presented perdition to the sinner with the hope of rousing him, but because he felt with peculiar force that it was *proper* that an impenitent sinner should be lost. Horror seemed sometimes to take hold of him on account of the wrongs which the Creator sustained from his creatures, and for a moment his faith appeared to stagger. His naturally cheerful mind thus acquired an occasional tinge of melancholy; and one of his friends mentions the community of his feelings with those of the writings of the prophet Jeremiah, as being at these times very distinct and remarkable.

About the midsummer of 1822 he went into the High Wycombe circuit to preach some occasional sermons. On the Sunday morning, when the congregation was assembled, he had not arrived at the chapel, and several persons were despatched in different directions to seek him. After the lapse of a considerable time, he was found in some solitary place out of doors, forgetful of all time, wrestling with God in mighty prayer for his blessing on the services in which he was about to engage. The result may be readily anticipated. Throughout the day, his mind appeared to be peculiarly impressed with the divine benevolence; and in one of his sermons he repeatedly, and with extraordinary vehemence cried out, "He is willing! He is willing! He is willing!" Many, on that occasion, had a blessed experience of God's willingness to save, and numbers of others were powerfully awakened to seek salvation. And as in the foregoing paragraph we have alluded to the first of those grand impressions which contributed to form Mr. Smith's character and to render him eminently useful, we may properly, in this place, speak of the second. To employ the statement of the friend to whom was addressed the letter from which our last quotation was an extract:

With these views of the holiness of the divine character was combined a conviction, not less absolute and vivid, of the unspeakable *compassion* of God. Hence, while on the one hand he was jealous in maintaining the rectitude and purity of God by asserting the exceeding sinfulness of sin, its guiltiness, and the necessity of humiliation, he was no less earnest, on the other, in insisting on his boundless mercy, and in leaving men burdened with the responsibility of their own continued impenitence. Accordingly, he was displeased when persons prayed as if God were unwilling to bless, or when they spoke of unbelief as a mere *infirmity*. "It is an abomination," he said, "when men talk as if *they* were more willing to bless than God." Thus he showed how the most awful sense of the divine sanctity and justice may accompany and grow with the deepest conviction of the divine compassion, being radicated in the same common sentiment. "There is no impediment on God's part," said he, in his own brief and energetic manner. "He has given us his Son." By thus firmly asserting the willingness of God to save, against all the temptations of unbelief, he urged and encouraged himself to plead with God for sinners. "It is by justifying God," said he, "that I sting and stimulate myself to contend." And again: "The necessity of wrestling arises not from the unwillingness of God, but from ourselves, or Satan. God is the same." And thus his resolute purpose to justify God and to believe, at all events, that there is no hindrance on his part, since he has given his Son, was to him like cutting off retreat. It left him no alternative but to wrestle and prevail. This was the principle which he would never suffer himself or others to call in question. But in following it out, in still tenaciously hanging upon it and pleading it in spite of every impediment, of all that Satan could oppose, or unbelief suggest; this was the conflict which we saw in him; this was that agony to believe which I have heard him describe as so severe that it has been as if soul and body were ready to part asunder.

Such were the discoveries by which Mr. Smith's unbending resolution was upheld in his arduous labors for the conversion of men: the purity and benevolence of God, alike infinite; sin, in its malignity, prevalence, and misery; and *salvation*, in its fullness, freeness, and power; the horrible condition and awful peril of the sinner; and the unspeakable tenderness, readiness, and ability of the Savior. Had this been merely an ordinary Christianity grafted on a naturally determined spirit, it would have been subject to fluctuations to which he was a stranger; and this would have been equally the case had he been the creature of animal and passionate impulse alone.[1] There are moments when the most powerful constitutional determination languishes and fails. Weakness of body, mental exercise,

---

1. The friend who has so largely contributed to illustrate Mr. Smith's character, remarks on this subject: "I have heard a doubt suggested by a clergyman who highly valued his ministry, and who acknowledged himself to have been more powerfully affected under his preaching than he had ever been under that of any other person, whether Mr. Smith might not, perhaps, depend too much on 'animal feeling.' From a thorough observation of the character of his mind, aided by all the advantages of daily and unrestrained fellowship for several months, I am fully convinced that he was utterly incapable of it. In his most animated moments, in the full tide and energy of a revival, I am confident that he might have replied, 'I speak forth the words of truth and soberness.'"

strong temptation, and other causes succeed in prostrating the most resolute; and such a reaction is often long continued and extreme. Who has not occasionally seen a mighty mind broken down, dissolved as it were into little more than infantile weakness? But Mr. Smith was too fully a Christian and a minister of sound and strong *principle* to be materially affected by the varieties of circumstances. Others I have known who have had very vivid impressions of the heinousness of sin, and they have so lived under their influence as to have become gloomy and severe; but I never met with a mind so happily balanced by these antagonist truths—so preserved, on the one hand, in its intensity of feeling, and on the other in its buoyant tenderness of hope. There were moments, it is readily admitted, in which one or other of his principles predominated; generally, however, these two impressions were, to his mind, like the centrifugal and centripetal forces in the planetary system, preserving it in its holy equilibrium, and impelling it around its center, "in glory and in joy," the fountain of benign and kindly influence.

Chapter 11

Frome

1822–1825

During the three following years, the Frome circuit enjoyed the advantage of Mr. Smith's ministry, in conjunction, first, with that of the Rev. James Heaton, and afterwards of the Rev. T. H. Squance. Of the confidence and friendship of each of these ministers he possessed a large measure, and their kindly feelings he most cordially reciprocated. Harmony was in their counsels, and success crowned their united labors. On the first Sunday evening on which Mr. Smith preached at Frome, an interesting young female obtained mercy at the prayer meeting. She was the youngest of three sisters, all of whom were members of the society; but neither of the others had entered into the enjoyment of the divine favor. A short time afterwards, the second sister called one morning at Mr. Smith's, and, according to his custom, he inquired whether she had received the blessing of pardon. Upon her replying in the negative, he proposed prayer; and they did not rise from their knees till she also was able to testify the power of the atoning blood; nor was it long before the eldest sister was likewise brought into the same happy state of experience. The parents of these young persons were members of the Society of Friends. Upon one occasion of Mr. Smith's visiting them, he was invited upstairs to see the mother, who was very ill. He found her surrounded by her weeping family and suffering under pain so severe that they apprehended her speedy death, unless it were mitigated. After making a few observations, he kneeled down and brought the case before the Lord. The answer was immediate. The pain entirely left her, and with the return of bodily ease came an extraordinary blessing upon her spirit.[1]

---

1. An answer to prayer of an equally remarkable kind was granted to Mr. Smith during the time he was at Brighton. Calling one day at the house of Mr.—, he

A few cursory extracts from Mr. Smith's correspondence during the years 1822 and 1823 will enable the reader to form some idea of the happy results of his efforts:

Oct. 8. A few weeks ago, at Nunney, we had a blessed love-feast. Nine found peace, and five the Tuesday following; seven on the Wednesday, one on Monday, and one on Friday. Yesterday week, at Warnstow, five found peace. Last Wednesday night, at Kilmington, I think ten found peace. A few others, in different places, have been saved since we came. I believe we shall see a great and glorious work.

Feb. 18, 1823. We admitted on trial, last quarter, upwards of two hundred and seventy. We had about the same number of conversions. Many obtained the blessing of entire sanctification. Since the quarter-day, we have given nearly a hundred notes of admittance, and we have had about the same number of conversions. The work is likely to go on. The people very generally are getting into action. They look for present blessings in their meetings. Some of the leaders and local preachers are very active and successful. I have frequently seen eight or ten saved at a meeting; I think twenty more than thrice; and once, at Frome, between thirty and forty. This blessed work melts me into grateful love to God.

March 22. I have witnessed many signal displays of the power and grace of God since I last wrote. At Badcomb, in the Shepton Mallet circuit, about twenty souls found peace with God in one night; and a person who does not relish a revival in what is called a noisy way says he believes forty souls were awakened. At our love-feast,

---

there found an infant lying on the lap of its distressed mother and writhing in a severe convulsive fit. It had frequently been affected in a similar way, even from the time of its birth. Mr. Smith took the child from the mother's arms, and sitting down, sang one of his favorite hymns. He then engaged in intercession on its behalf. Having risen from his knees, he gave it back to the mother and retired. From that time the affliction ceased; the child became strong, and, after the lapse of eight years, the grateful mother assured the relater of this incident that it had never since had a single fit. The same gentleman adds, from his personal knowledge, that the young person for whom this deliverance was wrought out is now in the bloom of perfect health; and he intimates that this was only one of many cases in which similar extraordinary effects resulted from Mr. Smith's prayers.

upwards of twenty found peace. In several of the country places, many have been saved. Glory be to God!

June 26. A short time ago, we had a prayer meeting after the missionary meeting at Shepton. Numbers were in deep distress, and many found peace with God. I was informed, on Monday last, by a pious young gentleman from that place, that the work is still going on, and that fifty have been saved since the missionary meeting. Several have been saved in various parts of our own circuit lately. We are trying to keep those whom God has given us and to get more converted. It is God's work; it must prosper.

July 30. The work at Shepton has been going on ever since. On the 20th, I preached there. There was much of the power of God among the people during the sermon. A special power came down in the last prayer. I called on a local preacher to pray. Some ran out with all speed; some were in great distress; some were taken into the vestry apparently senseless. I concluded, and commenced a prayer meeting; and I think nearly thirty souls found peace with God.

Oct. 8. The work of entire sanctification is going on in many parts of the circuit, particularly in Frome. We have a number of private bands, and have begun to meet them on the Saturday evenings. We anticipate much good from this. God is giving stability to the work already done. The backsliders are comparatively few. Some that sustained loss during the harvest are stirring themselves to take hold of God again. There is a blessed spirit of union among the people. Our leaders in Frome are one, and they are prepared to hail a continued revival. I have been at Bristol since I wrote last. I preached at Easton on a Sabbath evening. During the last prayer, a woman cried aloud for mercy. Others were in distress, and five or six found peace. We have had a friend of ours from London spending a week with us lately. He was one of eleven who were cleansed at one meeting in London; ten of the eleven, he tells me, have been made leaders. He went with me to several places and was astonished at the work. One evening six persons obtained purity of heart.

In the course of the year Mr. Smith paid several visits to Bath, and in that city his labors were greatly blessed. On one occasion, at a prayer meeting at Walcot Chapel, several were in distress, and seven or eight obtained mercy. On the following evening, Mr. Smith preached at King Street Chapel. Much divine power was present, and upwards of twenty penitents received pardon. "The work," says he, in one of his subsequent letters, "is going on still. At one meeting since, I have heard that twenty-two found peace." At one of the above meetings, there was present a medical gentleman who was a member of another religious community. At the conclusion, he came to Mr. Smith, and, taking him by the hand, said: "Well, Sir, you are a stranger to me, but I know your Master. I never witnessed such a night as this, but I perceive nothing here contrary to the Scriptures. I could not leave the place without saying this to you, and wishing you God speed!" adding, with other expressions of kindness, "and when your lungs are worn out, if you will come to me, I may perhaps be able to say something which will do you good." This instance of cordial and catholic feeling was very gratifying to Mr. Smith; and connected as it was with an unusual order of ministerial labor, seems to deserve record in these pages. After the missionary anniversary also, Mr. Smith, with his excellent superintendent, conducted a praye meeting in one of the Bath chapels, in which about twenty persons were justified and ten or twelve enabled to rejoice in the blessings of perfect love. In his own circuit, the success of his ministry was not confined to persons of moral habits. Not a few of the grossly wicked were awakened and saved through his instrumentality, and among others of this class were a considerable number of poachers. The Earl of Cork has some game preserves in the neighbourhood of Frome, and it was remarked by a person who knew the extensive results of Mr. Smith's labors that he was of more service to this nobleman than all his gamekeepers. But although the divine blessing thus remarkably succeeded his efforts, his own spirit looked higher for satisfaction and happiness. No outward events could afford him greater delight than the salvation of men; yet on one occasion, after expressing his gratitude for the good work going on in the circuit and neighborhood, he added, "But God is my portion." To employ his own phrase, his first object was to "obtain more of God"; his second, to "diffuse more of God." God was the beginning and ending of his meditations, his affections, and his labors: having received, he diffused, and in diffusing he obtained. But he never transposed the order of these duties, or allowed ministerial efforts to call forth any other than an interest subservient to the cultivation of personal holiness.

In the latter part of the year 1823, his robust health yielded to severe and long continued exertion. For some time he was wholly laid aside, and some of his friends feared that his lungs were seriously diseased. Dr. Parry of Bath, however, upon being consulted, gave them encouragement to hope that this was not the case, and thought that by relaxation and rest he might be fully restored to health. This, though very necessary, was to Mr. Smith himself a great trial. Yet with a strong desire to return to his beloved employment, his mind was kept in peace. In one of his letters he says, "I wish to be employed for God. I can stand hard labor better than sickness, but I want patience to have its perfect work." At another time he remarks, "I must rest a little longer yet, and proceed with great caution. Mr. Squance has acted the part of a father to me. The Lord reward him for his great kindness and affection." Then recurring to the ever present subject of his thoughts and concern, he adds,

> God is giving stability to his work in this circuit, and it is spreading a little. Eight souls found peace with God, I hear, in one of our country places last Sunday week. Several have been saved in Frome lately. Many of our people are looking out for signal displays of the power and grace of God. O, how ready is God to save!
>
> The gift of his Son unto death, his promise and his oath, ought to kill every doubt. "He that believeth not hath made God a liar." I hope I shall credit God more than ever. He is worthy. The connection between man and man is very close. God will do astonishing things for others in answer to our prayers. I want qualifying, especially as a minister, to take faster hold of the people—to be more like Moses, Samuel, Daniel, Paul, and the Lord Jesus. I must *wait in faith*, and then—.   •

In February, 1824, he went into Yorkshire with the hope of being benefited by his native air. After spending some time with his parents, he paid a visit to his friend Mr. Nelson, who was then stationed in the Birstal circuit. At the band meeting in that place, which he one evening attended, there were several seeking pardon, and he could not resist the impulse to labor, and thus risk the little strength which he had been two months gathering. The following Sunday, he with great difficulty persuaded Mr. Nelson to allow him to preach, by way of experiment as he said, promising at the same time that he would be very cautious. For a little while his exertions were moderate; but at length, warmed by the subject, he forgot his engagement, and gave way so fully to his generous ardor that it seemed as if he would have fallen in the pulpit. Of course, he was not again to be trusted. He returned to Cudworth; and finding that he was there in danger of expending his strength as he gathered it, he judged it prudent to travel home. He soon after resumed his labor, and witnessed still greater displays of the grace of God than he had before seen. The effects of this illness, however, he never fully recovered; and though his exertions in public were still almost unexampled, yet the prostration of his strength immediately consequent upon them was, in nearly all instances, more severe and long continued than at any previous period.

In the latter part of the year he was again afflicted. Under the date of Oct. 18, he thus writes to his father:

You would have heard from me sooner had I not been unwell. I have had a touch of a fever which has been making dreadful ravages in Frome and its neighborhood. I providentially attended to it in time, so that I have had but a slight attack. I think it likely that I took the fever through visiting some who were ill in it. I had for a few days much pain in my head. Thank God, it has been to me the best affliction with which I was ever visited. It has brought me much nearer to God. I was so touched with the divine goodness, while in an agony of pain, that I was constrained to shout the high praises of God. We had a blessed baptism of the Spirit last night at family prayer. We have devoted ourselves afresh to God, and he accepts us.

Nor was this a solitary instance of peculiar divine blessing upon Mr. Smith's family worship. In domestic life he was a happy and an interesting man, and the uniformity of his personal religion exerted a perpetual influence over his home. But it was especially when the members of his household accompanied him to the throne of mercy that the piety of the husband, the father, the master, and the friend was presented in its most impressive and touching aspect. Many who have had the privilege of uniting in these solemn engagements can never forget the emotions which were then excited. Mr. Smith's pertinent observations on the portion of Scripture, the reading of which formed a regular part of the service; the singular sweetness of the family music, succeeded by powerful and appropriate prayer, could not fail to affect a mind endowed with any measure of religious feeling. After the family worship of the morning, which Mr. Smith usually prefaced by several hours of private devotion, he returned to the exercises of the closet, and, sometimes on his knees and often on his face, wrestled with God till not infrequently a considerable part of the floor of his study was wet with his tears. In his unreserved disclosures of feeling to his friend Mr. Clarkson, he once remarked that he was sometimes engaged in prayer for two or three hours before he enjoyed that unrestricted communion with heaven which he always desired and which he generally succeeded in obtaining. "Often," says another of his friends, "when I have gone to his house with those who were seeking salvation, I have interrupted his devotions, in which he would be engaged for seven or eight hours at a time." He occasionally spent the whole night in prayer; sometimes the greater part, if not the whole, of several successive nights; and when he has been from home, the members of the families by whom he has been entertained have, at various hours of the night, been awakened by his groans, when his desires became too big for utterance and his emotions too mighty to be controlled. Of his public and social prayers, perfectly simple and inartificial as they were, multitudes have testified that the divine influence attending them exceeded anything that they ever experienced. The author of these pages, in common with many others, has seen persons so affected under them that nature itself has sunk, and they have been removed from the scene of action in a state of insensibility. And these results were as observable when his manner was placid as when it was peculiarly impassioned. Indeed, as some of his friends have remarked, there were seasons when his physical exertions were peculiarly violent, in which there was less accompanying influence than when he exercised more command over himself.

A similar power appeared to accompany his conversations, his reproofs, and sometimes even his looks. A woman in Frome, who attended the chapel, was in the habit of keeping her shop open on the Sunday morning. Mr. Smith several times faithfully warned her of the impropriety of her conduct; but though she promised amendment, her heart was too fully wedded to worldly gain to be persuaded to abandon the sin. One Sunday, as Mr. Smith was going to the chapel, he stopped at her house. Leaning over the half-opened door, he fixed his eyes intently on her as she served her customers, and shaking his head, silently withdrew. Had a bolt from heaven fallen at her feet she could scarcely have been more affected. The shop was never again opened on the Sabbath, and in a short time she herself, having joined the society, became savingly converted. "Truly," says Mr. Clarkson, who relates the incident, "this circumstance may remind us of the ineffable look which our compassionate Redeemer cast upon Peter." A sinner within the sphere of Mr. Smith's influence was perpetually exposed to the holy compulsion of his expostulations and prayers; and few who were resolved to cleave to their sins ever had the hardihood to endure a second interview with him, if it were possible to be avoided. At a prayer meeting in the Frome circuit, where several were in distress, he once remarked an old man looking on with much surprise. "Well," said Mr. Smith, "do you intend to leave off your sins and be saved tonight?" "Why no," replied the other with great coolness, "I think I will wait till next time." Had this been his real design, his policy would have been immediately to have left the place. He remained, however, and presently the hand of God came upon him. He cried aloud in anguish and horror, and in a short time the Lord gave him "the garment of praise for the spirit of heaviness." About twelve months since, he died in peace. The following incident also, which belongs to the same class of facts, deserves insertion here. A young lady of Frome, who was very ill, expressed a strong desire to see Mr. Smith. Her state of weakness, however, was such that it was with difficulty her friends were prevailed on to comply with her wishes. At length he was admitted to visit her, and he had the happiness of leading her into the enjoyment of the peace which passeth all understanding. For two or three days she retained the assurance of her acceptance, and her spirit then returned to God. Shortly afterwards, her sister, who was religiously disposed, remarked to a pious female that she feared Mr. Smith's visit had hastened the death of her deceased relative. The person to whom this observation was made replied that if this was her feeling, she would recommend her to go to Mr. Smith and express it to him, at the same time offering to accompany her. They went and found him at home. He immediately addressed the young lady on the subject of personal salvation. "Your sister," he said, "has gone to heaven; are you preparing to follow her?" She was much affected; and when he inquired if she wished to obtain the present pardon of her sins, she replied in the affirmative. They then united in prayer; and before she had the opportunity of stating the object of her visit, the light of God's countenance broke upon her soul, and she was filled with unspeakable delight. No person for whose salvation Mr. Smith was particularly interested could be secure from his efforts. If they even sought the resorts of drunkards and harlots, it did not at all cut them off from his influence. Sometimes, when he discovered them, he succeeded in leading them away; and I have a letter now before me which refers to his having, in more than one instance, kneeled on the floor of a haunt of intemperance till the individual for whom he interceded obtained the salvation of God in the presence of those who had been the companions of his excess.

In the beginning of 1825, Mr. Smith spent a fortnight in London. Here his labors were attended with extraordinary success. In what is now the second London West circuit, nearly a hundred and twenty persons obtained peace with God through his instrumentality; and about half that number entered into the enjoyment of purity of heart. Many of these received salvation at tea-parties and other social meetings of a similar kind; and it was one of the excellencies of this devoted servant of God that he rendered the parlor a sanctuary, and occasions of ordinary fellowship means of grace. In Frome and its neighborhood he will long be remembered with peculiar delight. One of his intimate friends[1] on that circuit says, "In every love-feast that I have attended or do now attend, many rise and declare with heartfelt gratitude that Mr. Smith was made a blessing to them.

---

1.   Lieut. Clarke, who with his wife was converted through Mr. Smith's instrumentality. An account of the experience and happy death of the latter will be found in the *Wesleyan-Methodist Magazine* for October, 1828.

CHAPTER 12

Nottingham
1825–1826

A t the Conference of 1825 Mr. Smith was appointed to the Nottingham circuit. His colleagues were the Rev. Messrs. Aver, Hanwell, and Parker, men to whom he was strongly attached and with whom he labored in delightful harmony. Among the people, his ministry was awaited with great expectation, which was strengthened by his first public appearance among them at the meeting of the bands. A person present on that occasion remarks:

> He professed in striking language what the blessed God had done for him, the deep concern he felt for the divine honor, the state of the world, and the salvation of souls, after which he engaged in prayer. Never shall I forget the impressions made upon me by his fine athletic figure, his open and majestic countenance, his powerful and sonorous voice, and above all his fervent and mighty prayer. It seemed as if heaven were opened, and we all believed that success was certain.

On the following Sunday evening, he preached with great power at Halifax Place Chapel. His subject was the love of God, and on this (to him) most delightful of all topics, he dilated in "breathing thoughts" and "burning words." "I preach in faith," he cried in one part of his discourse. "God will answer prayer and save souls tonight." About twelve persons at the prayer meeting that evening professed to receive the blessing of pardon.

This was an encouraging presage of the great work which succeeded, for perhaps in no place were Mr. Smith's labors attended with more remarkable results. The spirit in which his ministry was at this time conducted may be gathered from the following facts. Shortly after his arrival in the circuit, a pious friend remarked to him one morning that he looked very unwell. In reply he said that he had spent the whole of the preceding day and night in fasting and prayer, and that he was assured that God would shortly begin a glorious revival in Nottingham and its neighborhood. Some time afterwards a few friends called at his house one evening and found him in a state of deep depression of mind. He had been meditating on the condition of the sinners in the town and its vicinity and lamenting, with many tears, their dishonor of God and his laws. He invited his friends to join him in prayer. One or two engaged in this exercise, and then Mr. Smith himself poured forth his sorrows before the Lord, confessing and bewailing the sins of the people with great minuteness and indescribable emotion. His vehement agony was so extraordinary that Mrs. Smith, accustomed as she was to witness his exertions, was at length unable any longer to endure the sight, and left the room. His friends rose from their knees and gazed on him with astonishment mingled with apprehension. One of them ventured to expostulate with him, and besought him to cease. Mr. Smith turned to him, and in a tone of inconsolable grief exclaimed, "Go, man, kneel down, and cry and sigh for the abominations of the people." For nearly two hours did he continue to call on God with his utmost strength of body and of mind, and it was by sheer exhaustion alone that he was at last induced to desist. These extraordinary exercises were accompanied and followed by signs of a coming revival, and in a short time "there was a great rain."

I subjoin a few extracts from his correspondence during the former part of the year 1826, which will serve in some degree to exemplify his success.

Jan. 13. A few weeks ago I was at Ilkeston. In the evening we had a very interesting time. Many were in deep distress; and after a good deal of labor, I think eight persons found peace with God. The following morning, I learned that there were several very unhappy who had been at the preaching on the preceding evening. I agreed with a local preacher to go to a lace warehouse where some of them were working. We went. I made a few observations respecting the importance of salvation, etc. Many were much affected. We sang, "Take my poor heart," etc., and began to pray. The distressed souls cried aloud for mercy. Such anguish as some of them were in for more than an hour I have seldom witnessed. After considerable struggling, six found peace with God. May God give stability to his good work! We want more nurses in the church of Christ. Last Tuesday evening I was at Draycot, in the Derby circuit. We had much of the power of God among us. Many were in distress, and I think about twelve found peace with God.

April 8. God is blessedly moving among the people in various parts of our circuit. More than one hundred and fifty were added to the society the last quarter, and upwards of two hundred and twenty are on trial. In two or three places, the awakening influence of God seems to be general. The people are distressed in their houses without any outward means, doubtless in answer to prayer. At New Basford the people appear to be panic-struck. Some of the most notoriously wicked characters have been converted to God. I gave fourteen notes of admittance to persons in one class at that place a few weeks ago, all of whom professed to have found peace with God. We had a blessed time there last Thursday. The glory of God filled the place, and five obtained mercy. Many souls have been saved there every week for some time past. I gave seventeen notes at Old Radford a short time since; all who received professed to have obtained liberty. The work is going on. In several places it is spring. Hallelujah! At Nottingham souls are saved every week. More than a dozen were saved after Mr. Dawson had preached a few weeks ago; and six found peace with God on the morning of the same day, in a private house. I have seen some signal work also in the Mansfield and Ilkestone circuits.

June 29. Although our increase of members has not been very great—two hundred—we have four hundred and forty-seven on trial. In some places, the work astonishes the old members; they never saw anything equal to it. Numbers have trusted God for a full salvation, and many more are panting for it. It is the *good pleasure* of the good God to save—to save fully. How important it is to hold this truth fast through everything!

July 12. Many backsliders are returning to the Lord, and cleansing work is going on. Last Sunday night at Carlton, upwards of twenty, I think, either found peace with God or obtained a clean heart. We had a still greater night on Monday, at Halifax Chapel, and last night, at New Sneinton, many souls were saved. Glory be to God! I have not time to enter into any particulars.

It is, of course, impossible to trace the good which was effected primarily through Mr. Smith's instrumentality, as it extended and still extends in numerous ramifications. There are many instances in which whole families were brought to the knowledge of the truth, in consequence of the influence which, in the first place, he had exerted upon individual members of them. The following case is too remarkable to be omitted. A young man left his home and his friends in Derbyshire in rather a discreditable manner and came to reside at Nottingham a little after Mr. Smith's appointment to that circuit. A pious female, one of our tract distributors, had occasion to call at the house where he lodged, during the time of Nottingham fair. With her he was very jocose, and pressed her to go with him to the fair. She agreed, provided he would first accompany her to the chapel. Having gained his consent, she took him to hear Mr. Smith. During the sermon, he was deeply convinced of sin; and at the prayer meeting that followed, he obtained peace with God. He soon after returned home and surprised all his family by his seriousness and consistently pious deportment. One day, his mother, with an appearance of much concern, asked him how it was that he was so constantly happy. He told her his experience, and assured her that God was willing to make it equally hers. Upon this, they betook themselves to the throne of grace, and mingled their prayers and tears, till the God of all consolation revealed himself in her heart; and mother and son rejoiced together in unspeakable joy. Some time afterwards, her other son was married. The young man besought the Lord to grant that on the day of the wedding one soul might be saved; and though up to the very morning there was no appearance of any answer to his prayer, he felt assured that his request would be granted. Upon the return of the bridal party from church, he retired to renew his suit before the Lord. He then came back to the company and solemnly called upon them to join him in prayer. They did so; and before they rose from their knees, the bride was awakened and clearly converted. The youth once more withdrew and confessed and bewailed his sin in only asking for *one* soul, as he was convinced that God was far more desirous to save the whole than he could be. As he came down from his devotions, he heard a noise in one of the chambers, and upon entering, found his brother in deep distress, crying to God for the pardon of his sins. In a little while, he also was filled with peace in believing. Shortly after, two musicians, who had been hired to contribute to the hilarity of the party, came in. The bridegroom, in the fullness of his joy, told them that they were not wanted. "We have other music," he said, and invited them to unite in it. Again they had recourse to prayer, and once more the Savior answered. Before they had ceased their intercessions, one of the musicians was convinced of his sins, and brought into the enjoyment of the favor of God. The melody of renewed hearts celebrated their espousals to Christ on that happy day, and the burden of their chorus might well be supposed to have been, "Unto him that loved us, and washed us from our sins in his own blood; unto him be glory and dominion for ever and ever! Amen."

The strength of Mr. Smith's faith was probably never more fully displayed than in behalf of dying sinners. The condition of many of these is such as to extinguish all hope in the mind of an ordinary Christian; but I never heard of a case which he looked upon as hopeless, and what discouraged others appeared only to give to him an additional stimulus. The following is an example. He was called to visit an aged woman who was dying in the most miserable circumstances. Her heart seemed shut up in despair, and she expressed herself as having made up her mind to be damned! Mr. Smith spent several hours with her, exhorting, praying, and reading appropriate portions of Scripture. She repeatedly begged him to desist, assuring him that his efforts were of no sort of use; but every rebuff seemed only to increase his zeal for her salvation. At length she confessed that for many years she had been a backslider. She added that she had sinned away her day of grace, and her salvation was utterly impossible. He now renewed his exertions; his faith appeared to gather fresh strength, and he wrestled yet more mightily with God in her behalf. He considered the infinity of the merit of Christ, that his atonement was available even for her aggravated guilt, that the

Holy Spirit was purchased by the blood of the Savior, that a sufficient measure of his influence might be exerted upon her to meet her case, and that this influence might be obtained by believing prayer. He persevered, therefore, in the contest of faith with despair, and at last the dying sinner began to yield, to relent, to weep, to hope that it was yet possible that she might be saved before the eleventh hour expired. Shortly afterwards she ventured to cast her soul on Christ, and the Holy Spirit witnessed in her heart that God had accepted her. She was filled with gladness and thanksgiving; and having praised the grace of Christ for a few hours on earth, went to join the remembered thief in Paradise.

Many other similar examples of the unfailing character of Mr. Smith's faith might be quoted. I have before me an account of his successful labors in behalf of a malefactor of the name of Wood, who was executed at Nottingham for murder. This person had some pious friends, by whom he was recommended to Mr. Smith's attentions. The afternoon before he suffered, Mr. Smith was with him for some time, and then engaged to return and spend the night in the condemned cell. It was with considerable difficulty, and only at Wood's earnest wish, that he obtained admission. He then assiduously set himself to declare to the unhappy man the evil of his sins, and had the satisfaction of bringing him, through the agency of the blessed Spirit, into a state of deep and sincere penitence. Next he pointed him to Christ. Much time was employed in calling on God; and at length his divine mercy beamed into the darkness of his dungeon, and the still more dense darkness of his heart, and he testified that all his sins were taken away. In the morning Mr. Smith accompanied him to the place of execution; and, at his particular and repeated request, commended him by earnest prayer to the grace of that God into whose presence he was ushered a few moments afterwards. The popular feeling against Wood was unusually strong, and many were very sceptical as to his repentance. Mr. Smith himself, however, had no doubt of his acceptance at the last hour; and the error, if it were an error, was amiable and characteristic.

In the course of the year, a pretty little chapel was built at New Basford, and there were several events connected with the work of

God in that place sufficiently striking to demand insertion in these pages. The first exhibits faith resulting from effort. Mr. Smith called on a person who had been a Socinian. After some conversation, he complained that he was unable to believe the doctrine of the divinity of our blessed Savior. It was one of those cases with which every minister is familiar, where argument would have availed nothing. "We will pray about it," said Mr. Smith, "and if you will only *try to believe*, I will forfeit my head if God does not give you the power." The result answered his anticipations. The man became there and then a true believer, and forthwith united himself to the society. The following illustrates the soundness and clearness of Mr. Smith's practical counsels. Mrs. M. had the happiness of seeing all her children except one converted to God. He was the subject of many prayers and admonitions; but he persevered in his sins, seldom attended any place of worship, and assiduously avoided meeting with Mr. Smith, of whose faithful expostulations he was greatly afraid. The distressed mother proposed the case to Mr. Smith and requested his advice. "Lay your hand on one thing at once," was his reply, meaning that she should define to her own mind a distinct object of petition and not cease till her prayer was answered.[1] She did so, especially in reference to her ungodly son; and a short time

---

1.   One of Mr. Smith's friends relates an instance in which Mr. Smith gave, with remarkable good effect, advice similar to the above. It was during a visit which he paid to the metropolis, while he was stationed at Windsor, alluded to on page 115. He had attended a prayer meeting where many had been pardoned and purified. On the following day, which was Sunday, he had engaged to preach several times; however, a little before the previous midnight, he set out to assist at a watch-night "It was," to use Mr.—'s own words, "an overwhelming time." At first, nothing was done; the hearts of the people seemed hard, and prayer was accompanied with little power. Mr. Smith himself prayed after almost everyone who engaged. Now and then he gave a short exhortation, showed the way of faith, and urged the praying men to believe for the people. Particularly he called on the congregation to wait solemnly before God and to apply to the throne of grace "for something definite, to determine in their own minds what blessing they wanted, and then plainly and perseveringly to come to God for it." Several hours elapsed before the happy results of this counsel were apparent. At length, between two and three o'clock, the Lord whom they sought suddenly came to his temple. One person was then cleansed from sins; five minutes after, four others; then two more; and so the work proceeded. Six of these persons were subsequently made leaders.

afterwards, returning from the chapel where Mr. Smith had been preaching on the subject of prayer, she said to the young man, "Now I believe that the Lord will have mercy upon thee, for he has heard my prayer on thy behalf." The impression which these words produced was indelible. In about a fortnight afterwards, he was brought into the enjoyment of true religion, and is now an active leader and local preacher. I add a singular instance of the result of Mr. Smith's intercession. He was one evening preaching at New Basford, and a very holy influence rested on the people. In the congregation was a woman who had recently began to seek the Lord, whose husband was proverbial for wickedness. During the sermon, this man came to the door of the chapel and in a furious tone exclaimed, "Is Mary C. here?" adding that if she did not come out he would break her legs. Mr. Smith stopped in his discourse and cried, "Lord, lay thy hand on that man; put thy hook in his nose, and thy bridle in his mouth," etc., and then proceeded. A prayer meeting, as usual, followed; and before it was concluded, the man returned to the chapel. But he was now a different character. He came to tell the people that God had forgiven all his sins. It appeared that when, at the conclusion of the first service his wife returned home, accompanied by a pious female, they found that in the interval God had powerfully wrought on him; and he now gladly joined them in prayer for pardon. Some persons were sent for to pray with him, and in a short time the Lord answered and poured out upon him the regenerating and adopting Spirit. When he thus publicly declared the mercy of God to him, incredulity sat on almost every countenance, nor could the people be persuaded "that he was a disciple" till his Christian deportment manifested the greatness of the change which had been effected in him.

Much fruit of Mr. Smith's labors in New Basford still remains. Some of his spiritual children have left the place, and others have preceded him to a better world; but after all deductions, I am informed that there are now thirty persons living in the village who were converted through his immediate instrumentality.

I conclude this section with the relation of another characteristic incident which occurred in the early part of Mr. Smith's residence at

Nottingham. While on one occasion he was preaching at a village in the circuit, the whole audience appeared to be moved and cries and groans resounded from every part of the chapel. The extraordinary scene which followed at the prayer meeting attracted a considerable number of careless or scoffing spectators, who crowded in at the door, producing much confusion by their behavior, and arresting the progress of the work of God by their unhallowed spirit. Mr. Smith went to them and begged them to kneel down with the rest of the congregation and to join in the worship. To this request they paid no attention. He then fell on his knees before them, and with remarkable earnestness renewed his entreaties. Finding, however, that they were unmoved, he rose, and, stretching out his arms, drove them all out of the place, at the same time declaring with strong emphasis that he would not suffer God to be insulted in his own house. The Lord then wrought a great deliverance. Fifteen persons were that evening enabled to trust in Christ for pardon, the greater part of whom still adorn their Christian profession in the same village.

Chapter 13

Nottingham—Beeston
1826–1829

In the year 1826 it was my happiness to be appointed to the Nottingham circuit, and here I became intimately acquainted with the subject of these memoirs. It will not, therefore, I trust, be offensive to my readers, if, without circumlocution, I lay before them the results of my personal observations on his character. I do this with the less hesitation as, after the lapse of several years and with the maturest judgment which I am capable of exercising, I see no reason to alter or even materially to modify the opinions which at that time I formed. And here, in the first place, I candidly acknowledge that my prepossessions were decidedly unfavorable to the discernment and admission of Mr. Smith's excellence. I had heard of him as a zealous though singular minister. In a degree I had been informed of his success; and I had learned that this was to be attributed principally, if not wholly, to his personal piety and the power of his prayer. The shadows of the picture I had myself supplied from the characters of others whom I supposed to resemble him; and, with a want of liberality, in which I fear I was not singular, I had invested him with qualities which went far to neutralize the charm of his acknowledged virtues. In this state of feeling, I met him for the first time; and I had scarcely been five minutes in his company before I was ashamed and humbled on account of my prejudices. His amiableness at once commanded affectionate respect. I use the term amiableness because, though it is somewhat vague, it is the only expression which includes the ideas of his character which immediately presented themselves to my mind. Of his native qualities which may be comprehended under this phrase, the preceding pages have given the reader a cursory view. I therefore, in this place, allude principally to particulars which have not before been expressly noticed.

I soon discovered the infinite spiritual disparity which existed between us. But his religion was of an order which conveyed no sort of discouragement to those who contemplated it. It was neither mystical on the one hand nor exclusive and repelling on the other. There was about it no spiritual empiricism, if I may so express myself. No one who perceived the power of his faith (which was all but impossible to overlook) could for a moment hesitate to admit that it was perfectly adequate to the production even of his maturity of Christianity. The eminence of his virtue, therefore, exerted a stimulating influence on those who came within its reach. His experience supplied the most satisfactory reply to the popular objection against the doctrine of entire sanctification—that by setting the standard of Christian perfection so high we necessarily discourage Christians from seeking to attain it. It was at once perceived that to the simplicity of his faith no spiritual blessing was difficult or remote, and no one could discern the nature of that faith without being convinced that it was, in its gradations, readily attainable by every sincere and childlike spirit. And this I cannot but consider a principal cause of Mr. Smith's success as a preacher of the great doctrine to which I have just alluded. Hence, also, he himself sought out the most perfect models of Christian experience with the rejoicing consciousness that what one believer has succeeded in obtaining was equally within his reach. "When I read Fletcher's life," said he, "I saw a narrow way; not that I had not chosen a narrow way, but I saw one still narrower." And thus he not only recommended to others a high degree of Christian holiness, but likewise urged the best methods of attaining it. "Get signally blessed," was one of his common advices. At a love-feast which he conducted in the neighborhood of Nottingham, several persons spoke of their trials doing them good by driving them to prayer. At the close, Mr. Smith made some striking remarks on what had been said. He thanked God on behalf of those whose afflictions had been so beneficial to them. "But," said he, "there is a more excellent way: that state of mind is to be attained, in which a man shall not need to be whipped to his knees, but shall go to his duty, attracted by the delight which he feels in it." He then exhorted all to seek this happiness, at the same time assuring them that he himself enjoyed it.

And while his views of the omnipotence of faith gave to his own experience the aspect of simplicity and ready attainableness, they also supplied a singular unity to his theology. Hence, his profound and painful discoveries of the depravity of the sinner were combined with the most lively and practical perceptions of the high vocation of the saint. The sinner and the saint, in some schools of theology, are two isolated characters; and generally it is impossible to perceive with any degree of clearness how one individual can, at different periods of his life, sustain them both. The impression on the mind of a partially instructed reader, after rising from the perusal of some popular evangelical treatises, is of a fearful and insurmountable distinctness between man in his natural condition and the elevated privileges of the New Testament. Heaven and earth could not have been more remote before the promise of a Mediator beamed from the one to enlighten the despair of the other. But Mr. Smith's faith, boundless, untiring, undelaying, perpetually grasping a present promise in its illimitable breadth, brought the deepest depravity into contact with the fullness of evangelical purity, and seemed continually to cry, "The word is nigh thee, even in thy mouth and in thy heart."

His extraordinary humility gave a peculiar charm to all the other graces of his character and not infrequently assumed a most affecting prominence. During the time he was at Windsor, he had a rather severe illness, and with emotion he directed that, should it terminate fatally, his coffin should have no inscription but

UNFAITHFUL JOHN SMITH

There was in his mind, to use a happy phrase of one of his friends, "a springing forth to meet instruction"; and with it was combined a prompt and extensive sympathy for the infirmities and even unbelief of others. At a missionary meeting I recollect, one of the speakers, after having descanted upon the mass of corruption and the total alienation from God which exists in the world, remarked that sometimes when his own mind had been deeply and painfully impressed with these facts, he had for a moment doubted whether it were possible for the world to be converted. Mr. Smith, who was seated immediately behind him, instantly replied, loud enough for several on the platform to hear, "Yes, and so have I too." The man remembered the feelings of the child, and dealt accordingly with those who, in a peculiar degree, still "saw in part, and prophesied in part." It is here proper to notice also his remarkable liberality, especially in reference to different schools of ministers. On the subject of his own duty, he never had the slightest hesitation. And he sometimes expressed himself with a tone of determination amounting almost to severity when anyone questioned the correctness of his principles as they respected himself. These were fixed; and the law of gravitation in the natural world might as easily have been annulled as his mind should be turned aside from the course to which he had bound himself. "Sir, you are in error," said he with calm decision to a person of high respectability who once in his presence attacked one of his principles. The other was considerably irritated, and in a tone which was intended to repress all further discussion, replied, "I will not be told that I am in error by a young man, Sir, and before this company." "Then, Sir," said Mr. Smith, "you must not make such assertions when I am present."

The quiet resolution with which this was uttered silenced his antagonist, and the conversation took another direction. But with this decision was united the most noble admission of the excellencies of those whose style of preaching was totally different from that which he himself cultivated. He never made his own conduct a rule for that of others. "He was aware," says one of his intimate friends, "of the diversity of minds, as well as of gifts, which 'the same Spirit has divided to every man severally as he will'; and never did I know conscientious strictness combined with more liberality of thinking." He deeply regretted, it is true, that his own strong and serviceable views of divine truth were not generally received, especially among the more intellectual agents of the church; but wherever he saw a sincere desire to do good, he hailed it with unequivocal demonstrations of pleasure. He often remarked that the man who took pains to mend the world had his hearty thanks. In short, I may venture to affirm that there never was an individual whose character was more diametrically remote from that of the sour censorious zealot.

Of the tenderness of his spirit, mention has already been made; and this rendered him a peculiarly welcome visitant to the chamber of affliction. I remember accompanying him to see one of our leaders in Nottingham, a poor but pious man, who was near his end. When we arrived at his house, he was in the article of death. His eyes were glazed, and there was in his throat that awful sound which announces the immediate and inevitable approach of the king of terrors. We stood for some time gazing in stillness, but not in sadness, on the solemn spectacle. I looked on my dear friend; the tears were chasing each other over his face, his chest was heaving, and the whole of his athletic frame was agitated by irrepressible emotion. At length he broke the silence, and in a tremulous voice repeated, with a pathos and freshness with which I could scarcely have conceived it possible to have invested so hackneyed a passage:

> The chamber where the good man meets his fate,
> Is privileged beyond the common walk
> Of virtuous life—quite in the verge of heaven

and truly it was so at that hour as we successively commended the soul of the departing saint to the hands of God. And this susceptibility Mr. Smith preserved at all times to a remarkable degree. No sort of personal gratification seemed to have the power to shut up his heart in selfishness, or even at all to take off the sensitiveness of his feelings. Walking, for example, one day in the streets of London with a friend, the conversation took some turn which he highly enjoyed. In the midst of his full flow of pleasure, he casually turned his head and saw, slowly moving along, a young man who appeared to be in the last stage of a consumption. The smile instantly forsook his face, and he burst into a flood of tears.

It is difficult to determine whether Mr. Smith's energy or amiableness were the most striking. Perhaps the former generally impressed those who knew him only, or principally, as a public man; the latter, those who were more fully admitted into his personal friendship. It certainly is rare for these qualities to be so remarkably

combined in one individual. Men of strong resolution and independence often seem alone in their sphere, bending all others to their
will, but submitting their wills to none—cut off from the charities of
mankind and wrapped up in their own plans and their own power.
Several circumstances, besides his natural constitution, contributed
to render Mr. Smith so interestingly different. The first, and most
important, was the peculiarly tender tone of his personal religion;
and the second, the expectation of success only by the cooperation
of others. His plans it is true were his own; but, as we have already
remarked, it was for the church to succeed in them. This brought
him continually into intimate association with good men at their
very best moments. To them he delighted to expound his principles;
and when his own glow of feeling had infected their hearts, to carry
them off, all warm and inspired, to some scene of hallowed and
successful action. It will be easy to perceive how these and the like
causes operated on a mind naturally open and susceptible.

Mr. Smith's manners, though plain, were kind and inviting. His
good nature was unbounded; and in his conversation there was often
a quiet and harmless but shrewd humor which gave to his remarks
on human nature an unusual vivacity. His relations of incidents,
principally of course those which respected the work of God, were
strikingly graphic, though no one had a greater contempt for the
stringing together of anecdotes merely for the purpose of amuse-
ment. Yet, with all the playfulness of his natural disposition, it was
impossible not to perceive that there was a constant and powerful
undercurrent of religious feeling; and he never allowed himself to
diverge from the most solemn topics to a degree which rendered his
instant return to them either difficult to himself or harsh and star-
tling to those who enjoyed his society. In this respect, his character
was marked by a perfect harmony. He was

> A creature not too bright or good
> For human nature's daily food:
> And yet a spirit still, and bright,
> With something of an angel light.

Mr. Smith seldom refused an invitation to a tea-party or any
social meeting of a similar kind. He was of the opinion of a great

man, that "parlor preaching" was a very important part of the duty of a minister. Many were the seals to his labors in this department of Christian exertion, some of whom have already sat down with Abraham and Isaac and Jacob in the kingdom of God. His usual custom was, first, to give out a verse of a hymn and to engage in prayer. Then he proceeded to inquire into the spiritual state of each in the room; and in general, the experience or wants of one or more supplied subjects for suitable advice and for subsequent intercession. Were I not afraid of swelling this work to an improper size, I might relate many cases of this kind. One will suffice. It occurred at the marriage of one of our local preachers in the Nottingham circuit. Having by direct inquiry ascertained that the sister of the bride was seeking the Lord, Mr. Smith, in an earnest and concise way, pointed out God's method of saving a sinner and then called on all present to unite in prayer. For more than an hour they importuned the throne of grace till that same Savior appeared who, in other days,

> Did not refuse a guest to be
> At Cana's poor festivity

and the bitter waters of penitence were exchanged for the wine of the kingdom. In the same house, a few weeks before, another member of the family had been brought into the enjoyment of the divine favor through Mr. Smith's instrumentality.

In addition to those features of his piety which have been already noticed, there were two others which particularly struck me. The first was his luminous insight into the invisible world. On this subject, it is not for me to dilate. The veil is on my heart; nor are there many Christians who are capable of estimating this part of Mr. Smith's character. I take this opportunity, however, of confirming the remark of one of his friends, "that he was able to judge of the state of those for and with whom he interceded by an influence perceptible to his own mind." He had also a peculiar sense of the agency of the powers of darkness and of the resistance they offered to the exertion of faith and the consequent salvation of men. Sometimes this was so impressive that he actually addressed them as if visibly present and, in a tone of solemn and mysterious but unwavering confidence, defied their utmost efforts. He once, in private conversation, expressed it as his fixed conviction that their motions were periodical.

In common with some other eminent Christians, he enjoyed distinct fellowship with the blessed Three; and it was not unusual for him to commence his prayers in public with adoration, severally and successively, of the persons in the Godhead, and acknowledgment of the proper divinity of each. Nor was this species of distinction confined to the commencement of these addresses. Other passages in his prayers were addressed to the Savior and the Spirit, as well as to the Father; and to these no one who had spiritual ears could listen without perceiving that the mind of the speaker was engaged in clear and distinct communion with the glorious beings on whom he called. To this practical recognition of the mystery of the Trinity may possibly be attributed, in part, the peculiar impressiveness which frequently accompanied his administration of the ordinance of baptism. Such services were often with him seasons of unspeakable unction. One gentleman states that the divine influence which attended the baptism of one of his children by Mr. Smith exceeded anything he ever witnessed. Another similarly memorable incident which has been mentioned to me occurred at New Basford when Mr. Smith baptized one of the children of Mr. H. Beeson. Having with deep solemnity dedicated the infant to the Father, and the Son, and the Holy Ghost, he lifted it up towards heaven, as far as his arms would extend, and with abundance of tears presented it to the Holy Trinity. The impression upon the crowded congregation cannot be described.

The second particular of which I proposed to speak was the *style* of Mr. Smith's devotions. I cannot but ascribe the effect of his public and social prayers partly to their—shall I say—*logical* unity and connection. This was remarkable and well worthy of imitation. He first laid down certain premises in the most simple and perspicuous manner. For example, he would acknowledge the purity and justice of God; and when the minds of the people had accompanied him thus far, he proceeded with many tears to confess and bewail their impurity, their ingratitude, and rebellion. Then turning to the divine compassion, he would, to use his own phrase, "fasten on the truth of God" and plead some particular and apposite promise. Thus would he carry to the throne the penitence and faith of a thousand hearts, till the answer descended like a mighty wind, and the priest himself could scarcely stand to minister for the glory of the Lord. But in all this there was a perfect coherence, without any thing of rhapsody or rant. His prayers were specimens of reasoning which his congregation could understand and feel; and when their judgments were convinced, it was scarcely possible for them to resist the power of the ardent and vehement pleading which succeeded.

Mr. Smith's reverence for the Lord's prayer was very great; and in the use of it he was always impressive, sometimes extraordinarily so. One occasion in which this was the case will long be remembered by many who were present. It was at a love-feast in Nottingham. He had prayed with unusual power; and when he proceeded to repeat the Lord's prayer, the effect was beyond conception. Multitudes responded with peculiar fervor to each petition as it was pronounced, till he came to the doxology, at each clause of which he raised his voice and ascribed to the Almighty "the kingdom, and the power, and the glory, for ever and ever" in a tone and with an unction which fell on the congregation with irresistible force. A glow of heavenly feeling pervaded the whole assembly; many gave vent to their emotions by bursts of tears and some in irrepressible shouts of praise. Others laid hold of the sacred words, repeating them again and again even after he had ceased; and whispers of "for ever and ever," mingled with sobs, passed from one lip to another, till it appeared as if they had been under a spell, from which escape was impossible. In fact, it was some time before the regular business of the meeting could be resumed.

Another feature of Mr. Smith's character, which I was not prepared to expect, was the vigor of his understanding. I do not mean to say that he was, as the phrase is commonly understood, an intellectual man; but the calibre of his mind was considerable, and his judgment remarkably sound. And here I cannot do better than avail myself of the statements of that friend of Mr. Smith whose remarks have already so much contributed to the illustration of his character:

As one instance of the soundness of his judgment, I might cite the high esteem in which he held the character of Cecil, and the value he set upon his *Remains*, a work that he frequently quoted, which exerted no inconsiderable influence in modeling his character, and which is distinguished as much by its sober and solid cast of thought as by a deep insight into men and things. His own mind was eminently manly and judicious, and resembled in several respects that of his admired author. No one can have formed an adequate idea of the vigor of his intellect, nor consequently of the self-denial which was content to forego the credit of it, who has not enjoyed the opportunity of frequent and familiar fellowship with him. The topics to which he restricted himself were so few that, joined to his simplicity of manner and exclusive devotedness to one object, it is no wonder if, in their reverence for his piety, many have overlooked his mental superiority. I have known instances of this being the case; nor should I have been undeceived myself if I had not afterwards enjoyed for some time the opportunity of almost daily interaction with him.

One indication of vigor and independence of thought may be traced in language. As soon as anyone ventures to think for himself, instead of acquiescing in conclusions thought out by others, there will be a healthiness, a raciness, and even originality in his conceptions which will demand and create to themselves appropriate forms of expression. The *material* may be the same in both cases; but in the former it has been melted down and delivered to you with the stamp of the individual mind upon it. This was the case in no small degree with our late friend when speaking on that subject which most occupied his thoughts and heart—the work of God; many of the expressions employed by him being peculiarly his own; and yet such at the same time as immediately recommended themselves by their fidelity to the conceptions they were designed to express. Another remark which I have to make refers to his use of single words, or, to adopt the language of logic, simple terms. Everyone who has reflected much on the subject is aware of the confusion of thought which results from an indiscriminate and careless use of words; and will esteem it no slight proof of the strength of his mind that his conversation exhibited many instances of acute discrimination in this respect.

His collection of books was considerable [both in theology and in general literature], and he showed his enlightened regard for knowledge not only by setting himself to inculcate on all who had leisure for it the assiduous improvement of their minds; but by such a spontaneous readiness to lend his own books to persons in the humblest ranks of life, and when no motive, even of courtesy, required it, as fully proved that his love of knowledge, like everything else in him, was a *principle.*

Of his style and diction in preaching I will only add that it was chaste and unaffected, simple and perspicuous; and on subjects which had much exercised his thoughts, eminently vigorous and energetic. Clear and acute in his conception of any subject, he was distinct and intelligible in his enunciation. In general, his discourses were distinguished chiefly by their vivid exhibition of the fundamental truths of the gospel, and an earnest and powerful application of them to the cases and consciences of the hearers. Accordingly, they were hortatory rather than didactic, characterized by the force and persuasiveness of their appeals rather than by any regular exposition of doctrines or discussion of principles. The spirit and power, rather than the talent, of the preacher were seen and felt. But why do I multiply words on such a subject? SALVATION—the *end* of preaching, and that alone, was the object ever present in his mind. He had no heart for anything that did not tend directly to this result. He knew that the truths necessary to salvation were simple and few in number; and that the great difficulty to a preacher is not to make them clear to the apprehension, but to bring his hearers under their influence and power.

"There was not to be found in Mr. Smith's system of preaching," says Mr. Clarkson, "the gigantic mind exerting its power in a long connected chain of metaphysical reasoning on the subject he undertook to elucidate. Nor did his discourses shine with many and various illustrations, furnished by a rich imagination, on the great evangelical truths he was ordinarily accustomed to exhibit.[1]

---

1. He sometimes however employed, for the purpose of illustration, some trifling incident, in rather a happy manner. Preaching, for example, one evening, from John 14:21, he spoke of the delight arising from God's manifesting himself to the souls of his people, and added the following anecdote. When he resided at Windsor, he said, he once had an opportunity of seeing His late Majesty, George IV, receive

Nor were they delivered with any studied graces of gesture and elocution. Yet if eloquence, as defined by an eminent minister, be 'vehement simplicity,' Mr. Smith possessed its essence.... He was very urgent on penitent sinners to come immediately to Christ and believe on his name."

"God's *short* way of salvation," he was wont to say, "is the best. *He will make it sure.*" Mr. Clarkson adds:

> He was convinced that *it was easier for a penitent to lose his convictions and sink back into his former state of sin and darkness than for a believer to lose the saving grace of God*; and therefore, by the force of divine argument and the ardor of holy importunity, he compelled sinners to make haste to Christ for salvation. And thus

> He tried each art, reproved each dull delay,
> Allured to brighter worlds, and led the way.

Whenever I have had an opportunity of hearing him, his discourse has been regular and systematized, and in the most correct, simple, and unadorned taste. Some short time before his last illness, he destroyed almost the whole of his manuscripts, lest they should afford him any sort of apology for inattention to the composition of his sermons. I am therefore unable to offer the reader any adequate specimens of his preparations for the pulpit. The few skeletons which still remain, however, cursory and meager as they are, afford sufficient evidence of his regularity and coherence in the treatment of his subjects. He was accustomed to remark that "thought only could produce impression"; and he was convinced that arrangement and unity were necessary to give thought its proper and intended effect. I am quite ready to admit that there were occasions in which his ardor led him away from his preconceived plans; but in these

---

the sacrament. As the king walked down the aisle of the Chapel Royal, he (Mr. Smith) made a deep and reverent obeisance to His Majesty. The king, with his accustomed graciousness, bowed in return; and this slight act of condescension, he remarked, filled him with so great a delight that it was with difficulty he repressed the benediction which rose to his lips. "And O," said he, "if a monarch's notice of one of his subjects thus affects him, how transporting must be the revelations of God to the heart of the believer!" etc.

cases he rarely preached with his accustomed power, and the results by no means encouraged a repetition of such irregularity.

At the commencement of his public addresses, Mr. Smith usually spoke with great calmness and deliberation, though there was always an emphasis at the conclusion of his sentences which intimated the inflexible conviction of the speaker as to the truth and importance of the statements which he was making. But when he thought he had convinced the understandings of his audience, he broke forth with a vehemence which I never saw equalled, and addressed himself to their hearts and consciences, alternately in terror and tenderness, determined, if possible, to save some. To subjects of this latter class his heart often turned with an affecting abruptness. Sometimes I have heard him denouncing sin with words and tones and gestures positively terrific; and then in a moment his voice has faltered, and with a burst of tears he has proclaimed the boundless mercy of God and the infinite prevalency of the blood of Christ. Mr. Calder says:

> One of the most striking instances of his power over a congregation, I witnessed at Sheffield. His subject was Rom. 5:8. I had heard him some years before preach from the same words, but the difference in the composition greatly surprised me. It was rich in sentiment, full of the most striking truths, while the mode of exhibiting them was highly impressive and singular, being sententious, pointed, and I might say, amounting to the epigrammatic. The first part of the discourse dwelt on man's state as a sinner needing the love and pity of God. His descriptions of sin were awful; but when he came to point out its fruits, he was indeed terrific. Then, having demonstrated that each individual of his congregation was exposed to the torments of hell but for the interposition of the mercy of God, he abruptly asked in a melting tone if they were not thankful that they were out of hell; and, weeping, he added, If you are not, I am; but I believe you are; and as we all feel alike, let us praise God together. Then giving out,
>
> Praise God, from whom all blessings flow, etc.
>
> he with his own finely musical voice pitched the Old Hundredth Psalm tune. The effect was beyond all description. Two thousand people rose to join him in singing, and each person seemed to wish

to turn aside his face to hide the tear and smother the swelling throb of his heart. It was indeed a memorable scene, and to many amounted to an era in the history of their lives.

On the subject of revivals, Mr. Smith's opinions may be expressed in a few words. He believed that they were the results of the Holy Spirit's operation, and that faith and prayer would certainly secure that operation at all times and to an unlimited extent. The latter of these principles, I suppose, is the only one likely to be questioned, though with what show of reason it is difficult to conjecture. The terms on which the influence of the Holy Ghost are granted are clear and unalterable: "If ye then, being evil, know how to give good gifts to your children, how much more shall your heavenly Father give the Holy Spirit to them that ask him?" Here is no restriction, either as to the time or degree in which we may expect our prayers to be answered. It is the presumption of unbelief alone, therefore, which can suggest any other restriction than the wants of men or the measure of their prayers. Nay, more, as if to anticipate all objections, and silence all cavils, the promise is that we shall receive whatsoever we ask in the name of Christ;[1] so that unless it can be proved that no man can pray in faith for the reviving influence of the Holy Spirit, it must be admitted as one of the gifts which the veracity of God is pledged to grant to the intercession of his people. Can it for a moment be supposed that man's exposition of the divine promises can exceed in comprehension the benevolence of "him who is able to do exceeding abundantly above all we ask or think"? Is the atonement of Christ so exceedingly circumscribed in its validity that it is within the power of the lowest Christian daily to seek for blessings which it is unable to procure? It is not to be supposed.

But arguments in favor of Mr. Smith's views on this subject are abundantly supplied by every analogy which can be brought to bear upon the case. It is not to be denied that, in answer to prayer, God will vouchsafe grace sufficient for the sanctification of an individual believer, or the awakening, repentance, and justification of an

---

1. A promise repeated, in various forms of expression, no less than five times in Gospel history. See Matt. 21:22; John 14:13; 15:16; 16:23; and especially Mark 11:23, 24; which compare with Isa. 65:24, and 1 John 5:14, 15.

individual sinner. He who questions this makes all intercession for spiritual blessings idle and profitless; and he is confronted by the evidence of thousands of examples in which immediate salvation has been procured by this means. And if one soul can be saved in answer to prayer, why not a hundred? All that is required in the latter instance is a proportionate increase of the pleading of faith. God cannot change. The principle upon which prayer is answered in the one case must be maintained inviolate, and when brought to bear on the other must induce similar results. The *mode* of the divine working is dictated by sovereign wisdom, but the *degree* depends on the faith of the church. God himself determines whether he will descend as the dew upon Israel, or as the burning flame; but it is for his people to decide whether he shall come upon the single fleece, while the rest of the floor is dry, or whether the whole of the camp shall be surrounded and gladdened by the scattering forth of angels' food.

It is certain that God will convert the *world* by the agency of the Holy Spirit. Every missionary society goes upon the principle that this agency will be secured to the efforts of the church in answer to prayer. No member of such a society—which is almost equivalent to saying no Christian—can, therefore, without the grossest inconsistency, deny that a smaller measure of divine influence will be granted upon the same terms. It is no matter of doubtful disputation whether Christ shall indeed have the heathen for his inheritance, and the uttermost parts of the earth for his possession; that is determined. But, it seems, it *is* matter of great doubt and grave argument whether the covenant, which hereafter in its ample provision is to embrace all the families of the earth, can now be made available for a few hundred people in Great Britain, where the gospel has been preached for centuries! There is no question whether the wilderness will become a fertile field; but it *is* very dubious whether the champaign, already partially cultivated, can be at present raised to any higher degree of productiveness! The desolate woman shall bring forth children, but the married wife must be childless! For remote events, our faith is mighty; but when it is called for to achieve any considerable good now, we take refuge in some vague notion of the divine sovereignty, and refuse to avail ourselves of the unlimited promise of the Spirit.

Nor is it any objection to Mr. Smith's views that some revivals have arisen where, so far as we could trace, there previously existed no ardent spirit of believing prayer, and where, in fact, there was every indication of a very low spiritual condition. It would be strange reasoning indeed that, because in some cases God had transcended the express terms of his engagement, he would therefore, in others, fall short of them. As well argue that because he, of his spontaneous compassion, gave his Son to die for the sin of the world, he therefore will not fulfil the covenant procured by his death; or that, because he is found of some who seek him not, he will refuse to be found of those who do seek him. No, the argument manifestly tends to the directly contrary conclusion. If God gave his Son, he will with him also freely give us all things. If his grace comes to those who are comparatively indifferent about it, much more will it upon those who long and labor after it; and if some revivals occur where there is no importunate spirit of faith and prayer, it is the more certain that if such a spirit can be produced in the church, a revival will succeed.

A spurious faith is to be distinguished from the genuine and scriptural, first, by its want of success, and secondly, by its hurtful reaction upon its possessor. Now let us, by these infallible indications, try that faith which respects revivals. Of it, Mr. Smith was a man who made experiment, and what was the result? In every circuit in which he traveled, from the time he went to Brighton, it was productive of great *effects*. God owned and honored it, and that in no common degree. And would this have been the case, had it been a presumptuous interference with the divine prerogative? It must have been, if revivals be a mere question of the sovereignty of God. Let no man venture to impugn this order of faith unless he himself has tried it and found it to fail. To him who has *in vain* believed on the promise of the Spirit, we will listen as a rational opposer of Mr. Smith's principles; but it is sufficiently obvious that the mere assertion of any other person is worth nothing in the argument. The only question which remains, therefore, is whether those individuals and churches whose faith immediately respects revivals are really less holy and prosperous than their neighbors. The inquiry is not whether a man may neglect personal religion upon the plea of public duty—this every one admits. But is the reaction of the faith in question of spiritual prejudice to its possessors? Suppose the case of two men, of similar character and condition in other respects, who gave equal diligence to make their personal calling and election sure; would he who prayed and believed for a present revival of the work of God be an inferior Christian to him whose benevolence was vague and undirected, and whose prayers on the subject were general and indistinct? On the contrary, all experience testifies that he would be very far superior. Indeed, it must be so, in the nature of things. The Spirit which inspires a purely benevolent longing for the present salvation of men must be of God; and such a desire, if properly cherished, is, in its reaction, nothing less than a revival of personal religion. Again we say, let those who have made the experiment be the witnesses. Would to God that all opposers of these views would only submit them to the trial! Were all Christians daily to devote but a small portion of their time to intercession on this particular subject; were they resolved to obtain, without delay, all that God had engaged to bestow, both for themselves and others, there would be no moral enterprise too great to be achieved, nor any moral hindrance too stupendous to be overcome. The day *shall* arrive when this spirit shall prevail throughout the church, and then "the desire of all nations shall come, and I will fill this house with glory, saith the Lord of Hosts."

Holding these principles, Mr. Smith, of course, decidedly rejected the popular maxim, in its common acceptation, that "we must do our duty, and leave the result to God." This is, on all hands, admitted to be a correct rule in respect to temporal blessings, since for them the Scriptures offer no unqualified promise. But Mr. Smith maintained that while it was folly and presumption to suppose that any success could attend the Christian ministry except through accompanying divine influence, it was equally contrary to the reason of things to make God responsible for that which he has put into our own hands. In other words, as it is within the power of the church to secure a certain measure of the Holy Spirit's operation, it

is irrational and unrighteous to impute the absence of that operation to anything but the want of effort and faith in the church. It is
therefore, he argued, for every Christian minister in part to decide
the measure of his own success; nor is it possible to avoid this conclusion if the foregoing reasoning be correct.

A few extracts from Mr. Smith's correspondence may perhaps
not be unacceptable to the reader in this place, principally to illustrate the state of the work of God in Nottingham and its neighborhood, during the years 1826–27.

> Oct. 7, 1826. I trust that there may be many who will actively
> concur with the Spirit. The Spirit is grieved both with opposition
> and inaction. Some scores have been set at liberty since I was
> at Cudworth, and many have obtained clean hearts. During the
> feast week at Ratcliffe, I think about thirty souls found peace.
> Last Tuesday, Mr. Hannah opened a chapel at Hyson Green. In
> the evening, at the prayer meeting, I think five souls were saved.
> Two years ago we had no society in that place. Now we have fifty
> in society and ten on trial, and a chapel that will hold more than
> three hundred people.

> Feb. 21, 1827. God makes some little use of me in awakening sin-
> ners and in leading them to Jesus, the sinner's friend, for which I
> praise his name. Last Sunday fortnight, at Arnold, eight or nine
> found peace with God. At Granby, in the Grantham circuit, three
> weeks ago, nine souls obtained pardon and two were cleansed.
> At Ruddington, in our circuit, about fifty have joined the society
> within the last quarter, most of whom have peace with God. The
> cleansing work is also going on. This will secure permanency and
> give extension to the church.

> March 22. I am still choosing God for my portion and his good
> service for my employment. I wish to be used much, and God
> to have all the glory. I cannot, I will not, be easy without see-
> ing *effects*. Nay, I must not, I dare not, thanks be to God! And I
> am determined that he shall have all the praise. God is working
> mightily among us. I think we have about four hundred and fifty
> on trial this quarter. Laboring, pleading men are increasing. God
> will stand to his engagements. The work must go on. About a

hundred have begun to meet in class at Arnold during the last quarter. The last time I was there, not fewer, I think, than twenty found peace. God seems to be agitating nearly the whole village. Lenton, which has long been desert, is fresh and green. The society has been more than doubled; Burton, the same. At Bulwell, last Monday night, my very dear father preached. Two were cleansed from sin, and eight or ten found peace. On Tuesday, at Old Basford, one obtained a clean heart, and twelve or fourteen found peace. We had about eight saved at Hockley chapel last Sunday night. Glory, glory be to God!

April 24. At Old Radford, last Wednesday night, sixteen or eighteen obtained entire sanctification, and eight were pardoned. At Halifax chapel last Sunday night, ten or twelve found peace; and last night two were pardoned, and one was cleansed. The work is sure to go on, for God and we are agreed. Labor, labor is absolutely necessary.

May 19. At Normanton, the last time I was there, twelve found peace. The following evening, I was at Wysal, in the Melton circuit. After a mighty struggle, about twelve were saved. I heard this week that in that place, last Sunday and Monday nights, thirty were set at liberty. A short time ago, I saw nine or ten saved at Epperstone in the Mansfield circuit. Last Sunday week, I was at Mount Sorrel, preaching for their Sunday schools. I think nearly twenty got liberty, and some others were awakened. Glory be to God!

July 11. Last night, at Old Basford, many were pardoned, and several cleansed. On Monday night, at Bulwell, I suppose between twenty and thirty were either pardoned or cleansed. Our increase this year is about six hundred, and we have about three hundred on trial. I have been in the Loughborough and Derby circuits, and saw many cleansed and pardoned.

Mr. Smith's correspondence supplies many other equally striking details of a similar kind, which are only omitted from the fear of swelling the work to an improper size. The following incidents, however, seem worthy to be preserved.

Among others converted through Mr. Smith's instrumentality, in a country place of the Nottingham circuit was one of those persons who, even in their sins, appear to be the subjects of peculiar providential care. He was at the battle of Waterloo and had two horses shot under him, but himself escaped unhurt. Some time afterwards, four ruffians assailed him, and, having beaten him severely, left him for dead. He recovered, however, and the persons who ill-used him were transported for the offence. Only three days before he was awakened, he was fighting in the streets of Nottingham and had his shoulder dislocated through a fall. In this condition Mr. Smith's ministry was made the means of giving him to feel the anguish of a wounded spirit. After he left the chapel, he spent nearly the whole of the night in inexpressible anguish; and on the following morning, through the directions and prayers of Mr. Smith, he was as a brand plucked out of the fire, and made happy in the divine favor. That evening, he led a person who had been awakened at the same time with himself to hear Mr. Smith at an adjacent village, where he also experienced the pardoning love of God.

A visit paid by Mr. Smith to the Newark circuit in the year 1827 is perhaps also worthy of record. On the Sunday afternoon and evening he preached the anniversary sermons for the chapel at Balderton, a village about two miles from Newark. On the former occasion, the congregation was so large as to render it necessary for the service to be conducted in the open air. At the outskirts of the assembly was a group of young men who appeared to have come to scoff. Mr. Smith addressed them in so solemn a manner, however, that they were overawed, and induced to listen with attention to the sermon. One of them was cut to the heart by the truths which he had heard, and not long after, in a love-feast at Nottingham, made a public profession of having obtained pardon for all his sins. At the tea table the same afternoon, at or about the time of taking tea, five persons entered into the enjoyment of peace with God. During the evening service, much divine power was present; but for some time it was resisted, and to use Mr. Smith's own words, "the struggle was awful." At length, seven were awakened, three of whom were set at liberty before the meeting concluded. On the Monday evening, Mr. Smith preached at Newark, and there was a melting influence under the sermon. A prayer meeting followed; but nothing remarkable occurred till about nine o'clock, when a woman in the gallery uttered an exceeding bitter and piercing cry; and in less than two minutes, the awakening power swept across the chapel, and all hearts seemed to bend before it, as corn beneath the sickle. Upwards of thirty persons were that evening converted to God, and several were cleansed from all sin. The next morning at breakfast, after some delightful pleading with God, six others entered into the enjoyment of entire sanctification; and in the evening, at the prayer meeting, fourteen penitents were filled with that peace which passeth all understanding.

At a love-feast in Halifax Place chapel, Nottingham, which Mr. Smith conducted in the month of July, 1827, an extraordinary divine influence prevailed. There was much good speaking; and towards the close of the meeting, Mr. Joseph Taylor, a local preacher, who has since died in a most triumphant manner, rose to relate his experience. He said that he had once enjoyed the blessing of entire sanctification, but through unwatchfulness had in this respect suffered loss. With much feeling he added that he was now earnestly longing and waiting for the restoration of this great privilege. Mr. Smith instantly started from his seat in the pulpit, and cried, "The cleansing power is on you *now!*" For a moment he hesitated; it was but a moment, and he then exclaimed, while the whole of his body quivered with emotion, "It is; I feel it in my heart!" The congregation then united in thanksgiving and prayer; and in a short time the windows of heaven were opened, and there was a rush of holy influence such as by the majority of that vast assembly was never before experienced. It seemed like a stream of lightning passing through every spirit. At one time, twenty persons obtained the blessing of perfect love, and rose up rapidly one after another, in an ecstasy of praise, to declare that God had then cleansed their hearts from all sin.

The following incidents will exemplify Mr. Smith's tact and courage in reproving sin. We were walking together in the streets of Nottingham, and overtook two men in conversation, just in time to hear one of them say, "I'll be damned if I do." Mr. Smith touched him on the shoulder, and with a mingled air of severity and compassion said, in a low, expressive voice, "It is a serious thing to be damned!" The man turned pale, and instantly replied, "You are right, Sir; it is so." "Then do not talk so fluently about it," returned Mr. Smith, and passed on. On Saturday evening, soon after he had retired to rest, he was aroused by the outcries and execrations of a number of persons who had come into the street to decide a public-house quarrel. Mr. Smith threw up his window, and with an overpowering voice exclaimed, "Who is that swearing and blaspheming the name of my God? I cannot allow such language in the ears of my children." Then slipping on his clothes, he hastily mingled with the crowd, and began to remonstrate with the combatants. Finding, however, that they would not listen to him, he seized the more athletic of the two by his arm, who feeling the force of his grasp, cried out, "You are too strong for me, Sir!" He then suffered Mr. Smith to lead him through several streets from the fray, confessed that he was a backslider, and solemnly engaged never to fight again.

During the time he was in Nottingham, he engaged to accompany Mr. Alderman Carey to Alfreton and preach to the people there. Mr. Carey states:

> I wrote to my friends there, requesting them (as it was my native town) to join me in fervent prayer to the Lord, that he would accompany his servant and pour out his Spirit upon the people. I believe they did so, and the Lord made the visit a blessing. After dining at my brother's, we called upon a good man who had been brought to God under the ministry of the late John Nelson. Mr. Smith was greatly interested while the good man related the particulars of his awakening and conversion. At the close of the conversation, Mr. Smith, turning to the man's son (a young man in bad health), said, "Well, young man, have you got salvation?" to which the young man replied in the negative. Mr. Smith then said, "Well, do you think God is able to save you?" The young man replied, "Yes, I do believe he is able." "Then do you believe he is willing to save you?" "Yes, I do." "And do you believe God is willing to save you now?" The poor young man, as though he had anticipated Mr. Smith's coming to Alfreton that he might be shown the way to be saved, said, "Yes, I believe God, for Christ's sake, is willing to save

me now." "Then," said Mr. Smith, "let us pray"; and falling upon his knees, he cried to the Lord in an agony. The young man soon found Jesus, to the joy of his soul. His affliction terminated his life in the course of three months after this change. He died most triumphantly, shouting praises to God and the Lamb to the last. On the same day that we visited the above young man, we called upon a friend who had been a local preacher and leader for more than thirty years. His daughter being under some concern, Mr. Smith proposed prayer. We kneeled down and continued in supplication until she found peace with God. She continued a pious and consistent member of society for ten years. Several years after her marriage with Mr. Nuttal, a draper of Belper, she sickened and died, a believer in Jesus Christ. Her death was a most happy and triumphant one.

To several members of a large family residing in the neighborhood of Nottingham, Mr. Smith had been rendered very useful; and the greater part of them were members of the society. The mother, however, lived without any sense of religion, and had a particular dislike for him. Her pious children had frequently solicited permission to invite him to the house, but this was strongly refused. One Sunday morning, he ventured to call. The moment she saw him, she said he seemed to look through her; and she felt that he knew all that was in her heart. After he had taken some refreshment, and while a hymn was sung, she was smitten with deep conviction of sin; and when prayer was proposed, she was glad to kneel down, that she might not be observed to weep. While Mr. Smith prayed, a peculiar divine influence rested upon all present; and when another person began to pray, he went to her and said, "Well, Mrs. B., you feel yourself a sinner!" "O yes!" she replied. "And are you willing to give up your sins?" Wringing her hands in deep anguish, she rejoined, "O yes, Sir, I am." He then exhorted her, without delay, to believe on Christ for present pardon. She instantly cried, "O Lord Jesus, I *will* believe! O Lord Jesus, I *do* believe!" She was at once filled with a joy so extreme that, for a time, it seemed to overwhelm her faculties; she immediately united herself to the people she had once despised, and still remains an example of God's abundant grace.

In the beginning of the year 1828, Mr. Smith's health began to decline. One day, when he was very unwell, a person called and said he must see him, as he had come upwards of twenty miles for that purpose. His urgency procured him admission to the chamber where Mr. Smith was confined to his bed, suffering at once from weakness and pain. The man told him that he had been a backslider and that, for some time past, he had been under deep convictions of sin; that he had sought the Lord with many tears, and had fasted and prayed, but still remained without comfort. "Yes," said Mr. Smith, "and you may do so a long time, and be no better, unless you believe God. You do not need to leave this room without salvation. God would rather save you *today* than tomorrow. You may die today, and if you die unpardoned, you are lost for ever; but God wishes to save you. *He* says it, and he means what he says." "But," said the man, "if I should believe and not get the blessing!" "Do not meddle with God's business," replied Mr. Smith. "But it is God that saves the soul, is it not?" "Yes, but it is not God's work to believe; that's your business. Do your part, man, and God will do his. Go down on your knees, and ask God to save you at once." He did as he was directed. Mr. Smith then turned himself in bed and began to pray; but finding that his strength was gone, he stopped and said, "We cannot get a step farther unless you will believe. How long is God Almighty to wait for you?" "I will believe," cried the penitent. "I will believe; I cannot do wrong in believing. I *do* believe." God answered in a moment and filled him with such joy that he literally danced on his knees. "Did I not tell you," said Mr. Smith exultingly, "that God would attend to his own business?" The poor fellow rose, kissed Mr. Smith's hand, and hurried home in unspeakable delight.

The following is about the only notice of Mr. Smith's personal experience during the time he remained in Nottingham which I find among his papers.

> Dec. 21. 1826. Yesterday I had a very signal baptism of the Spirit, which had connected with it an assurance that the body of sin was destroyed, and that God had full possession of my heart. This assurance I retain; glory be to God! I feel indescribable pleasure in surrendering my all to him. I have had today a very affecting

view of the shattered and miserable state of the world; but I have also had a very relieving view of the efficacy of the atonement of Christ, of the power of the Spirit, and of the covenant engagements of the blessed God. *He* willeth that ALL should be saved and come to the knowledge of the truth. I have a strong desire that I may be better fitted for the good service of God, that I may be employed much, and that he may get all the glory. Amen. My body has been out of order, but my faith has not wavered. God is mine, and I am his; glory be to God!

Mr. H. Beeson, of Sheffield, gives the following account of a visit paid by Mr. Smith in April, 1829, to a dying backslider in that town.

J. W. was the son of pious parents and a child of many prayers and admonitions. He had at one period of his life known the power of divine grace; but he had unhappily turned aside from following the Lord, and for a number of years had persevered in his rebellious course, when it pleased the Lord to afflict him—or, as Mr. Smith used to say, "God took him aside to remonstrate with him." His friends became very assiduous in their attention to his spiritual interests, but such was the carnal obstinacy of his heart that he appeared rather annoyed than profited. Several weeks passed; his disease was making fearful progress; he began to yield, was brought into bitterness of soul, and in this state Mr. Smith found him. He said that he was very unhappy, that he had been seeking the Lord but had not obtained mercy. Mr. Smith seemed to enter into a deep sympathy for him, and inquired whether he rested on Christ for salvation. He replied that he did. "Well then, God accepts you in Christ, and God accepts you *now* in Christ," said Mr. Smith, repeating the declaration again and again with much emphasis. He spoke and prayed for nearly an hour; and while he was pleading the promise, "I will heal their backslidings," etc., the man was clearly set at liberty; and notwithstanding his weakness, he rose up in bed and shouted the praises of God with such energy that his voice overpowered the voices of all present. In this happy state of mind be continued for three weeks; and then, while

His last faltering accents whisper'd praise,

he sweetly fell asleep.

At the Conference of 1828, Mr. Smith was compelled to become a supernumerary. His constitution was so broken up that it was manifest his life could be prolonged only by at least a partial cessation from labor. It was with great reluctance that he submitted to this arrangement; but of its necessity, he had in himself evidence too palpable to be resisted. He therefore took up his residence at Beeston, a pleasant village a few miles from Nottingham; and it is proper to be recorded that a handsome provision was made for him from the circuit funds, and that his friends were assiduous in supplying every alleviation of his affliction which was within their power. Yet with all the consolations which faith can command and friendship afford, the situation of a supernumerary is deeply painful. To Mr. Smith it was peculiarly so; and his mind was often exercised by powerful temptation, and deeply depressed. He could not be prevailed upon to remain entirely in a state of inaction when he was at all able to labor: that degree of relaxation which he allowed himself, however, was materially serviceable to him; and throughout the year his health gradually improved. I subjoin a few extracts from his letters at this period.

From Barnsley, where he was staying for the benefit of his health, he thus writes to Mrs. Smith:

Sept. 11, 1828: I am very glad that you are rising in your soul. There is no substitute for communion with God. Without divine communications, the soul droops and dies and becomes a corrupt thing. But with what life and beauty and blessedness God can impregnate the soul! Yes, before the mighty energy of God the Holy Ghost, everything that is foul and corrupt is driven out, and from the indwelling Spirit spring love, joy, peace, etc. Let us, my dear, pray on and pray hard. God will not disappoint "a feeble worm that trusts in him." I thank you for the help of your prayers. You have my poor prayers, and shall have them. Notwithstanding much unfaithfulness, I believe it possible for us to live to God as we never have lived. Let us try. God's blessing, his peculiar blessing, is always connected with entire devotedness to him. It will also be an inheritance to our children. O that the blessed God would send us speedy and appropriate help! I am in a fair way to come about again. Most likely I shall long be a delicate man with respect to bodily health. This may be the best for me. This I know: God cannot err, nor can he be unkind. Glory be to him! With a peculiar sense of the value of your affection, and wishing that you and your charge may dwell under the shadow of the Almighty, I am, etc.

Under the date of Dec. 26, 1828, he thus writes:

My soul has fast hold on God. He is mine and I am his. I have had, of late, some very gracious divine communications. I am looking for brighter, more penetrating and soul-transforming manifestations of God. I want, "beholding as in a glass the glory of the Lord, to be changed into the same image from glory into glory, even as by the Spirit of the Lord." The grand adversary has laid hard at me, but God has pitied me and rebuked him. Disorder is retiring from my body. Health and vigor are returning. With caution on my part, God seems disposed to build me up again. Much prayer has been made for me in this circuit, and in other places. God has heard and regarded. I am thankful. I mean to use my returning health for God and for souls. *He* will help. You are aware that I have commenced preaching again; and God is pleased to connect his soul-saving power with me.... I have raised a class, which meets in our house. God owns it. The first night, a local preacher, who has come from Shepton Mallet, got a clean heart; the second, four obtained pardon; the third, two others; the fourth, two more; and last Wednesday night, five were cleansed, as was another who came into our house just as we were commencing family worship. Glory, glory be to God! The cleansing God still lives and works. My wife is tolerably well, and happy in God. Ellen is under a divine influence. What a pleasing thought it is that our children are the Lord's. We must try to prevent the devil from making any use of them in the world. The provisions of the gospel are sadly overlooked and neglected. "The promise is to us and to *our children*." We will try that they may be a holy seed. May the Lord help you and me to claim the grace which is provided and offered in Christ.... I am loaded with the kindness of the people in this circuit. I trust God will reward them. My prayers they shall have. You and yours have my prayers and tears. I am, dear brother, yours, etc.

March 17, 1829. My Very Dear Father, A few weeks ago I spent upwards of a fortnight in London. I had liberty beyond my expectation in preaching at Hinde Street one Sunday night from, "As I live, saith the Lord of Hosts, I have no pleasure in the death of the wicked," etc. The strong power of God was among the people. One woman cried out while I was preaching, and a general burst was anticipated. This, however, did not take place, perhaps through not going to prayer at the time. A great multitude stayed at the prayer meeting. Many were powerfully wrought upon, and it was supposed about thirty were saved. Glory be to God! On Wednesday I and brother McD. went to Woolwich. I preached in the evening from, "Ask, and ye shall receive," etc. D. and I returned to London that night; but we afterwards learned that the pardoned and cleansed amounted to sixteen. Mr. Reece engaged me for Queen Street the following Sunday night. I had special liberty from, "This is a faithful saying, and worthy of all acceptation," etc. There was much of the cutting power of God among the people. According to a previous arrangement, I commenced the prayer meeting from the pulpit. Not fewer than fifteen hundred people stayed. The praying men then came forward well. Several got liberty; the high praises of God were sung, etc. Mr. Reece marshalled the meeting until after ten o'clock, and then requested all who were in distress to retire into the vestry. It was supposed that not fewer than forty were saved that night. Glory be to God! You would not be much surprised at this, were you to hear their mighty men pray. O what straightforward believing in God! What powerful wrestling! On the Wednesday following, I preached at Charles Street, a favorite place of mine, from "Wilt thou be made whole?" It was crowded, and again the Lord Jesus displayed his royal power and mercy in saving souls. The pardoned and cleansed, I understand, were not fewer than thirty. Glory be to God! By this time my body was shorn of its strength, and I was glad to seek rest by returning to Nottingham. In different places in our own circuit, I have seen several saved. To God be all the glory! Amen and amen.

July 2, 1829. I preached at Sheffield, according to appointment, to a large congregation; and there was a powerful influence connected with the truth of God. I should think twelve or fourteen hundred stayed to the prayer meeting. Many were in distress, and a goodly company either found peace or were cleansed from sin.[1] I preached out of doors at Chilwell a few days afterwards; three or four were awakened and have since joined the society. On Whitsunday, we had a good day at New Basford. Five found peace in the evening. They are going on well there. I was at Hickling, in the Melton circuit, a short time ago. Many were in distress, and five found peace. The week before last, I went to Clauson, where we had a very signal time; a crowded chapel, much power under the sermon, and after some powerful struggling in the prayer meeting, fifteen or sixteen were saved. We had one saved at our class last Tuesday night. So, you see, the Lord is still working among us. "O Jesus, ride on, till all are subdued." Through mercy, we are all tolerably well in health; and we are determined to try to get and diffuse more of God.

Then, in allusion to his temporal circumstances, he adds,

I would rather break stones on the road than pass another such a year as the last. I like to earn my bread, and that has sometimes made me labor when I ought to have rested. But I hope God will smile after bruising me a little. I am, dear father, etc.

July 21, 1829. For many weeks I have been laboring hard, and I have stood it well. Many seals have been given to my ministry, and to the agonizing prayers of God's people. Frequently four, five, six, have been saved in an evening—several individuals in families. Last Sunday I was at Hockley, perhaps for the last time; numbers went away who could not get into the chapel. The mighty power of God was among us. It is said that not fewer than thirty were saved. Last night I was at New Basford; such floods of heavenly influence I have seldom witnessed. Many were saved.

On Easter Sunday evening of this year, Mr. Smith preached at Hockley chapel; and, having commenced a prayer meeting, went into the vestry, intending immediately to return home. A poor man followed him, and with an expression of extreme disappointment, exclaimed, "What! are you going?" "Yes," said Mr. Smith, "what is the matter with you?" "O, I am a miserable man, Sir!" "Are you a

---

1. This was the service which Mr. Calder describes, p. 155, above.

backslider?" "Yes, I am, and I am a miserable man!" "Do you wish to come back? do you want to be saved again?" "I am come on purpose, and now you are going." "Go into the chapel, and get upon your knees," said Mr. Smith, "and I will be with you in a few minutes." He did as he was directed; and when Mr. Smith went to him, he found him in an agony of distress, exclaiming, "There never was such a sinner as I am." "You deserve hell," said Mr. Smith. "That's true," replied the other, with a deep groan, "I do indeed." "O man, God will not allow you to remain in this distress. He says, 'I will heal your backslidings, and I will love you freely.' Do you think God tells lies?" "No." "Then he will do it, will he not?" The penitent laid hold on the truth, and was instantly delivered, and filled with a joy as extreme as had been his previous anguish. The same evening, a poor woman went up to the communion rails, taking with her two others. She said, "This, Mr. Smith, is my daughter, and this other is my son's wife; they both want salvation." God gave them also the desire of their hearts, and several others were also saved.

Mr. Smith's health being sufficiently restored to enable him to resume his regular labors as an itinerant preacher, he was appointed, in 1829, to the Lincoln circuit, under the superintendence of the Rev. W. Clegg. On the last Sunday which he spent in Nottingham, he preached the anniversary sermons for the Sunday schools; and after the evening service at St. Ann's chapel, upwards of twelve persons obtained peace with God. On the Monday evening, he delivered a farewell discourse at Halifax Place chapel. The congregation was very large; and at the prayer meeting which followed, not fewer than twenty entered into the liberty of the children of God. Among these was a woman who had a persecuting husband. She had once enjoyed the divine favor, but had suffered her domestic troubles so far to prevail over her faith and diligence that for some time she had lost the evidence of her adoption. On this evening, she went up to the form usually appropriated to penitents, and, kneeling down, resolved not to rise till the Lord again lifted on her the light of his countenance. In a short time, the Comforter returned to her heart; and, with a face wreathed with smiles, she was retiring when she caught a glimpse of a man who had just obtained a similar blessing. It was her husband. She rushed into his arms, and fainted. It afterwards appeared that each of them was ignorant of the other having come to the chapel. The power of God laid hold of the ungodly man's heart during the sermon; and just at the time that his wife received the renewed assurance of the divine favor, he also had entered into the enjoyment of peace in believing.

Such was the closing scene of Mr. Smith's regular ministry in a circuit most tenderly endeared to his own heart, and in which his name will long be remembered with deep emotions of gratitude and reverence. Of his usefulness during the four years of his residence here, it is impossible to form an adequate estimate. A gentleman intimately acquainted with the circuit, and in every other respect qualified to form a correct calculation, states it as his opinion that there are now in its societies not fewer than four hundred persons who were converted to God through Mr. Smith's immediate instrumentality. And if to this extraordinary number we add those cases in which his ministry was powerfully blessed to neighboring circuits, and the other instances in which he was, in a still more extended, though less palpable and direct way, the instrument of good in his own circuit, we have an amount of spiritual service to the church, as the result of one man's labor, such as, in so short a period, has very rarely been surpassed. Upon the supposition that his principles were really incorrect, and his modes of effort unscriptural, the marvelous character of his usefulness is strikingly enhanced. What must have been the might of that piety, which, in spite of fundamental and practical error, achieved such an incalculable mass of good! What the energy of that faith which, with such serious hindrances, succeeded in bringing down heavenly influence so extensive and powerful! Nay, rather, we are compelled to say, blessed is the error which tends to lead such multitudes to the knowledge of the truth!—honorable is the heresy which establishes countless believers on their most holy faith! Sacred is the extravagance which from every side calls wandering sheep to the fold of Christ! and happy, thrice happy, is the man who, with the brand of error, heresy, and extravagance affixed to his character at the human tribunal, returns to God to be enshrined and exalted as a radiant and spotless star for ever and ever!

CHAPTER 14

Lincoln
1829–1831

Mr. Smith commenced his public ministry in Lincoln on Sunday morning, August 30, with a powerful and characteristic sermon from John 16:24: "Ask, and ye shall receive, that your joy may be full." On the evening of the same day, he preached, I believe, from Job 22:21: "Acquaint now thyself with him, and be at peace," etc. In both these discourses he gave his hearers distinctly to perceive the order of his preaching. "Whoever discredits my Master," said he, in one of them, "I do not. His promise is, 'Where two or three are gathered together in my name, there am I in the midst.' Jesus is here. Glory, glory be to God!" He thus speaks of the results of his early labors in this circuit in a letter to a friend:

Oct. 21, 1829. I am rather strong to labor; I am disposed to labor. I have plenty to do; and the best of all is, God is with me! I had been told that the Lincoln congregation consisted of a very still sort of people who were incapable of excitement, etc., etc. Caution, caution would be necessary. Well, pondering took place in my mind. The result was, I will strike the first Sunday. I did so; execution was done. God saved four; and he has saved, I should think, at least fourscore since in Lincoln. Hallelujah! Hail to the Lord's Anointed! The royal diadem belongs to him! We will crown him Lord of all! The floods are coming! Many drops, some showers, have already descended. How refreshing! But the *floods* are coming! If our people continue in agonizing, believing prayer, which has fast hold of them at present—and why not?—nothing can stand before them. Satan will fall as lightning from heaven. Hardness, levity, carelessness, and profanity are as chaff before the wind. God has risen from his holy habitation and speaks salvation in every direction. What an honor to be one of his attendants! To be one of his heralds! I cry out, "He is *coming*," and often, "He

175

is *here!*" His royal presence is known by his bounty distributed, pardons in great numbers, the frequent healing of backsliders, clean hearts, filled spirits go away rejoicing, and the arrows stick fast in the heart of the King's enemies. With tears, and cries, and groans, and rejoicings, I say,

> Live for ever, wondrous King,
> Born to redeem, and strong to save!

Good luck to thee; ride on, win, subdue, conquer, triumph, have the glory for ever and ever! What! Do tears of joy fill your eyes, and do you say, "Amen, my God! Let there be a sweeping work! And strengthen his body?" O, my brother, I have just had to wipe away my tears at the thought of your praying for me—body and soul. Thank you, thank you! Well, when we shake hands on the banks of the river, we will sing, "Hallelujah to the Lamb!" I should like to enter into particulars; but for want of room, I cannot go back far. Only some who were thought to be the most unlikely to get salvation have been saved, such as proud, high-spirited young men, etc. But what is all this before the omnipotent Spirit whose work it is to save? From four to twenty have been saved at one meeting in Lincoln, again and again. An uncommon stir there is in many parts of the circuit, and persons from nine to seventy-six years of age are among the saved. Last Sunday, I was at Bassingham. I preached at half-past one from, "Create in me a clean heart," etc. We then had a good love-feast. Just as I was about to give out a verse and commence a prayer meeting, a fine young man got up and told us that he had some time ago lost a clean heart, but that he had been powerfully acted upon again during the sermon, etc. I was on the point of speaking to him, when he said, "God cleanses me again!" It went like electric fluid. I said, "Now you see the cleansing power of God *is* in the chapel; you that want a clean heart may have one." One man exclaimed, "I have got it;" and looking round, added, "you may all have it." We began to pray, and the meeting did not conclude till I went to preach at six o'clock. I was told that thirty-three obtained entire sanctification, and many were pardoned. In the evening, the strong power of God was present. I suppose towards thirty were pardoned, and many cleansed. Glory be to God! I went on Monday to Besthorpe.

Seventeen found peace, several were cleansed, and others in distress. Yesterday morning, I saw two cleansed and one get into liberty. These are days of grace. It is God's will that they should continue. Hallelujah! On Monday night, at the prayer meeting in Lincoln, four or five and twenty were saved. Expectation is high, and God will not fail. Love to the praying men.

One of the young men to whom allusion is made in the foregoing extract had been accustomed to attend the chapel for some years; but, as he himself confessed, he listened to sermons in general, merely as he would have done to the rehearsing of a play. Mr. Smith's ministry, however, he could not treat thus. In spite of himself, it compelled him to reflect; the terrible denunciations of sin, and the accompanying representations of perdition with which it occasionally abounded, produced the most lively alarm in his mind; and he did not rest till he was brought to the knowledge of salvation through the remission of sins. Another individual of similar age and character occasionally went to the chapel to oblige some pious friends but evinced, in the most unequivocal way, his thorough scorn for religion and its professors. A sermon by Mr. Smith powerfully wrought upon his mind; but being naturally of a reserved disposition, he concealed his feelings for several days. His distress, however, became so great that he could no longer attend to his business. He retired to his room and was there overheard by a Christian relative, uttering his anguish before the Lord. She went to him; his agony was so great that she feared his reason would have left him, and the struggle was protracted and awful. At length, the sacrifice of Christ was presented to his mind. "If he will save sinners," he cried, "*can* I, *may* I hope that he will save me?" As if in distinct reply to this inquiry, there was immediately applied to his mind the promise, "Him that cometh unto me, I will in no wise cast out." He laid hold of it and was filled with gladness and thanksgiving. These two young men have already been made useful in the church of God. May they, with fidelity and perseverance, follow those "who through faith and patience inherit the promises!"

Nov. 4, 1829, he writes to his friend Mr. Alderman Carey:

God is with us; yes, he is mightily working. Not a week passes without some being pardoned or cleansed. Last Sunday afternoon at the prayer meeting after the sacrament, about twelve found peace; three more at night, ten others on Monday. Last night I was at Saxilby. Three found peace, six obtained clean hearts. Today I have seen one cleansed and two pardoned. I say to our friends in Lincoln, if they will only stick to it, if they continue in agonizing and believing prayer, there will be such a work in Lincoln as was never witnessed. Glory be to God! At our last leaders' meeting, forty-five were proposed to receive notes on trial, besides many more who have begun to meet in class. We have begun to confess the sins of the people, to plead the blood of the covenant, and the promise of the Spirit. The business, I trust, will be continued; the Lord will not fail. In many places in the circuit, God is working. Local preachers, leaders, and members are trusting God for a full salvation; they are also laboring for souls, and many sinners are awakened and turned to God. The set time to favor our Zion is come. Hallelujah! Does your heart warm; and do you say to your wife, "Hear, my dear"? I know you will rejoice with us. Come soon, and see and hear for yourself. A bed, something to eat and drink, etc., you shall have. And if Mrs. Carey can come, our pleasure will be heightened. You are among some others in the Nottingham circuit whose kindness loads us; and your faces will, I expect, kindle a fire that will melt us, because of what is past. Well, a cup of cold water will not be forgotten. You and yours are dear to me. My prayer shall go to heaven for you. Nottingham is dear, very dear to me. I hope to see it soon. I shall be glad some morning to surround the family altar with you and your family.... Henry,[1] live to God!

A few days after Mr. Smith's arrival at Lincoln he was made instrumental of good in a case of obstinate and protracted unbelief. The person who was the subject of it had been repeatedly visited by pious individuals, but every argument employed by them had failed to produce any effect upon his mind. Mr. Smith readily entered into a view of his state; and, having remarked that there was much satanic influence operating on his spirit, prayed several times, till at length the trembling penitent ventured to cast his soul on the atonement, though he still remained without much sensible comfort. Subsequently, he gave way to doubt, and again was brought

---

1. Mr. Carey's second son; at that time a pious youth, a member of our society, and now a useful class leader.

into total darkness; but through Mr. Smith's instructions, he had acquired such views of the way of faith and the simplicity of evangelical salvation that he speedily recovered what he had lost. His comfort increased; and, at a love-feast a short time afterwards, he stated these facts, and testified that he could then rejoice in God through our Lord Jesus Christ.

In January of 1830, Mr. Smith visited Nottingham to preach in behalf of the tract society in that place. The following is an extract from a private memorandum written at the time:

> My object in going to Nottingham is the glory of God, in, 1. The awakening of sinners; the bringing of penitents to Christ, that they may be pardoned, accepted, adopted, and regenerated. 2. The restoration of poor backsliders. 3. The entire sanctification of believers, their support and comfort under trouble and temptation, and their being filled with all the fullness of God. 4. Begetting and increasing, in God's people, concern for the salvation of souls in general, and of sinners in Nottingham in particular. Every soul in Nottingham was called into being by the blessed God and has been preserved and redeemed by him; and it is God's will that each should be saved. For the getting and cultivating sympathy for souls, consider that they are: 1. Immortal; 2. Accountable; 3. Capable of bliss or pain extreme; 4. Naturally corrupt; increasers of corruption in themselves, and propagators of it in others; also that they are acted upon injuriously by men and devils. God pities them and bids them welcome to the blessings of his house; Christ died and intercedes for them; the Spirit works upon them and is ready to furnish still more powerful influence; but they must use the means of God's appointing, actively concur with the Spirit, or perish everlastingly. They are our brethren; we have access to them in person or by proxy. We are capable of acting upon them. A divine influence is connected with every Christian. God and Christ require it of us. We have power with God for them. Their state must be looked at with as much particularity as possible. The atonement must be believed for them; promises of the influences of the Holy Spirit must be seized and pleaded for them; their hardness, profanity, pride, carelessness, will give way; and it will appear that God is with Zion, making her "a sharp threshing instrument, having teeth." Individual pleading in this way will do

much; united pleading will do more. Who will come up to the help of the Lord against the mighty? Allow not the work to flag; stick to it. Personal piety will improve, and there will be accessions to the church of Christ, etc. Who is sufficient for these things? No one, but the man whom God fits for the work. Lord, help *me!*

Mr. Smith's labors at Nottingham, on this occasion, were greatly blessed; and among other cases of his success, there was one meeting that he conducted in which not less than forty souls obtained the pardon of their sins. In his correspondence, he speaks of the Sabbath which he spent with his Nottingham friends at this time as a day never to be forgotten.

Meanwhile, in his own circuit, the work of God greatly prospered. Writing to a friend, in the month of March, he says:

> O how the Spirit has been poured out upon this circuit! It is spring in nearly every place. The wilderness has become a fruitful field; the desert, as the garden of the Lord. I think it certain that more than five hundred have been added since Conference. What may we not expect? For we have many men in full action.

Almost all the neighboring circuits appeared, in a larger or smaller degree, to share this holy influence. Some of them were visited by Mr. Smith himself; and individuals from others, who had been blessed through his instrumentality in Lincoln or its immediate vicinity, returned to their several places of residence, carrying with them a portion of his ardor, and becoming in their turn the partakers of his success. Thus the word of the Lord had free course and was glorified to a degree rarely, if ever, known in that country. Mr. F. Eggleston, one of the local preachers at Newark, gives the following account of a visit paid by Mr. Smith to that circuit.

> In March, 1830, we gave him an invitation to preach our anniversary sermons for Newark and Bennington chapels, I offering to supply his place at Besthorp on the Monday evening. His letter on that occasion I have before me:
>
> > I intend, God willing, to stay over the Monday, according to your request respecting Bennington. Our friends at Besthorp will, I doubt not, be very glad to see you. I will thank you, as

opportunity may serve, to caution the friends at Newark against looking too much to *man*. We must not forget that *all* good flows from God, and that he will not give his glory to another. May the blessed God hold me in his right hand and use me for his glory!

His labors were singularly owned of God on that day. After preaching in the evening, I requested him to leave the chapel, and I would conduct the prayer meeting. He reluctantly retired for a time. The altar rail was surrounded with penitents crying for mercy, and several found peace with God. I attended for him at Besthorp; and when I returned on Tuesday morning, I found a blessed change in my own family. My eldest daughter and my apprentice—who is now on the Lincoln plan as an exhorter—had found mercy. Mr. Smith spent the day with me; and such a day, he declared, he had not spent since he was born. His soul seemed filled with glory and with God. He wept, he prayed, and shouted aloud, "Glory, glory be to God!" Sometimes, as if holding communion with the Triune God, he for a few moments appeared abstracted; and then bringing his mind among us, he said, "Come, brother E., let us praise God." A favorite verse was sung, we prayed together, and then entered into conversation respecting the prosperity of Zion. Many penitents found their way to our house that day, that he might pray with them. Their anxiety—that of returning backsliders, and of others who had found peace—to see him was such that until he entered the coach to return, he had constant employment. He appeared to carry with him the spirit of his Master wherever he went. We have a great number who are members of our society at Newark who are indebted, under God, to John Smith as their spiritual father; and there is scarcely a society in the circuit which does not contain one or more of his spiritual children.

In the month of June, I had an opportunity of spending half an hour with Mr. Smith as I passed through Lincoln. I found him, as usual, absorbed in his great work. He related to me, with much delight, many pleasing instances of the power of grace which had recently occurred in the circuit. Among others, he mentioned one place in the country at which, a few evenings before, between twenty and thirty souls had been set at liberty at a prayer meeting. I was particularly struck with his powerful expressions on the subject of the divine benevolence, and more especially with the last sentence which he uttered before I took my leave of him: "If God will not save men, it is no business of *ours*"—a truth deeply momentous and interesting, since human exertions for the salvation of souls are only rational on the ground of the surpassing and infinite willingness of the Almighty.

In the character both of his preaching and of the success which attended it, Mr. Smith exceeded the expectations which had been entertained by the friends at Lincoln before his coming among them. On this subject, the following testimony of a respectable member of the society is appropriate and forcible; and it is here inserted the more readily because it goes strongly to confirm the views supplied by the preceding pages on the topics to which it alludes:

> He was not merely the means of filling our chapel and class books with the poor, to whom the gospel and (may I not say?) Methodism peculiarly has been sent, but with many of those also whose education and powers of mind were such that they required something more than excitement. Mr. Smith never preached a sermon that I heard in which there was not powerful, close reasoning connected with the impassioned appeals of one who felt deeply and keenly the dangerous state of many of his hearers. Nor was it only to the unconverted part of his hearers that his sermons were addressed. He fully displayed the way of salvation from all filthiness of the flesh and the spirit. He was not one of those from whose ministry, although rejoicing in its success, calm and experienced Christians would retire when personal profit was desired. No; without a dissenting feeling, his ministry was attended with delight by all our members; and perhaps the change produced upon us as a church was as visible as our increase of members gained from the world. It is often said of those who, like Mr. Smith, earn to themselves the honorable title of "revivalist," that they are fitted only for one department of the work of God, and that other talents are required to build up the church. However this may be the case with others, it did not apply to him. To many, whose names are fresh in my recollection, he was useful not only in conveying light to their minds, and healing to their consciences, but also in directing them to the acquisition of knowledge and general information, that they

might thus be employed more usefully and influentially for God and their fellow-creatures.

The subjoined instance of Mr. Smith's spiritual discernment is supplied by the writer of the foregoing extract. A sick woman in Lincoln was visited by him. She was under considerable concern for her spiritual condition, but the advices which she had previously received appeared to have produced no salutary effect upon her mind. It was difficult to conjecture what prevented her from entering into the enjoyment of the divine favor, but manifestly there was some material hindrance. Mr. Smith conversed with her cursorily; and then becoming thoughtful, he for a while sat in silence. At length he said, "But have you not at some time known the grace of God, and proved unfaithful?" With some hesitation the woman confessed that this was the fact. "O then," said Mr. Smith, "you must take your right character before the Savior. You are a backslider; you must come to God as such, and he will receive you." He then prayed with her, and she was enabled to exercise faith in the promises adapted to her state. She was filled with peace and joy, and shortly afterwards her spirit returned to God. Mr. Smith was a perfect stranger to her character at the time of his visit, and the friend who accompanied him, and who gives the relation, had not the slightest idea of the real state of the case.

Mr. Clarkson relates the following examples of the success which, about this time, attended Mr. Smith's labors in private. The latter is inserted as an illustration of his faithful and searching method of dealing with sinners. Mr. Smith was one evening at the house of a friend, and among the company was a young lady, the daughter of an eminent and exemplary deceased member of the society. He addressed her on the subject of religion and inquired whether she wished to go to heaven. She replied in the affirmative, but added that she thought she might succeed in arriving there without meeting in class, etc. "But that was not the way your father went," said Mr. Smith. "No," she rejoined, "it was not." "Then," said he, "you are wiser than your father." After some further remarks, he added, "The Lord has hold of you, Miss—." The next day she met him in the street and asked permission to come to his class. He inquired the reason of her wish. With much emotion she replied that his conversation the previous evening had made an impression on her mind so deep that she could not rest in her present state. She was resolved, she said, to go to heaven the same way as her father. She attended the class, and shortly afterwards entered into the enjoyment of the salvation of the gospel.

In one of the country places of the Lincoln circuit there resided an aged man who had employed the whole of his life in folly and sin. He was at length indisposed, and declined rapidly. In fact, it was manifest to himself and to those around him that his race was nearly terminated. Mr. Smith heard of him, was much affected by his condition, and resolved to visit him. When he entered the house, the old man was seated by the fire, bowed down by the united influence of infirmity and disease, and looking anxious and disconsolate. Mr. Smith, in an elevated tone, abruptly exclaimed, "Well, you are going to die!" "Yes," replied the other. "And then to hell?" said Mr. Smith. "I suppose I am," was the answer. "Why, you have been a great sinner!" "I have been a very bad one, and I deserve hell," rejoined the aged transgressor. "But God will save you," added Mr. Smith. "Come, let us pray about the matter." They had scarcely engaged in prayer for half an hour before the old man obtained the pardon of all his sins. Filled with transport, and forgetful of his weakness, he went out and invited his neighbors to come in and hear the wonderful tale of God's mercy to him. Mr. Smith then commended him to the attentions of two pious persons resident in the neighborhood; and a little while afterwards, he had the satisfaction of hearing that he had died happy in the love of God.

A respectable class leader of the Lincoln society has supplied me with an account of a visit which, in the early part of this year, he and Mr. Smith paid to a sick person, and which, as somewhat resembling the preceding narration, is inserted in this place. The name of the individual was Cooke. He had been the engineer of a steam packet, and, from what I can gather, a very profligate sinner. He appears to have had some serious impressions from the time that he was taken ill; but these were matured and rendered indelible by a dream which he had a few days before Mr. Smith called on him. He imagined that he saw four of his children, who died in their infancy. They appeared very beautiful and unspeakably happy. But when they passed the foot of his bed, they assumed a severe aspect and, looking frowningly on him, exclaimed, "Where we are, you can never come." He awoke in extreme agitation; strong convictions of sin seized upon him; and his past life, in all its defilement and rebellion, rose in vivid array before his conscience. His medical attendant finding him in great distress begged Mr. Smith to visit him. When Mr. Smith and his companion came into his room, they found him half sitting up in bed, crying earnestly to God: "Lord, have mercy upon my soul!" "Amen!" said Mr. Smith. "Lord, save my soul!" "Amen!" "Just now extend thy mercy to me." "Amen, my God!" "Canst thou pardon such a wretch as I am?" "O, man," cried Mr. Smith, "you are in a desperate condition; how long have you been thus?" The man told him, adding, "Sometimes I think God will save me, and at other times it is suggested to me that there is no mercy for such a wretch." Mr. Smith, in his accustomed simple and forcible way, then expatiated on the love of God, the fullness of the atonement, and the infinite willingness of Christ to save all who come to him. "Do you believe God is able to save you?" he inquired. The penitent replied in the affirmative. "O yes," said Mr. Smith, "he would much rather save than damn you. Come, let us pray." Having prayed himself, he called on his companion; and while the latter was engaged in intercession, he strove to induce the distressed sinner to cast his soul on Christ: "You deserve hell; you deserve hell," he said. "Hell is too good for me," cried the other. "But, glory be to God," continued Mr. Smith, "you are out of hell, and may still be kept out of it. Now try and pray for yourself." He did so, Mr. Smith at every interval urging him to take hold of the Lord Jesus. Hope began to beam on his mind, and his efforts for salvation became more resolute and confident. Mr. Smith kneeled once more and wrestled with God in mighty agony till the trembling penitent was enabled to cast himself fully on the atonement. He then rose up in bed, and cried, "I see him. He died for me. He is my Savior, nailed to the cross for me and my salvation. I do believe in him; yes, I do believe that God, for Christ's sake, has pardoned all my sins." His burden was all removed, and he united in singing the praises of that "God, from whom all blessings flow." He was afterwards partially restored to health; but he still maintained his confidence, and for a short time walked worthy of his high calling. It then pleased God to take him to himself. "Is not this a brand plucked out of the fire?"

But while Mr. Smith's labors in public and private were thus attended by the prospering blessing of heaven, his own constitution gradually gave way to exertions so disproportionate to the critical state of his health. The duties of the Lincoln circuit, even as he found it, would probably, at this period of his life, have proved too severe for him, especially as at first he had not many to cooperate in his plans; but now, augmented as the societies were, and requiring, as of course they did, increased attention and effort, no result could have rationally been anticipated but that which actually took place. It was with some difficulty that he was prevailed on to remain in the circuit a second year; and when he at length consented, it was probably with the hope that the assistance of a third preacher, which it was determined to call in, would afford him some relief. This, however, did not prove to be the case. The growing claims of country societies, which it was thought had before been inadequately met, actually increased the proportion of labor assigned to each preacher. It is not for me to dispute the propriety of this arrangement. There are cases in which, for the accomplishment of some great end, human life is deservedly held cheap; and the sacrifice of the most eminent men, though for the moment deeply to be regretted is in the event amply compensated by the magnitude of the good which their death achieves. Whether the present was one of those cases, I do not take upon me to determine. Whether that consideration was shown to Mr. Smith which so valuable a character deserved; and whether some sacrifices might not have been made which would have tended to the prolongation of his life—are questions which I leave to the decision of those more fully informed on the subject.

From the Conference of 1830, Mr. Smith frequently found his public duties painfully oppressive. His health continued to decline till it was past human remedy. Had he desisted from all exertion some months before he was compelled to do so, there might have been a hope that he would have rallied again. But the die was cast. The elasticity of his constitution was destroyed, and that fatal and flattering distemper which had before threatened him was now to fix its envenomed and triumphant dart in his debilitated frame to be no more withdrawn. Before, however, we terminate the history of his public life, we must avail ourselves of the few remaining incidents or characteristics which friendship has gathered up, or which his own correspondence can supply; which, however comparatively insignificant in themselves, become in their actual situation unspeakably dear and affecting, because—the last. Happy is the man who knows not the volume of melancholy meaning comprised in this one word.

The Conference of this year was held at Leeds. Mr. Smith attended it, and preached several times with much power and considerable success. To one of these occasions he thus alludes in a letter to a friend. "At the Conference, one Tuesday morning, the floods came down. Many were pardoned; many were cleansed. At the glorious coming down of Jehovah, the noise of the people was as the sound of many waters. It required strong measures to get order, but it was secured; and God stayed and worked signally and clearly. His hand was seen and adored. He will stand by his *own plan. His good pleasure is to save.*" Finding, however, that he was in danger of injuring himself at Leeds, he retired to Cudworth before the Conference concluded. Here he preached once, and several souls were given to his ministry. A gracious work began in the village from this time. Writing to his father a few months afterwards, he thus speaks on this subject:

> The tidings of your prosperity at Cudworth gave me great pleasure. Only stick to the work, and then.—This is a must be. There should be no flagging; in order to this, *lengthened meetings generally should not be encouraged.* If you mind, you may have a sweeping work this winter.—Try!

On the first Sunday after the Conference that Mr. Smith preached at Lincoln, seven persons were converted to God, and in general the circuit continued to present gratifying indications of prosperity. At the September quarterly meeting, sixteen hundred members were reported, being, after all deficiencies arising from deaths, apostasies, and removals had been supplied, about half as many again as twelve months before. Under the date of Sept. 24, Mr. Smith thus writes to Mr. Calder in reply to an invitation from the missionary committee at Leeds:

> Such is the state of my health that I must not leave my circuit for some considerable time. Indeed, at present I am taking rest. My windpipe is the failing instrument, and Mr. Harvey is trying his ability to mend it.... God is smiling upon us in this circuit still. Our people have stood well during the harvest—a good omen this. Expectation too is rising. I suppose you will join with me in saying heartily, I am sure *God will not fail*. No, it is the good pleasure of his goodness to save. Let us take fast hold of God's good will to man. Strong exhibitions of the superabounding goodness of God do much execution, and desponding man needs them. I love you much, and I should like you to have much fruit. Give my kindest love to your sweet family. My heart warms with good wishes for them, and tears fill my eyes while I am thinking of them. They are dear to me, as well as to you. Tell them so, and that we must have them to love the Savior. I forget not the kindness of Mrs. Calder during the Conference. My Christian love to her. Praying that God may hold you in his right hand, and employ you in saving many, many souls, I am, etc.

Shortly after this, Mr. Smith spent some time at Nottingham for the recovery of his health, and appeared to have derived much advantage from the change. In consequence of taking cold on his return, however, he was again laid aside. In a letter dated Oct. 22, he says:

> Ever since Conference I have been under my work. I have not been able to attend to it without considerable pain almost continually. At present, I am taking rest. My body is sadly shaken, but I believe it will be repaired again. God is doing us much good in the circuit. It is quite spring with us. Many laboring men have been made. Why do we dwell upon earth, but to get and diffuse God? Appropriate labor always tells. Labor we must use. I intended being in London this month, but it is over. My health has interfered. An idle or a resting man I could not be in London. Safety is connected with staying at home. I have had to say "No" to, I should think,

near twenty requests since Conference to visit other circuits. This has been painful, because God has used me in this way. I must and do submit. Much of the steel has been forced from my body; I still hope it will harden.

After passing a few weeks in rest at his native village, Mr. Smith returned to Lincoln sufficiently recovered to resume his beloved employment. To his father he thus writes immediately afterwards:

Dec. 10. You will be glad to learn that I got to Lincoln without taking any cold. I have taken my full work ever since, except one sermon. Two souls found peace on the first Sunday evening at Lincoln, and I have had some very gracious seasons in the country; some good has been done. I stand my work better than I anticipated; and I trust, with care, that I shall be able to go through my labors with tolerable ease. I think I shall not do wrong to say, "O health, thou sweetener of the blessings of life, return and stay with me and mine!" But I can say, through mercy, as heartily, "May all the dispensations of divine providence be sanctified to me and mine!" God is doing me much good, and I mean to aim at his glory and the salvation of souls. May I be favored with his heavenly guidance! Amen.... A few weeks ago, two young women came to see their sister at Skellingthorpe, and God converted them. They went home and requested permission to pray with their parents. Conviction seized the mother; she came to see her daughter at S., and returned happy in God. The father came in great distress, and he also was set at happy liberty. A few months before, I saw the husband of the sister set at liberty. God, you see, is blessing families. Glory be to him!

In the spring of 1831, there was a slight improvement in Mr. Smith's health; and strong hopes were entertained, both by himself and others, that he would once more be fully restored to his former vigor. Under the date of April 9, he thus writes to a friend:

Your kindness to me has far exceeded mine to you. In many things you are formed to excel me. I know you will receive my recommendation to sing, "O to grace, how great a debtor!" Through the tender mercy of our God, I and my family are at present in tolerable health. We have had some afflictions; but, thank God, they have given place to sweet rising health, which we receive from our heavenly Father as no small good. Health and strength to labor fit me well. I like labor in myself and others. God encourages it, and I think he should be able to fix his eyes upon it in his own world.

Then, after having stated that one hundred and forty members were reported on trial at the preceding quarterly meeting, exclusive of many persons under sixteen years of age, and that the circuit was in a state of great financial prosperity, he adds:

> Opposers of revivals are very unwise. Salvation has its appurtenances. Let us get souls saved, and we shall not lack other things. At P— we have a remarkable work. I was there six weeks ago. At the prayer meeting, seven got liberty. I was much concerned for the family that kindly received and entertained me, and had been concerned for some time. They were not saved, and seemed far off. I was distressed in my closet next morning about them, and went to breakfast in a pensive mood, pondering and pondering what to do. While we were at breakfast, the leader's wife came in and said, "Seven got liberty last night, and your charwoman was one." Mrs. S., my hostess, said, "She saved? She is as much saved as I am!" I said nothing. The woman came in to breakfast, and after reading, I said, "Well, some say that you got your sins forgiven last night, did you?" "No, Sir." "Then you are not happy." "No, Sir." "Do you wish to be saved?" "Yes, Sir." "When?" "Now, Sir." "Then God and you are agreed. Well, Mrs. S., how long is God to wait for you?" "I do not know, Sir. I do not think that either I or anybody else can come to God for salvation unless something particular come upon them." "Of course, the fault is God's, then," said I. "Now, I assure you, you are wrong; for God *would* have saved you long ago. Your conduct is telling God that he is a liar. We must pray." The charwoman and Mrs. S.'s daughter cried aloud for mercy. They soon found peace. "Now, Mrs. S., what will you do?" She shook as if she had four agues upon her, and cried for mercy till God saved her. I then went to the master. He said he could not believe. I prayed. He then said, "I can, I can believe." We arose and praised God for liberating the four. I was at the place this week, and they all stand. I believe not fewer than fifty have been brought to God there in a very short time. Upwards of twenty were saved that week. Glory be to God.... I am going to Leeds tomorrow week. Get your class to pray for me.

In a postscript he mentions a love-feast that had recently been held at Lincoln, "the fruits of which were about twenty souls pardoned or cleansed."

On the 17th of April, Mr. Smith preached the anniversary sermon for the Leeds old chapel; and on that occasion his ministry was rendered useful to many of his congregation. In consequence of traveling on the outside of the coach on his return to Lincoln, he took a severe cold. After a day's rest, however, he went into the country and preached. On the following evening, he attended a missionary meeting; and, though unwell, enjoyed the opportunity exceedingly. On his road home, he remarked, "It was a blessed time; the meeting was full of inspiration." Indeed, everything connected with Christian missions was to him the subject of deep interest. He carried to the platform those strong and absorbing principles which, in the pulpit, he so successfully labored to render prominent and impressive; and though his speeches had not usually either the enlivenment of anecdote or the sparkle of wit, they had—what was far better, and more in consonance with his real character— the gushing of intense compassion, the expression of mighty faith, and the accompaniment of plentiful unction. The topics on which he commonly dwelt were, the naked deformity of Heathenism, its avowed and audacious defiance of God, with the fullness of the divine compassion, and the certainty of the triumph of Christ, as displayed and ensured in the promises of the Scriptures. From their birth, his children were enrolled as subscribers to the Missionary Society; and it was pleasant to remark how the first workings of their infant compassion acquired direction and expansion from their father's conversation and habits. A correct judgment of the spirit of a household may often be formed from the manners of children; and it may exemplify the impressiveness of Mr. Smith's principles to add that one of his little girls, when very young (as if the range of human vice and sorrow had been too bounded for her benevolence) was once overheard lisping her prayers for the salvation of the arch enemy of God and man.

The above was the last missionary meeting which Mr. Smith was permitted to attend. The next day he found himself very unwell, and for more than a week afterwards did not attempt any public duty. On Sunday, May 1st, however, he could not be dissuaded from endeavouring to fulfil his appointment at Lincoln. He went from his bed to the chapel at the hour of the morning service, and in great weakness and much pain once more labored to enforce that comprehensive promise on which he had often before expatiated with such power and success: "A new heart also will I give you, and a new spirit will I put within you; and I will take away the stony heart out of your flesh, and I will give you a heart of flesh. And I will put my Spirit within you, and cause you to walk in my statutes, and ye shall keep my judgments, and do them."[1] It was with the utmost difficulty that he proceeded with his discourse; and at its conclusion, he told the congregation that he felt so ill as to be quite incapable of addressing them in the evening. He then closed the service and retired from the pulpit. This was his last sermon.

---

1. Ezek. 36:26, 27.

Chapter 15

Lincoln—Sheffield

1831

Several circumstances conspired to render the last six months of Mr. Smith's life a season of severe trial. His natural fortitude might have enabled him to have endured debility and pain; but to be cut off from his beloved occupation, to be subject to the continual alternations of hope and fear, and to have to contemplate the suspense and anxiety of a beloved wife, and of other dear friends—this was indeed sorrow! The painful interest of his present situation to those who loved him can only be estimated by such as have watched the desolating progress of disease on the objects of their warmest regard, and have ultimately seen the tomb close on their hopes, and repel their assiduities. The singular excellencies of him of whom we now write of course gave an intensity to these emotions, which in an ordinary case could not have characterized them. It was under such an impression that, at the time of a former illness, his venerable father exclaimed, "O how glad should I be to die for thee!" "For a good man, some would even dare to die." But no; the "good man" was now to endure his own suffering and privation; and as he had before instructed others how to conflict "with spiritual wickedness in high places," and to keep themselves "unspotted from the world," he was now to give the example of "suffering affliction with patience," and to teach us "how to die."

The dealings of God with his people in the last scenes of life are very varied and often not a little mysterious. Yet as a general rule it may, I think, be remarked that the abounding of divine consolation and joy is in an inverse ratio to the strength of their faith. To those whose faith is weak and whose piety generally is immature, it seems necessary that there should be communicated an unusual degree of the comforts of the Holy Ghost. Were the case otherwise, the solemnity of their situation, and the mystic awe of that state into which they are about to enter, would probably so oppress their spirits that it would be little less than a miracle for them at all to maintain their confidence in God. Hence their minds are graciously withdrawn from those overwhelming contemplations to which they would otherwise naturally revert; and they are often so filled with the joy and triumph of hope as to forget everything but the glory which, in its fullness, is about to be revealed in them. They earnestly desire to depart and to be with Christ. How many instances can those recall who are familiar with the sick chamber and the death-bed of individuals who, though "all their lifetime subject to bondage" through the fear of death, have at last gone down to the grave not merely without a cloud but with the effulgence of heaven beaming on their spirits. Nor is it too much to imagine that this merciful arrangement is intended not solely for the advantage of the dying saint himself, but partly also for the solace and encouragement of survivors. God thus removes from the minds of bereaved friends that bitterest aggravation of their sorrow—uncertainty as to the final destiny of those whom they mourn. At the same time, he thus declares to the church, not only that he will not break "a bruised reed" nor quench "the dimly burning flax," but that, in the case of those who have tremblingly but sincerely cast themselves on the atonement, he will "send forth judgment" to final, certain, and triumphant "victory."

On the other hand, there are saints to whom these extraordinary communications are not necessary. As therefore there is always a fitness without profusion in the divine dispensations, such persons spend their last hours in that elevated calmness which has usually characterized their Christian experience, without the glow of feeling and the singular joy which God vouchsafes to some others. Nay, not infrequently the enemy carries the battle to the gate. They have conflicts sharp and severe, even to the close of life; nor are they permitted to exchange the shield of faith for the garment of conquest till it has again and again quenched darts of the wicked one more thickly multiplied, and more fiercely fiery, than were ever before hurled at them. But death to them has long lost its terror, and he cannot now reinvest himself with it. In a less mature period of their experience, eternity was the object of their unmixed hope; and it cannot now be viewed with apprehension. They are more than conquerors through him who hath loved them. No assurance of their final safety is required by their surviving friends, or by the church, beyond the fidelity and elevation of the piety of their lives. And even if they be cut off suddenly, if they "die and make no sign," there is nothing of saddening uncertainty cast over the minds of those who knew and loved them on earth and who still remember and bewail them. The ill-manned, crazy, and scarce seaworthy barque must have daylight and fair weather to enable her to get into the harbor; but the gallant frigate with a crew of practised hands and unconquerable hearts, under the direction of an unerring pilot, with her guns bristling from her decks and the invincible flag nailed to her mast, may successfully attempt the entrance in the darkness of midnight, with a swelling sea, and in the face of an enemy.[1]

Mr. Smith's experience during his last affliction appears to have been marked by considerable variety; he had no fears of death, no apprehensions of eternity; but he had seasons of strong conflict. Nor was he privileged by those revelations which have often shed unspeakable rapture on the souls of inferior Christians in the like circumstances. His spirit generally rested with calm confidence in God; and more than this was not necessary, either to himself or his friends. None who knew him could entertain any anxiety as to his final safety. "That was settled." And had he, like the venerable Bramwell, been suddenly snatched away, all our mourning for him would have been mingled with "sure and certain hope." In his actual state of mind, however, he was fully alive to whatever aggravations of

---

1.   Since the above was written, I have met with a remark of the celebrated Arnauld which illustrates the same subject in a somewhat different way. "He used often to say," it is remarked by the authoress of the *Select Memoirs of Port Royal*, "that the deathbed of young converts is generally most bright; because their newly acquired sense of the mercy of God in some sort dazzles their eyes from steadily beholding his holiness," and he mostly added, "the experienced Christian has too solid a view of the mercy of God in Christ not to rejoice; but he has too exalted views of the holiness of God not to rejoice with trembling."—*Memoirs*, vol. 1, p. 244

affliction his circumstances might present; and I cannot but allude to the anxiety which he felt respecting the Lincoln circuit, as one which, it is to be feared, tended materially to increase the virulence of his disease. Some of his appointments were kindly supplied by local preachers, but no arrangements were made by which the claims of the country societies could be regularly and permanently met. This was to Mr. Smith a source of continual uneasiness at a time when it was of the highest importance that his mind and body should be kept in a state of the most perfect quietness. Whether such a provision *could* have been made, my acquaintance with the subject does not enable me to determine. I can only state the fact, and that I do with a regret as deep as it is unavailing.

Mr. Smith's disease in the first place was an affection of the mucous membrane of the windpipe. It terminated in real and rapid pulmonary consumption. No complaints, probably, are more fluctuating than disorders of the lungs and of the adjacent organs. None so frequently excite hope, nor so certainly blast it. Nothing, it is well known, is more common than for patients laboring under them, even to the last few days of their lives, to suppose that they are actually amending; and it will not therefore appear surprising that the subject of these pages cherished the hope of recovery to a period which, in another case, might have appeared irrational. Yet his was not a selfish love of life. If he spoke with earnest desires of the removal of disease, it was that he might prosecute the great work of saving souls; and with a mind unchanged by weakness, and unsubdued by pain, he maintained "the ruling passion strong in death."

The following is an extract from a letter written by him to his friend Mr. Herbert, of Nottingham, soon after he terminated his public labors.

> May 12, 1831. O, Sir! I did myself and you wrong in not uttering my thoughts and feelings to you on the death of your sweet little Anne. My mind was completely thrown to you; it lingered with you. I wept, I prayed for you; and strange to say, I rejoiced. I said, "Well, he has another attraction in heaven." These strong and pensive feelings gave way to something which I do not now remember; and what I had fancied a letter, never reached you.

Forgive me. Defectiveness seems to be a constituent of my character, and mixes itself prominently with my proceedings. Little fineness of spirit comes out of me.... What a blessed thing it is to have fast hold of God's *concern* to save man!

In the beginning of June, the district meeting was held at Horncastle. It was to be preceded by the missionary anniversary, in the services connected with which it had been arranged that Mr. Smith should have taken some part. This of course was impracticable, and without doubt it would have been prudent for him to have avoided every species and degree of excitement. His wish to meet his brethren once more, however, was so strong that he could not be prevailed upon to absent himself from the district meeting. On Tuesday, June 3, therefore, he left home; but when he arrived at Horncastle, he found himself so extremely unwell that, after a day's rest, he returned to Lincoln. He had taken a fresh cold. His cough was very much increased; he labored under an almost insupportable languor, and on the whole, his symptoms were much more alarming than at any previous period of his illness. Besides the medical gentleman who ordinarily attended him, a physician was now called in who, however, held out very encouraging assurances of his recovery. To Mr. Herbert, June 8, he thus writes: "The doctors pronounce me improving. But I am low. When I shall resume my labor is quite uncertain." And then as if forgetful of his own critical condition, he adds, "Go on, man! God is with you. He will be with you to the end, and I hope to hail you on the banks of the river, and with you sing of salvation," etc.

About this time Mr. Smith was seized with violent inflammation of the passage leading to the lungs. The most decisive measures were immediately resorted to. Forty leeches were applied to the chest, and were succeeded by cupping glasses, and a large blister. These, with the use of calomel internally, produced the desired effect; and Mr. Smith began again slowly to amend. To his father he thus writes, June 14:

I am still ill, but have a turn for the better.... I am in the hands of God—good hands! He is with me, giving me peace and rest of soul, and a hope that in a while I shall make known, with power, his will to the sons of men. I thank you for your prayers.

July 1, writing to the same, he says: "I am yet on the shelf—an awkward place for me; but perhaps it is the best place for me. God knoweth. I wish his will to be done. His will is best.... I think our circuit is in a good state, from accounts at our quarterly meeting. Thanks be to God." In reference to his next year's appointment, he remarks, "What God will do with me, I know not, nor am I anxious about it. All will be well." This was Mr. Smith's last letter to his parents.

Yet although he himself was happily delivered from anxiety, it became a question of interest whether he would be able to undertake the regular labors of a circuit after the approaching Conference. Through a considerable part of the month of July, his health so obviously improved that he was himself very sanguine on the subject. His medical attendants also, upon being consulted, stated that if he would submit to be perfectly quiet for a short time longer, and spend a few weeks at the seaside—the southern part of the kingdom they particularly recommended—it was probable, by the time his services were required, that he would be quite fit for the duties of an ordinary circuit. This, of course, was very cheering; and Mr. Smith proposed immediately to set off for Brighton. To this step there were several objections. The distance was considerable. Mrs. Smith was in circumstances which rendered it impracticable that she should attend her husband; and, most of all, it was to be feared that in Brighton he would be peculiarly liable to excitement and exposed to temptations to exertion—as indeed the sequel unhappily proved. All these objections, however, were overruled; and on Friday, July 15, Mr. Smith left Lincoln. Upon his arrival at Brighton, he thus wrote to Mrs. Smith:

> More than half of my journey to London I stood well, but the rest was attended with subduing weariness. I, however, arrived safe, and had a few hours' sleep at Mr.—. I was so unwell on Sunday as not to allow of my going to chapel. On Monday, for ease and safety, I started for Brighton. There would have been no end to talking, etc. My journey outside the coach greatly refreshed me.

But I still feel the effects of the overcoming weariness. I took a warm bath yesterday, which produced a powerful effect on my shoulders, etc. I rather confidently expect much good from bathing, but I must give it a fair trial. I intend to bathe every other day.

In his second letter to the same, dated July 28, he says:

I am, I think, substantially better. My cough is greatly mitigated; I sleep better; my appetite is tolerable, and I can walk pretty well; but I perceive that strength comes but slowly. I have had some difficulty in escaping danger from visitors. I am obliged to be rather rough, but it is a must be. One soul has been saved, and another cleansed; yet it rather shook me. I have made a stand, such as I know you would applaud if you knew all about it. I am rather singularly beset almost wherever I go.

I know not how my readers may be affected in perusing the foregoing lines, but to me they are unspeakably melancholy. I do not, at any time, claim for Mr. Smith the praise of prudence respecting his own health; there can be no doubt, indeed, that he was a self-sacrificed man. But there was now no one near him who had friendship enough to lay upon him, in God's name, the strong arm of restraint. When he was at home, he was forbidden even to conduct the family worship. His only chance of life was in his being kept perfectly still. Exertion was suicide. And to many of his friends besides myself, it must ever be matter of deep regret that, at every risk, he was not at this time shut out from all excitement and compelled to remain in complete retirement. The results of his imprudence soon showed themselves. In his third and last communication to his family from Brighton, he says:

Some time ago, I was looking forward with pleasing anticipation to the time when we should again be placed in a circuit, and I resume my labors. But last week, a dreadful bowel complaint seized me, devoured my strength, and reduced me to feebleness itself. It seemed to have subsided, and I fancied health was again springing; but a second slight attack dashed my hopes to the ground. I was so perplexed in my mind respecting my appointment, that, if possible, to get something like satisfaction, I consulted Dr. King, an eminent physician at Brighton. He seems to understand my case well; and he says that there is no chance for the recovery of my health unless I abstain from all vocal exertion in preaching and praying, and as much as possible in conversation, for at least three months. I am now attending to his prescription and have already derived some benefit, I think. But I am exceedingly weak. I have communicated these tidings to Mr. Clegg. I expect to sit down. I have requested to be put down for Sheffield, that I may have opportunities of breathing my native air, and consulting Dr. Dawe. I intend leaving Brighton next Tuesday or Wednesday and, God willing, seeing you at the close of next week. Hanging upon Jesus, and commending you and the children to his sympathy and care, I am, etc.

In accordance with the wishes of his friend in that circuit, Mr. Smith was appointed by the Conference to Sheffield East, as an effective man, with the hope that a short time would render him actually such. He left Brighton as he proposed, on Tuesday, August 9, and after resting in London, Northampton, and Nottingham, he arrived in Lincoln on the Saturday of the same week. As he passed through Nottingham, his friends were deeply affected by the alteration of his appearance. He was pale, emaciated, and oppressed by extreme debility; and they too certainly foreboded that they should see his face no more. On the day he spent there, a large party, among whom were the preachers, dined at his friend Mr. Herbert's. Mr. Smith, overcome with languor, was reclining on the sofa when the Rev. H. S. Hopwood, then superintendent of the circuit, who had for some time been subject to sudden attacks of a disease which he every day expected to prove fatal, said to him, "Whether do you think, you or I will go first? Shall we either of us live till next Conference?" Mr. Smith, with that deceitful hope so characteristic of his complaint, replied that his constitution was not yet broken up, and that he expected he should recover. He died about a fortnight before Mr. Hopwood.

After resting in Lincoln for a few days, Mr. Smith and his family removed to Sheffield. He bore the journey better than had been anticipated. According to the Rev. Alexander Strachan of Barnsley:

When he arrived in Sheffield, the disease under which he had for some time labored—a disease unquestionably induced by extraordinary exertion—had made a deep impression on his constitution. The friends in Sheffield, believing that, should he remain there, it would be impossible to restrain him from public and active duties, and justly inferring from his extreme debility that the least exertion would not only extinguish all rational hope of ultimate recovery to health, but also speedily terminate his life, kindly urged upon him the necessity of retiring into the country, to his father's house at Cudworth, where he was likely to derive benefit from his native air and to enjoy uninterrupted repose. In this instance, he yielded to the wishes of his friends; and I had the pleasure of seeing him at his father's on the morning of Sunday, August 28, 1831. I found him in bed, apparently inclined to sleep, and but the shadow of what he had been. He instantly recognised me and sat up. But alas, the keen glance of his eye and the bold expression of his countenance were gone. The eyes were dim and deep in their sockets, while the face was exceedingly thin and pallid. "My dear brother," said he, "since we last met I have experienced the goodness and severity of God; but in patience I have possessed my soul. You are expected to preach here this evening; may God come with you! O how I should rejoice to lift up my voice once more in the sanctuary of my God; but you see that I am confined here as his prisoner. Well, God is with me, and I must not complain. The sinners of this village have been much upon my mind ever since I obtained mercy myself; and wherever I have been stationed, they have had an interest in my prayers. The time to favor them is surely come. May many of them receive the message of salvation which you are come to deliver." After proposing several questions relative to the state both of his body and his mind, to all which he replied with his usual frankness and candor, I prayed with him. In prayer, I expressed strong confidence in the sufficiency of Christ's atonement to justify the ungodly who believe in him; in the willingness of God to sanctify the unholy who continue in the faith; in the competency of providence and grace to preserve the soul, thus sanctified, "blameless unto the coming of our Lord Jesus Christ." I concluded with especial reference to his condition. During prayer he frequently said, "Glory be to God!" but, when I was rising from my knees, he gave free utterance to the strong and lively feelings which he had been endeavouring to suppress. He took up the above topics and enlarged upon them in the most animated manner.

To Mrs. Smith, who by family circumstances was compelled to remain at Sheffield, he addressed a short note, dated August 29th, in which he says, "Dr. Dawe and Mr. Hare came yesterday and very minutely examined my lungs. The doctor rather exultingly said, 'All is right.' You will unite with me in thankfulness for this. I said, 'But I fear the membrane is terribly diseased.' He replied, 'Never mind, we will put it to rights.' The blister on my throat has done its work well. Let us look to Jesus."

Mr. Smith's mind, at this time, seems to have been in a state of delightful tranquillity. He was filled with grateful resignation to the will of God; and though his sufferings were often very severe, no murmur or complaint ever escaped his lips. The attentions of his friends he acknowledged with peculiar sweetness; and the whole of his piety exhibited a mellowness and maturity that seemed like the pluming of the angel-wing of his spirit for the region into which he was about to enter. The day after his arrival at Cudworth, he was especially happy. He said to his friends, "If the Lord have a little more work for me to do, and I think he has, I shall be restored to my family and the church of God. What blessed lessons have I learned in this affliction!" The Word of God became increasingly dear to him; his soul seemed to long for its blessed truths as a parched land for the refreshing shower. The Scriptures, he used to say, were the food of his soul. On one occasion, he expressed himself as peculiarly delighted with the first chapter of St. Peter's first epistle, which his sister had just read to him. "O," he remarked, "the Word of God is such a comfort to me!" Then observing his mother weeping, he said, "Mother, why do you weep? *All* is right. Praise the Lord!" At another time, when in severe suffering, she exhorted him not to be so anxious about recovery, but to yield himself fully into the hands of God. "Bless the Lord!" he replied, "I have done that; I still give myself to him. He is my portion."

Often in the night—for he was very wakeful—the voice of his thanksgiving sounded sweetly through the house; and many were the seasons of delightful communion with heaven which he and his pious father enjoyed while others slept. His soul dwelt in the repose of love and peace. In his experience there was nothing of the

tumult of rapture. There were none of those bursts of ecstatic joy
of which we sometimes hear in such cases. And herein we cannot
but recognise the arrangement of divine wisdom. In the scenes of
active life, his principles and labors had often been deemed extrava-
gant. He was now cut off, not only from all external, but also from
all internal excitement. There was nothing to interrupt the calm
examination, the sober, deliberate testing of his personal experience
and his methods of exertion in the church. Had his principles been
unsound, they now would have certainly failed him. In the severe
scrutiny of the hours of sickness and of ebbing life, when all that
tends to warp the judgment is done away, and with no extraordinary revelation of ravishing joy to withdraw his thoughts from the
subject, he was qualified, more fully than at any former period, to
form a calm and candid opinion of his past life, and to afford to
those who questioned the correctness of his views the most decisive
evidence which the nature of the case would admit. But he never
wavered. No shade of suspicion that he had been wrong appears
ever to have darkened his spirit. On the contrary, he distinctly mentioned those opinions and modes of action in which he had been
considered singular as subjects which, at this time, called forth his
special gratitude to God. They had before proved themselves practically beneficial; and they now not only could bear a dispassionate
view, but proved also sources of consolation in weakness, in suffering, and in death.

Mr. Strachan remarks that:

> On my return to Cudworth, a fortnight after my first visit, he
> informed me that during my absence he had been alternately
> better and worse in health, elevated and depressed in mind; but
> that for several days past his strength and spirits had returned
> in a surprising degree, and that a short time, he believed, would
> complete his recovery and enable him to resume his labors in the
> pulpit. His appearance certainly indicated a change for the bet-
> ter; but it was equally evident that the wound which his general
> health had received was too deep to be healed in so short a time
> as he supposed. I expressed a doubt as to his ultimate recovery,
> and asked him how he could reconcile the extreme anxiety which
> he felt, in reference to the final issue of his affliction, with that

perfect submission to the divine will which he professed to enjoy. He replied, "I have many reasons for wishing to regain my former strength, but none weighs with me so much as a desire to improve the opportunity that would thus be afforded for *saving souls*." He then remarked on the various methods adopted by the mercy of God to bring sinners to repentance, illustrating these methods by examples that had come within the range of his own observation. He described some of the plans which he himself had employed to revive, extend, and perpetuate religion among the people in the different circuits in which he had traveled—exalting, how- ever, above all prudential means, the ministry of God's Word, and meetings for social prayer. On another occasion he gave me a brief narrative of his experience, from the commencement of his Christian profession, from which it appeared that his path had been "as the shining light, that shineth more and more unto the perfect day." He alluded with peculiar emotion to the time of his admission into full connection at the London Conference in 1822. "It was," he said, "a time never to be forgotten. I look back with great satisfaction, I assure you, on the entire surrender which I then made of myself to God. This act of self-dedication is well described in those comprehensive and expressive lines:

> Take my soul and body's powers,
> Take my memory, mind, and will:
> All my goods, and all my hours,
> All I know, and all I feel;
> All I think, or speak, or do;
> Take my heart—but make it new!

From that day to this, I have been enabled to serve God without fear. Return unto thy rest, O my soul; for the Lord hath dealt bountifully with thee."

On that evening a remark was made by one of the young men which produced a deep impression upon my mind and has been of immense importance to me. Brother Smith, in describing the manner of his justification, observed that while wrestling with God for the pardon of sin, he obtained such clear and believing perceptions of the atonement of Christ as constrained him to exclaim: "O God, if all the sins of all the individuals in the world were charged to my account, here is a fountain in which I could wash them all away in an instant." With these words the Spirit presented before my mind the atonement of Christ in all its infinitude of merit and efficacy, and filled my soul with the love of God.

While conversing one day on the necessity of constant communion with God in order to further our personal happiness and the success of the ministry, the difficulty of discharging, with uniformity and fidelity, the important duties of self-examination and self-denial, our proneness to lukewarmness and self-deception, I used an expression [inadvertently, of course] which conveyed to his mind the idea that I doubted the sincerity of his motives and the soundness of his faith. He took no notice of it at the time; but afterwards, while engaged in prayer, I happened to use the same expression. He then rose up, and with one of those piercing looks which he always assumed when under excitement, said, "Lord, thou knowest all things, and thou knowest that I love thee. Living and dying, I am thine. Were I to depart now, I should go to glorious happiness. My heart is fixed, O God, my heart is fixed. I will sing and give praise." After pausing for a few moments, he said, "My dear brother, as I felt a little drowsy at the time, and heard you indistinctly, it is possible that I misunderstood you."

Returning from the country one Sunday evening, I called and found him very feeble, but sitting by the parlor fire, and truly "in the Spirit on the Lord's day." Numerous friends had visited him in the course of the day, some of whom he faithfully warned to flee from the wrath to come, and others he exhorted not to rest satisfied without a "clean heart." We united in prayer and felt it good to wait upon the Lord. Soon after I left, his father arrived from a neighboring village, where he had been preaching. While engaged in family worship, their expectations were raised and their faith wonderfully strengthened, so that the service was prolonged; and each person present pleaded for some special manifestation of God's condescension and love. In a short time, their prayers were turned to thanksgivings and hallelujahs. It seemed as if they had been suddenly "raised up together, and made to sit together in heavenly places in Christ Jesus," or that the full tide of heaven's glory was poured forth on their souls. Mr. Smith, mentioning these circumstances when we met, observed that on that night he believed that the sanctifying power of God penetrated every part of his nature, expelled every degree of evil, and filled him with perfect love.

I subjoin extracts from his two last letters to Mrs. Smith.

Sept. 19. During the last week, I was somewhat alarmed by a rather violent attack of inflammation in my left lung. Leeches were applied without giving me any relief at all; but the application of blistering ointment, which worked mightily, has caused it to retire, and enabled me to breathe freely without any pain in my chest, except what is occasioned by the prodigious soreness of the outside. Glory be to God! This morning the glorious light of the sun caused the fields (which I could see as I lay in bed) to smile, and the sounds produced by the cattle were such music in my ears as I have not heard for a very long time. When the doctor was last here, I saw from his manner that he believed me to be much better. I expect he will begin to build me up immediately. I have great confidence in his skill, and God's blessing upon it. The prayers of God's dear people are an inheritance to me. May his abundant blessing be poured upon them, for their kindness to me and mine! God signally blesses me in my soul. Prayer is offered up here for you, my dear, and for the family; and it will continue to be offered up. Do not droop, my dear. Despondency bites the body. Look steadily at our kind, and loving, and chastising Father. He will help you. I feel much for you. Give my love to the children, and tell them it will help to make me better if they are good, and I hear of it.

Sept. 24. MY DEAR ELLEN—I invite you to join me in giving warm thanks to the blessed God for his great kindness to me. This is the third day I have been downstairs, and I am much better today than on either of the preceding [days]. The doctor was here yesterday and seemed very much pleased with my state. I said, "Sir, I feel it is life from the dead." "Bless the Lord, O my soul!" The Lord has blessed me exceedingly in body and in soul. He has again and again richly baptized me with his blessed and Holy Spirit, and called forth from me songs of thanksgiving. I have had some most delightful seasons in thinking on his most blessed Word. It is exceedingly sweet to my taste. I shall be more a *Bible man*. My dear, we *must unite* in giving ourselves to God and his good Word;

and he will help us in this. We must try to have every room in our house perfumed with God. We will be fully his. I long to exhibit and offer to the dear people in the Sheffield circuit the salvation of God. Well, wait a little, and then! Hallelujah to God and the Lamb! Amen. My heart warms, while I am writing, with love to God and universal love to man. Do you not catch a little of the holy flame, my dear? God will restore comforts to many who have mourned for me. Give my kind love to my beloved colleagues. My lovely children tell, father loves them much, and it will give him great pleasure to learn that they are good.

Yet, while Mr. Smith was thus hopefully anticipating his recovery, as indeed were his friends also, his disease was actually making rapid progress. A few days after the foregoing was written, hectic fever fixed on his brain; and, with some short intervals, he was for several weeks afterwards under the influence of delirium or stupor. The following memorandum was written about this time, and betrays, as the reader will perceive, a slight wandering of mind. The manuscript gives affecting evidence of the writer's physical weakness. It is blurred and blotted. The handwriting is very tremulous, and many of the words are misspelled. Yet there is in it a glow of feeling not unworthy of the last literary act by a right hand which was about for ever to forget "its cunning." I give it entire, only correcting the errors in orthography, etc.

In my dear and honored father's house at Cudworth, near Barnsley, about a yard and half from the spot where God, in his endless mercy, set my soul at gospel liberty and adopted me into his heavenly family; having just recovered from a painful and protracted affliction, by the skill of Dr. Dawe and his assistant Mr. Hare, I feel exceedingly grateful to both of them for their prompt, constant, and kind attention to me during my stay at Cudworth for the good of my health.

Never had I so penetrating [a sense] of the importance of an overruling and beneficent Providence superintending, directing, and controlling all things among the sons and daughters of men, for the honor of his adorable name, which is a strong tower, into which the righteous runneth and is safe. The upspring and spontaneous language of my heart is that of the Psalmist, Psa.

103:1, and that of Isa. 12, also of Mr. C. Wesley's hymns on the 322d, 358th, and 360th pages of the large hymnbook used in our chapels; and, finally, of all who have been brought out of deep and bitter waters, restored to the bosom of a most lovely and beloved family, with the delightful anticipation of being better fitted for God's good service. I wish to be eminently a minister of the Spirit. Christ says, "Without me ye can do nothing"; also, "It is the Spirit that quickeneth: the flesh profiteth nothing." Well; "I will circumcise thy heart."   "Ask, and ye shall receive, that your joy may be full."—"If ye then being evil," etc.— "What things soever ye desire," etc.—"But let them ask in faith," etc.

I propose visiting Leeds, Nottingham, and Northampton; partly on business, partly for the establishing of my health; and, finally, for the gratification of conversing with some of the excellent of the earth on divine subjects; that our spirits may be refreshed together; that they may see the exceeding and abounding kindness of the blessed God to one of the most unworthy, worthless, and unfaithful creatures among the progeny of man; but one whom the Triune God is intensely concerned to bless with a present, a free, a full, and everlasting salvation, in sharing in his own ineffable and endless bliss, in his eternal heaven. Who is a god like unto our God? None in heaven, or upon earth; who has set his heart on man, and manifested his intense interest for his present, constant, and everlasting happiness, as ought, and must, and will fill angels and men with delightful astonishment, admiration, and gratitude through endless ages. Glory be to the ever-blessed and Triune God for ever and for ever! Amen and amen. So says John Smith, from the very bottom of his heart, which is warm with universal love—love to God and universal man. It is the deep and strong, and, he trusts and hopes, will be the constant and lasting wish of his heart to get and diffuse as much of God in the world as he can. Who is sufficient for these things? No one but the man whom God fits for the business. But nothing is too hard for the omnipotent God who has promised to be with them that seek to promote his glory upon earth. I will try for one, by the help of God. May I be graciously helped by divine strength, without which all human efforts, however splendid and conspicuous, must be for ever in vain. My trust is in a promise-keeping God, whom I wish to adore and enjoy through endless ages. I hope and wish to adore among angels, and archangels, and all the redeemed of the Lord. This glorious consummation I ardently long to be realized. May God put forth his strength!

Mr. Smith's state was now so alarming that it was thought necessary to send for Mrs. Smith. She was deeply affected to find him in a condition of such extreme weakness, both of body and mind. When she went to his bedside, consciousness revived for a moment; and with a smile illuminating his still expressive countenance, he said, "This is what I have long wished to see." Upon being asked if he knew who it was, he replied, "Yes, it is my dear wife." He immediately relapsed into stupor, and it was nearly a week before he was again sensible. He then expressed some anxiety about his dear children, and begged Mrs. Smith not to protract her stay. On the day following, therefore, she returned to Sheffield. During nearly the whole of his delirium, he imagined himself occupied in the duties which he had so much loved. He was almost constantly engaged in preaching, praying, or praising God. One morning, after having been delirious during the night, he began to sing with extraordinary sweetness. He had always been remarkable for the taste and music of his singing, but never before had it sounded so rich and melodious. Both the words and the tune were unknown to those who heard them, and it seemed as if he were preparing to assume his place in the mystic chorus of a world of peerless and immortal harmony.

Before this time, he had experienced strong conflicts "with the principalities and powers and the rulers of the darkness of this world." On one occasion he requested that he might be left alone for some time. When his father returned to the room, he said, "Father, I have had a mighty conflict with the powers of darkness; but, praised be the Lord, he has delivered me. I have come off 'more than conqueror' through the blood of the Lamb." He then broke forth in an animated strain of praise. But it was now, while his physical powers were oppressed with fierce disease, and his mind generally was weak and wandering, that the foe was permitted to make the most terrific and the last attack. Yet, though fever raged in his veins, and his body was tossed and writhed in frenzy, his soul was enabled to collect its energies for the shock; and, as nearly as could be recollected, he thus addressed his spiritual assailant:

Thou art a *devil!* How thou didst become one, I do not know, but God did not create thee so. The blessed God cannot be the author of evil. God made thee an angel of light! Thou didst not keep thy first estate! Thou didst become a devil; but how I do not know. But thou art a devil now! It pleased the blessed God to create man a happy creature—and place him in paradise—and *thou* hadst the impudence to go to paradise and tempt our first parents to sin against the blessed God. They hearkened to thy suggestions, disobeyed the command of God, fell into transgression, and brought down the curse of God upon themselves and their posterity. It pleased the blessed God to send his Son Jesus Christ to die for the sin of man. And I am John Smith, was born at Cudworth in Yorkshire of pious parents who brought me up in the nurture and admonition of the Lord. But I was a bad lad, was led captive by thee, and loved my sins. I caused my parents much grief— they prayed mightily to God in my behalf—with many tears. It pleased the blessed God—of his infinite mercy—and in answer to prayer—to connect his Holy Spirit with me—to convince me that I was a miserable sinner—in the road to hell—and under his curse. I resolved, through grace—to leave my sins. I sought the Lord in my distress—he heard my prayer. I was encouraged to believe on Jesus. God was pleased for the sake of Christ—to pardon all my past sins—and to put his love in my heart—and to grant me the witness of his Holy Spirit that I was adopted.

And I believe that Jesus Christ, the Son of God—is a divine person, equal with the Father—and that it pleased God the Father—of his spontaneous kindness—unsolicited—to send his Son—into the world. And I believe that Jesus Christ became incarnate, and was born of the virgin; that he was a man of sorrow, and acquainted with grief; that he lived three and thirty years in this our world; that he died a shameful and accursed death upon the cross; that it pleased the Father to bruise him for the sin of man; and that he rose again from the dead on the third day. Death had no power to hold him; and he triumphed over *thee* and all thy power, and he ascended into heaven; sat down on the right hand of the Father, to make intercession for man; and all power in earth and heaven is committed into his hands. And I believe—that he, by his sufferings and death—made a full and sufficient atonement for the sins of the whole world—and purchased for mankind the Holy Ghost. And I believe that God is pleased, in answer to the intercession of Jesus—to connect the Holy Spirit with every soul of man—with saving purpose and intention, in order to bring them to Christ for salvation. And I believe that there is salvation to all who apply. The blessed God is unwilling that any should perish. And I come by faith to Jesus Christ—I believe that his precious blood avails for *me*—and I cast my soul upon him; I rest upon his atonement, and I defy thee, Satan! Thou art a malignant being—the enemy of God and man!—and thou art seeking to destroy me; but I defy thee! I commit my soul to Jesus, and I defy thee! Thou canst not hurt! In the name of Jesus I defy thee, Satan![1]

This remarkable contest with his spiritual adversary continued from ten o'clock at night until three in the morning, with loud and distressing cries, moans, and prayers. Much of the address to Satan, particularly the former part, was repeated many times; for whenever an interruption occurred, either in his own mind or from without, he recommenced it; nor would he cease till he had delivered it throughout in an unbroken form. His voice was as strong as it had ever been known; and his body was so violently agitated by the agony of his mind that it was with difficulty that the united strength of five men detained him in bed. It was unutterably distressing to behold him, and to hear him, many times successively, crying in the most pathetic tone, "Jesus!—Jesus!—Jesus!—Je—e—sus!—help!" At length deliverance came; the enemy was overcome; peace returned; and there is reason to believe that from this time his heart was uninterruptedly glad in the light of the divine countenance.

After having spent about six weeks at Cudworth, Mr. Smith was removed to Sheffield. He still entertained the hope of recovery. Several of his friends endeavoured to cherish a similar expectation and held a weekly prayer meeting for the specific object of intercession on this subject. But the decree had gone forth, sanctioned and sealed by infinite wisdom and mercy; and it was irrevocable. Mr.

---

1. My informant vouches in general, for even the verbal accuracy of his report of this extraordinary address.

H. Beeson, an attached and kind friend of Mr. Smith, was one of
those who watched with him during some of the last nights of his
life. In a conversation with Mr. Beeson upon the various orders of
intellect, he said of himself, "I am a minister of the Spirit. Soul-
saving is my business. God has given me a heart for it. I will go on
in his name, and believe for effects." Of his labors in the Lincoln
circuit, he remarked, "I was always anxious to get as much business
done as possible; so I worked while God was working, and his arm
was made bare in many places." He added, "I ought to have given
over preaching three months before I did." And after some further
observations on the same subject, he broke forth, "Hallelujah to the
blessed Jesus! I have not had one pain too much, not one stroke too
heavy. All is right. God can do without me."

This last remark Mr. Smith repeated several times to persons
who visited him. He appeared to apprehend that an undue value
and dependence had been placed upon his labors; and his trembling
sensibility for the honor of God led him thus to endeavour to check
a feeling so erroneous and sinful. Nor was this fear without reason.
It is indeed a difficult thing to give all the respect which they appear
to demand to the zealous and successful efforts of a minister, without in a measure losing sight of him through whom alone the most
splendid capacity and the most perfect devotedness can avail anything. To us it seems very desirable that the lives of such men as the
subject of these memoirs should be prolonged; but, O, it is of infi-
nitely higher moment that God should have the undivided homage
and dependence of his church. When therefore the creature is made
the object of a confidence which wholly belongs to the Creator, and
the accomplishments and successes of a minister are regarded with
an unscriptural complacency, it is an act of mercy to all parties to
withdraw such an individual from the sorceries of an idolatry which
may go far to charm away his own simplicity, and which already
encroaches on the awful circle of divine glory. Thus many ministers
of distinguished promise have been snatched away in the bloom of
life and of service; and in the blank and desolation which succeeds,
the hearts of God's people have turned, in an exemplary degree, to

honor that hand, which, while it smites, is ready to distil the healing balm and pour the full tide of reviving power.

It was not till the last week of his life that the truth broke on Mr. Smith's mind, and he felt that he was now to die. But it was no shock to him. His spirit did not for a moment quail in the solemn certainty. He rested confidently on Christ, and calmly awaited the end. To a kind friend who attended him, he said, "It appears I shall die." "Yes, Sir," was the reply, "there is no other prospect." "Well," rejoined Mr. Smith, "God can carry on his work without me." He continued, "I want more prayer," and begged his friend to pray with him. "What shall I pray for?" returned the other, "for I cannot pray for your life." "Pray," said Mr. Smith, "as the Spirit shall direct you. 'Prayer,' as Mr. Bramwell once remarked, 'always brings one out on the right side.'" They then prayed together, and the Lord blessed the soul of his afflicted servant. At another time, he said to one of his medical attendants, with his accustomed promptness of expression, "Shall I die, doctor?" Observing that Dr. Young hesitated, he added, "You need not fear to tell me; I am not afraid." Mr. Wild, his other medical friend, observed, "You must keep your mind constantly fixed on eternal things"; to which Mr. Smith answered, "My mind *is* constantly fixed there."

The friend to whose communications this work has already been so much indebted remarks:

> The prospect of meeting in heaven with Wesley, and Whitefield, and Fletcher, and Bramwell, and Nelson, and others, whom he loved for their distinguished excellence, was peculiarly dear to his thoughts, and often furnished matter for enlargement and glad anticipation in his acts of devotion. The thought of not recognizing the saints in the eternal state never appeared to have any place in his mind; as it is, in fact, one of those refinements which busy speculation has built upon the *silence* of Scripture respecting subjects which are only not distinctly enunciated because nothing but the credulity of unbelief could have ever called them in question. "By faith, when he was dying, he gave commandment concerning his bones," that they should lay them beside those of his friend Nelson; thus attesting not only his assured hope of a

joyful resurrection, but of a glad recognition, also, of him whom he had known and loved on earth.

To a person who visited him he said, "Mind your business, and take care of your family; but above all, see that you keep the love of God in your soul. Be firm, and let nothing for a moment lead you to think of giving up your class or declining any exertion in behalf of the cause of God." To a young man whom he believed to be called to the ministry, he said, "Do, my brother, be diligent; play the man; play the man." Of his experience and feelings, he remarked, "I rest in the atonement; I am hanging on the cross of Christ; this is my only hope." To one of his colleagues, he said, "All is clear. I have had some success in my labors; but my happiness does not result from that, but from this—I have now hold of God. I am a very great sinner, and am saved by the wonderful love of God in Christ Jesus. I throw my person and my labors at his feet."

When, on one occasion, Mrs. Smith was speaking of his being about to be removed from her, he replied, with solemn and tender emphasis, "The widows and the fatherless in Israel are God's peculiar charge." At another time, observing her extreme emotion, he would not rest satisfied without a promise from her that she would claim the special consolations promised to those in her circumstances. One evening, when it was thought that he was about to enter into rest, she came to his bedside and inquired, "My dear, do you think the Lord is about to take you home?" "Not just yet, perhaps," he replied. Then clasping his hands, and lifting up his eyes towards heaven, he exclaimed, in the most impressive tone, "I commend to the care and protection of the Triune God, my dear wife. May she be supported and consoled. I commend to the same God my Ellen Hamer Smith," and then proceeded to name all his dear little ones separately, and to place them thus solemnly under the charge of a faithful and merciful God. He continued, "This body I give to be committed to the dust, in sure and certain hope of a joyful resurrection to eternal life, through our Lord Jesus Christ. This immortal spirit I commend into the hands of Him who gave it." He then appeared exhausted, but in a short time revived again.

The salvation of souls was almost constantly the subject of his meditations and intercession. One day, when he supposed himself alone, he was obviously engaged in fervent mental prayer; and at length he broke out, "Glory be unto our God! Glory be unto our God! What god can deliver like unto our God?" Then extending his arms, while his countenance was lighted up with joyful confidence, he exclaimed, "Glory be to God! Sheffield circuit shall rise! Sheffield circuit shall rise! Sheffield circuit shall rise!"—a prediction which, during the succeeding year, was most happily fulfilled.

On Thursday, November 3rd, the Rev. Messrs. McLean and Holgate visited him; and while they engaged in prayer, a heavenly influence filled the room. Prayer was turned into praise; and although Mr. Smith was in the last agony, his spirit caught the strain, and an expression of sacred joy lighted up his pale countenance. When prayer was ended, he beckoned Mr. McLean to him, and labored for several moments to give expression to something which he wished to say. After a repetition of unsuccessful efforts, he abandoned the attempt as hopeless, and condensing what he had purposed saying into the fewest possible terms, and concentrating his whole strength to the single effort of expressing them, he exclaimed with an energy almost equal to his former self, "You said, Praise God; and *I said Amen.*" This was the last articulate sound that he was heard to utter. It was the sealing of the volume, the closing testimony of an unwavering spirit, the echo of which he was to catch from myriads of immortal and redeemed intelligences in a world where the song shall never languish nor the festival ever terminate. In the course of the morning, the medical gentlemen called. Mrs. Denton, an affectionate friend who was present, followed them out of the room. Dr. Young then told her that it was probable that Mr. Smith would not live an hour longer. Upon her return, he beckoned to her to tell him what they had said. For a moment she was silent. She then replied, "In less than an hour, Sir, it is likely that you will be in eternity." A heavenly and triumphant smile played on his emaciated face. He turned his head on his pillow; and, about a quarter before ten o'clock, while several of his friends, in an attitude and spirit of prayer, commended his soul to God, he entered the realms of eternal praise.

His remains were deposited in the vault which encloses those of his friend Mr. Nelson. In the same place lies the body of his youngest infant, who, in the early part of the year, was called from this world of trial to mingle with the "angels who do always behold the face of our Father which is in heaven." Thus with the dust of his ministerial father at its side, and of his kindred according to the flesh at its feet, his body (sanctified in life and death, and precious and reverend even in decay) reposes till the Conqueror of the grave shall kindle it to immortal beauty and crown it with everlasting honor.

The intelligence of Mr. Smith's death was received by his numerous friends with every expression of lively emotion. Funeral sermons on the occasion were addressed to large, attentive, and deeply affected congregations. In Sheffield and Leeds, by the Rev. F. Calder; in Lincoln, by the Rev. T. H. Squance; and in Nottingham and its vicinity, by the Rev. Messrs. T. Harris and W. H. Clarkson. Several of these services were attended by the special presence and blessing of God. May the good impressions thus produced prove permanent and indelible!

The following notice appeared in the *Sheffield Mercury*:

Died, on Thursday week, aged 37, the Rev. John Smith, Wesleyan Preacher, in the Sheffield East circuit. This individual, so highly esteemed in the denomination to which he belonged, and who was previously stationed at Lincoln, had been appointed to this town by the last Methodist Conference, at the earnest solicitation of many of the principal members of the society in the circuit; in which he was expected to have labored with that degree of zeal and usefulness for which he had been elsewhere distinguished. A state of ill health, however, prevented him from so much as once preaching to the people whose desires had been consulted in his appointment. He had indeed only been residing in this place about three weeks when he was cut off in the midst of his life, leaving a wife and six young children to sustain their irreparable loss. His end was in accordance with the experience of that religion of which he was the ardent preacher; [some of] his latest words being, "All is well; all is peace." His remains were interred on Monday morning, in the vault connected with the chapel in

Carver Street, and about two hundred persons were in attendance to pay a last tribute to a man who was generally termed "THE REVIVALIST."

This last epithet—employed probably, in the first place, as a mere playful distinction—has now become the serious designation of that class of men to which Mr. Smith belonged. It is not, I think, a happy appellation. To say nothing of its barbarism, it has too often been associated with a spirit of partisanship; and by men who differ from those it is intended to describe, is sometimes used as a term of reproach. Yet it is at least proper for those who sustain it to inquire whether that reproach be altogether unmerited. Do they make the Word of God the subject of diligent study, and is it exclusively the rule of their labors? Are they ambitious to be mighty in the Scriptures, and do they endeavour to infuse the taste for scriptural research into the minds of those who are, through their instrumentality, converted to God? Do they strive to repress that factitious excitement which is almost invariably attendant upon real revivals, which tends to provoke the prejudices of other sincere Christians, and to confound the work of the Spirit with mere passionate and momentary emotion? Does the scriptural character of their own piety manifest itself by *continual* exertion for the salvation of men, or are they only fervent occasionally, and by fits? Is their zeal an essential attribute of their Christianity, or is it a quality which they can sometimes, without much regret, lay aside till a more convenient opportunity? Are they willing, in all humility, to sit at the feet of those whom they believe to be taught by the Spirit, or are they self-seeking and self-opinionated? Do they ingenuously admit the excellencies of other Christians, or is their temper exclusive and censorious? These, and the like queries, involve the accusations usually brought against this very useful class of Christians by those whose opinions and labors are dissimilar from their own. Let such as bear the name of revivalists, or desire to attain the character supposed to be implied in it, candidly inquire how far they merit these accusations. The example of one to whom, in general, they may honorably seek a resemblance, is sketched in these pages; and though the outline is faint and inadequate, it is yet sufficiently distinct to show how fully, and by what means, he shunned many of those errors from which some who partially resemble him are supposed not to be entirely free.

Men of sanguine temperament are not generally qualified to attain distinction. They do not possess sufficient body and depth of character. Hence when, as in Mr. Smith's case, we find a Christian of this class truly eminent, it is important and interesting to inquire what causes foreign from the native elements of his own mind conspired to support the impulses necessary to excellence. To excite persons of this character to action in the first place is easy; the difficulty is to give their motives a regular and increasing power. It may readily be shown that the duties to which naturally they are the least disposed tend most fully to this result; and these undoubtedly are the calm, scrutinizing, and meditative. Mr. Smith was unusually assiduous and diligent in his closet; and in this fact, I think, is to be found the explanation of his steadiness, uniformity, and consequent eminence both as a Christian and a minister. It was thus that he was made the subject of those penetrating discoveries which continually urged him to action. It was thus also that he was brought into those deep and painful exercises which rendered his experience and his principles so solid and established. Here it was that he made those daring experiments of faith, by the repetition of which, in society, he succeeded in drawing down such uncommon blessings from on high. He had a thousand times watched the fire of heaven play around his sacrifice in solitude; it was not for him to doubt that the sign would be repeated before the eyes of all Israel, though the altar and the offering were alike surrounded by the waters of indifference and unbelief.

To be more particular, however, persons of the class to which allusion has just been made are not only likely to be betrayed into rashness and precipitancy, but they are also peculiarly disposed to be satisfied with what is crude in doctrine and superficial in experience. Mr. Smith's enlightened piety and well-digested principles appear to have especially resulted from his continual and prayerful researches into the Scriptures and his perpetual recurrence to them. Nor is it too much to say that no person of this character can attain a maturity of Christian virtue, or an extensive degree of scriptural usefulness, who does not constantly and peculiarly make the Bible the subject of humble and devotional study. "You must search and dig into it," said Mr. Smith to one of his friends, "as the miners do for treasure in the bowels of the earth." He who is most active in the church has need of the largest measure of scriptural knowledge and understanding. Without this as ballast, he will never be able to bear up against the varying winds to which he is continually exposed, nor even to take advantage of the favoring breezes with which heaven may swell his sails.

Yet let me not be understood to propose Mr. Smith as a perfect example. To admit that his character was not without alloy is only to allow that he was a man, and as such, liable to error and frailty. I readily grant that he was sometimes wanting in prudence, but it was a rare thing indeed for that want to injure any but himself. His modes of exertion in some cases, also, even if perfectly justifiable in him, cannot be proposed as a safe example for others. Indeed, it should be remembered that, whatever has been rationally questioned in the conduct of a man of such acknowledged excellence, becomes doubly doubtful in the behavior of those whose spiritual attainments are but low. Yet when we speak of his spirit—of its tenderness, its sympathy, its humility, its ardor, its devotion, its resolution, and its heavenliness—we feel that we are on secure ground. Here no cold qualification is required. It is indeed a bright example. It is truly worthy of imitation; and those who were most perfectly acquainted with it—be their differences of opinion upon other matters what they may—will cordially unite in the desire that it may prove powerfully and increasingly influential.

He has returned to Zion with singing. It is our privilege to follow him in our contemplations. We are not only called to profit by the example of distinguished saints while they remain on earth, but also to accompany them in spirit to that land of perfection, where everything of infirmity and error, where the possibility of lapse or decay, is for ever removed. Our faith is invited to listen to their solemn songs and to anticipate their holy joy. As those objects in nature which, when minutely inspected, are in many respects coarse and unsightly in the distant landscape, are softened into perfect beauty, so are our recollections of the departed faithful to rise on our spirits in fair and unsullied vision. All that was worthy of our esteem here, we are to contemplate as now expanded and sublimed—all that was earthly and questionable, as shaken off for ever. We are to witness their love wake up to undying and rapturous ardor; their zeal enkindled in a pure, untrembling pillar of ascending flame; their praise multiplied by the echoes of countless spirits, pure and ethereal as themselves; their intellects, with unwearied wing expatiating over eternity, and finding new matter for wonder and adoration in every line of light which radiates from the throne; and then, when our thoughts are ravished with the glorious and pure scenes which present themselves to our faith, we are to kneel before our Father and their Father, and, lifting up holy hands and a sincere heart, to breathe forth the comprehensive and mysterious prayer: "Thy will be done in earth, as it is done in heaven."